BMW   Motorcycles of the Century

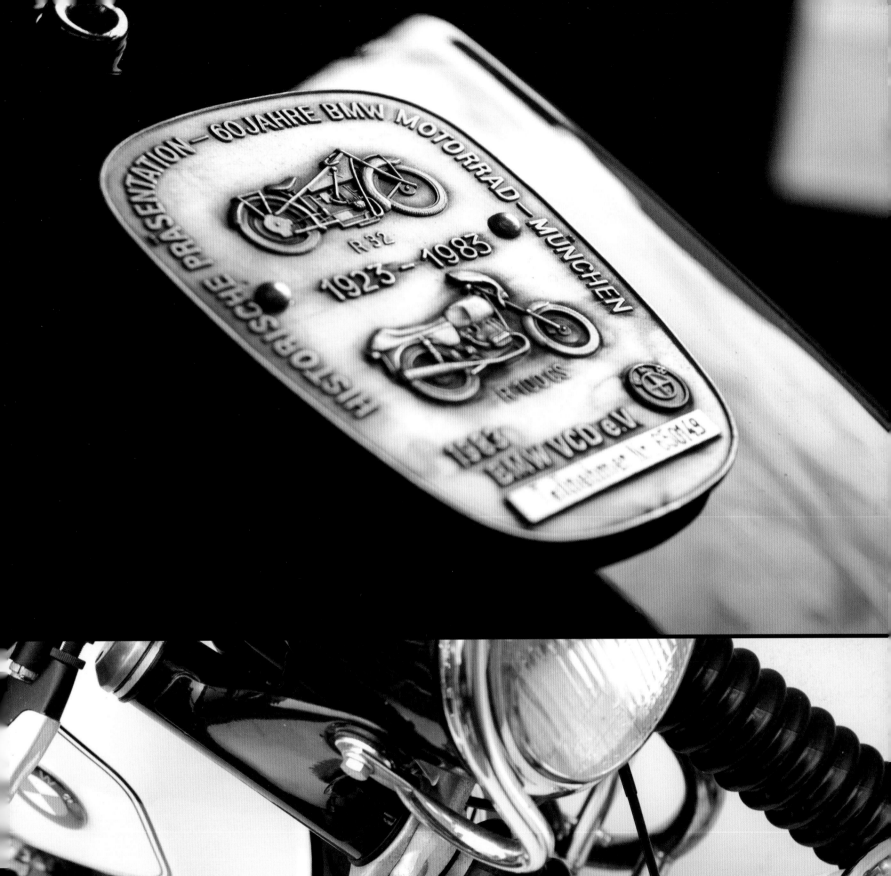

Claudio Somazzi, Massimo Bonsignori

BMW
Motorcycles of the Century
Guide to Models 1923–2000

SKIRA

Art director
Marcello Francone

Design
Flavio and Paola Ranzini

Editorial coordination
Eva Vanzella

Copy editor
Christian Cavaciuti

Translation
Robert Burns for Language Consulting
Congressi, Milan
Catherine Bolton, Conor Deane and Karen
Tomatis for *Scriptum*, Rome

First published in Italy in 2013 by
Skira Editore S.p.A.
Palazzo Casati Stampa
via Torino 61
20123 Milano
Italy
www.skira.net

Printed and bound in Italy. First edition
ISBN: 978-88-572-1954-7

Distributed in USA, Canada, Central & South
America by Rizzoli International Publications,
Inc., 300 Park Avenue South, New York,
NY 10010, USA. Distributed elsewhere in
the world by Thames and Hudson Ltd.,
181A High Holborn, London WC1V 7QX,
United Kingdom.

Photo credits
Bayerische Motoren Werke Historic Archive,
Munich: 22 bottom, 25 bottom, 26 bottom,
28 bottom, 29 top right, 30 top and bottom,
31, 32 centre (second from top), 34 bottom,
36 top and centre (third from top), 39 top,
centre (third from top) and bottom left
and right, 64 bottom, 79 bottom right,
80 bottom, 102, 142, 147 bottom left and
centre, 150 bottom, 161 top, 186, 187
bottom, 189 top, 216 top, 217 bottom, 222,
223 centre and bottom, 230, 231 bottom,
232, 235 bottom, 237 bottom, 238–39,
241 bottom, 242–43, 245, 246–47, 248–54,
255 top, 256 bottom, 258 centre left
and bottom right, 260 centre left, 262
Bonhams Ltd: 29 centre, 32 centre (third
from top), 35 top, 37 bottom left, 63 top,
64 top, 65 top left, 68, 69 top and centre
right, 70–73, 76–78, 79 top, 80 top, 81, 83
top and bottom right, 84 top, 91 centre right,
93 bottom, 94–96, 97 top, 99, 101 top, 104,
105 top right, 106, 107 top, 110 centre,
111 top right, 112 centre (first from top),
117 bottom right, 118 bottom, 119, 121 top,
125 top, 128–29, 134–35, 137 bottom,
138–39, 143 top, 144 top, 163, 165 centre
and bottom left and right, 171 top, 173,
175 bottom, 176–77, 181–83, 185, 187 top,
189 bottom, 190 bottom, 192, 194 right,
199 top, 203 bottom, 210–14, 220–21,
225 top, 226, 260 centre right, 261 centre
right and bottom left, 265 top
Paolo Pulga: 2–14, 26 top and centre, 40–41,
50-51, 67 centre, 116, 117 top and centre,
122–23, 126, 127, 137 top and centre, 158,
162–63, 166, 178–79, 199 bottom, 200–02,
203 top and centre, 204–07, 234, 235 top,
240, 241 top, 258 centre right, 259 centre
left, 260 bottom left, 263 top, 270–71
Petra-Dubrava Museum Complex Archive
(www.motos-of-war.ru): 100, 108 bottom,
110 bottom
Massimo Bonsignori Archive
Paolo Conti Archive (Legend Bike)
Nonsolomoto Archive, Milan
Claudio Somazzi Archive
Ubaldo Bellan Collection
Gabriele Dallatana Collection
Sergio Mancuso Collection
Willy Neutkens Collection

Texts
Claudio Somazzi
Massimo Bonsignori

Assistant and general coordination
Gianni Lucini

*The authors wish to thank
the following for their assistance
during the preparation of this book*
Ettore Bonsignori
Helen Buckingham (Bonhams)
Marco Cirilli
Andrea Frignani (BMW Italia)
Antonio Frova
Marco Gualtieri
Paolo Pulga

Contents

18   Why this book? Why a vintage motorcycle? Why a BMW?

20   A story of transformations, achievements and revolutions

42   Buying a vintage motorcycle

50   Suggestions for a correct maintenance of the vintage motorcycle

52   Purchase guide

56   Bayerische Motoren Werke production figures, by year

61   **the 1920s**

89   **the 1930s**

115   **the 1940–50s**

153   **the 1960s**

169   **the 1970s**

197   **the 1980s**

229   **the 1990–2000s**

258   The joy of sidecars

262   BMW Racing Team

Why this book? Why a vintage motorcycle? Why a BMW?

Over a decade has elapsed since we published our first book, *BMW Passione d'altri tempi*, which we devoted to our great passion: the vintage motorcycles made by Bayerische Motoren Werke. The book, published on the Italian market but purchased all over the world (Italian must be easier to understand than we think!), was a gesture of love towards these beautiful road machines. Above all, however, it reflected a "conscious foolishness" that has led us to work night after night, for months, to find the material that could fulfil the desire for knowledge and the need for evaluation of all those who, like us, love classic BMW motorcycles.

Ten years have elapsed and many things have happened. We have enjoyed more years of research, collected materials, bought and sold beautiful motorcycles. We have seen our book become a key instrument for countless collectors, experienced and neophytes alike, in helping them choose which motorcycle to buy, whether from a friend or at one of the countless markets. We have received letters and e-mails with compliments from many countries, from the United States to Australia. And we were delighted to receive requests for a new book after the first one completely sold out.

It took ten years to understand that this book, written out of passion, had left an important mark and that it thus merited a sequel. So, between tightening bolts (Massimo), a start-up and an app (Claudio), we decided it was time to make that leap: to take the best of the first book, enrich it with twenty years of new classic motorcycles (1980–2000), update assessments and recommendations for the collection, share the countless photographs and emotions we have amassed since 2003, and, above all, produce an "international" book – this time finally in English, for collectors from Europe, the United States and around the world, where the legend of Bayerische Motoren Werke continues to hold sway.

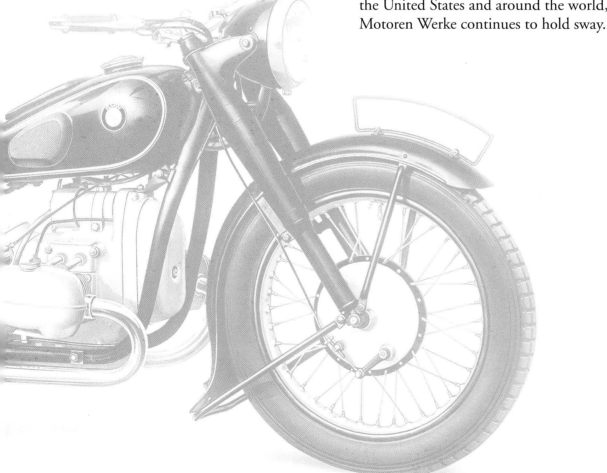

This was the starting point of *BMW. Motorcycles of the Century*, a fantastic "effort" that took months to complete, with countless friends who worked on it with us. But now, as we open it with the same emotion of the first film we saw as children, all our efforts have been fully rewarded.

What you are holding now is a book to read, leaf through and, above all, consult. It is a book that can help the neophyte who is about to enter the world of vintage BMW motorcycles for the very first time, but at the same time it is a reference for even the most experienced collector, prey to doubts or simply unsure about a frame number. Having a guide is important above all to orient you in choosing the motorcycle of your dreams, giving you greater agility in the jungle of the now-weekly markets, aided by full knowledge that will help you avoid impromptu sellers who, dazzled by the chance to earn easy money, are willing to invent anything to sing the praises of their product. The texts in this book have been written with extreme humility, but, above all, extensive research, so that they can be consulted confidently by those who have any doubts.

Now the book is finished. At this point, it is no longer "ours", but "yours".

We wish everyone a good journey. To us, to you, who have decided to trust our "blue-and-white nights", to our travel companions Gianni and Paolo, to all our collector friends who have lent us their fabulous motorcycles, and to the extraordinary professionals at Skira, who believed in our "conscious lie" that an R 69 S is as much of a masterpiece as a Munch painting.

See you on the road!

Claudio Somazzi and Massimo Bonsignori

A story of transformations, achievements and revolutions

Collecting Bayerische Motoren Werke motorcycles means taking an exciting trip through time, savouring forgotten atmospheres and experiencing nuances lost forever. It is also about getting in touch with our past, and not just as it applies to motorcycles. BMW motorcycles have gone through ten decades, surviving two world wars and the worst crises of the last century. We'll discover more about the brand with the "propeller" logo – and our own history – through the models, anecdotes, curiosities, historic dates, important moments and the people who made the history of Bayerische Motoren Werke. In the next pages you will read about the "milestones", the pivotal moments in BMW's industrial and racing adventure, from its foundation to the triumphs in the African deserts. And the story continues...

1916. Bayerische Flugzeug-Werke is founded

On 7 March 1916, the Bayerische Flugzeug-Werke (BFW) was founded following a merger with Otto-Werke, a small manufacturer of aeronautic engines and parts. BMW, for Bayerische Motoren Werke, considers this day as its founding date, given the following merger of the two companies in 1921, made by the Viennese financier **Camillo Castiglioni**.

Camillo Castiglioni

The Austrian financier, born in the city of Trieste in north-east Italy, came into contact with what would become the BMW founding team in 1916, when he helped Rapp Motoren Werke get a key contract with Austro-Daimler, a company he later became the majority shareholder of, developing the automobile business along with the lead designers at Puch and Porsche. In the late 1910s, Castiglioni also acquired several banks and newspapers in Vienna, and at the beginning of the First World War, aware of the potential of the BMW project, he invested heavily to let the company grow, sustaining also its post-war production activities. He later moved away from BMW to manage and invest in the fledging automobile industry, coming back on stage at the beginning of the 1920s at the request of Franz Josef Popp. Castiglioni bought back the BMW brand from Knorr-Bremse, and started over the engine business for the company. Until the early 1930s, he was a supervisory board member, the president and the major shareholder of BMW. Then in 1929 some financial difficulties forced Castiglioni to hand over his shares to a consortium of banks.

Franz Josef Popp

The first general director of BMW, and later chairman of the Board of Directors, the engineer and lieutenant Franz Josef Popp, a native of Vienna, was hired by Rapp Motoren Werke and placed in charge of the aircraft engines quality. Curiously enough, Popp came into contact with Rapp when he was sent there as an inspector by the Austro-Daimler to assess the suitability of the Rapp plants for the construction of aircraft engines under license. A man of great skills, he can be credited with the transformation of BMW from a small German aircraft factory to a leading engine company

1917. Bayerische Motoren Werke, BMW is born

On 20 July 1917, Rapp Motoren Werke – named after the founder's name, designer Karl Rapp – a company in Munich that made aviation engines, changed its company name to "Bayerische Motoren Werke" (Bavarian Motor Works). It was the outcome of a strategic decision made by the technical director of the company, **Franz Josef Popp**, who could not find investors because of Rapp Motoren Werke's bad reputation, especially among German military officers responsible for army contracts. A new name would have guaranteed greater prospects. The new company opened a large plant, proportionate to the growing demand for military aircraft engine production, close to a military airfield of Oberwiesenfeld, in Munich. For the occasion, a completely new logo for the company was created: a simple two-colour (white and blue) design representing a stylized propeller in motion. The logo was registered on 5 October 1917.

1918. BMW enters the war and becomes a joint-stock company

In May 1918, following the decision of the United States to enter the war, the German military leaders had to stimulate the production of military material, with a particular effort in building aircrafts. The initial contract for the construction of a six-cylinder engine gave BMW a decisive boost, and on 13 August 1918 it was transformed into a joint-stock company, with an initial share capital of 12 million German marks, four million of whose came from Camillo Castiglioni. The technical direction of the company was entrusted to Franz Josef Popp, whose primary mission was to develop the new engines. In this sense, the hiring of engineer **Max Friz**, coming from Daimler in Stuttgart, gave a huge momentum to the Munich design department.

in Europe. He left the scene in April 1942, when he was removed from BMW over a disagreement about orders from the Reich's Ministry of Aviation.

Max Friz

Engineer Max Friz was hired by BMW on 2 January 1917, after working at Rapp as a specialist in aircraft engines. He is regarded as "the father of the first BMW motorcycle", having designed and led to production the celebrated R 32, in 1923. Among his major innovations, Friz designed the carburettor with which BMW established its first world record in 1919. With the production of the R 32 under way, followed shortly thereafter by the creation of other models, in the 1930s Friz mainly focused on building engines for BMW cars. From 1925 to 1937 he was chief designer, and ended

his career in 1945 as director of the Eisenach plant, which built aircraft engines.

1918. The first boxer engine, M 2 B 15

Among the engines developed by BMW in the post-war period, the one that gave the company led by Franz Josef Popp the greatest satisfactions was unquestionably the M 2 B 15 motorcycle engine, the first boxer engine in BMW history. It was created by the 34-year-old engine expert **Martin Stolle** under the supervision of Max Friz. The two had been asked by their boss to develop non-aeronautic engines possibly leading to new business opportunities for BMW, in a time of economic crisis and also of strategic confusion. The M 2 B 15 did its part remarkably well, becoming the forebear of one of the true legends in motorcycle history: the Bayerische Motoren Werke boxer engine.

1919. BMW after the war

Soon after the armistice between France and Germany was signed on 11 November 1918, the German army stopped supporting with contracts BMW, which entered a difficult period culminated in the closing of the factory, until February 1919. The peace agreements stipulated in France included a ban on the aeronautic production in Germany, a decision that could have marked the end of BMW. Therefore Popp looked for new lucrative business outlets, leading the factory to build even small tools, or to manufacture and repair small engines for road and agricultural vehicles. In the end he was forced to stop all engine development in favour of a new project that would allow BMW to survive. Dusting off some old contacts, he then got in touch with the Knorr-Bremse company in Berlin, which commissioned BMW to manufacture 10,000 brake systems per year for the Royal Bavarian State Railways, starting in 1920.

Martin Stolle

Born in Berlin, not only a polished expert but above all an engine enthusiast, Martin Stolle was the man behind the design and realization of the first BMW boxer engine, the celebrated M 2 B 15. Having worked his way up, he had started his own machine shop in Munich, which he closed when the German army called him to service, along with his trusted flat-twin, two-cylinder Douglas 350. He then began working for Bayerische Motoren Werke in autumn 1917. Rewarded by Popp with increasingly important roles, Stolle rapidly embarked on a collision course with his direct superior, Max Friz, who refused to leave him any room for design creativity. Popp's choice not to invest in the development of the M 2 B 15 eventually forced Stolle to leave BMW in January 1922. This did not stop his career, as he continued to develop his own projects as the lead designer at a small company in Munich called Wilhelm Sedlbauer. His perseverance was rewarded soon after, when the manufacturer Victoria of Nuremberg discarded BMW's engine from its KR II to mount it with Stolle's new engine.

1920. Castiglioni saves BMW

While Knorr-Bremse's production order gave BMW some breathing room, at the same time it forced the Bavarian management to transfer ownership to the Berlin company, which had no interest in developing engines. It did allow BMW's production traditions to continue, but only to manufacture brakes. Popp soon understood that the only possible solution to keep alive the company founding mission was to take the majority of the holdings back in the hands of people he trusted: starting from Camillo Castiglioni. And so, at the end of 1921, the Viennese financier bought the BMW name and logo back from Knorr-Bremse. He also obtained the rights to build engines and all the machinery that was not implied in the manufacturing of braking systems. Furthermore, he allowed Popp to transfer his most trusted collaborators, led by Max Friz, to the "new" BMW. Castiglioni then lend over to Knorr-Bremse the plants of Bayerische Flugzeug-Werke, of which he had just become the majority shareholder. Though only a few know this move made by Castiglioni, it had an historical importance, because it saved Bayerische Motoren Werke from becoming an anonymous manufacturer of train brakes.

1921. Victoria KR I lays the groundwork for BMW

Thanks to Popp's unconditional support and in spite of the ongoing disagreements with Max Friz, who did not see it welcome the rapid rise in the company of his former right hand, Stolle developed the boxer engine using his own motorcycle as a prototype for testing. It was an English bike, the same Douglas he had used during the war. In the winter of 1920, BMW began production of about 100 M 2 B 15 engines, bought by a bicycle maker in Nuremberg called Victoria. In 1921, the Victoria KR I was launched on the market and enjoyed a good commercial success. It was the first motorcycle in the world equipped with a BMW engine.

The forerunners of the R 32: the Flink (above) and the Helios (below)

1922. BMW equips the Helios

A new enthusiasm for motorcycles pervaded Germany in the early 1920s, fuelled also by the abolition of restrictions on the import and of the rationing of petrol. It brought about the birth of a single-cylinder motorcycle made by the Bayerische Flugzeug-Werke (in fact, Castiglioni's new BMW). Little more than a motorized bicycle, this light motorcycle was christened "Flink" and reached the market just a few months before a more advanced motorcycle went into production. It was called the Helios and was equipped with a BMW M 2 B 15 engine mounted transversely. This new gamble, the result of Victoria cancelling its orders for BMW engines, drove the company towards its future in the motorcycle business. On 5 June 1922, Castiglioni – the sole shareholder – officially brought BMW back to life after the Knorr-Bremse "hiatus". He re-established the company under the name Bayerische Motoren Werke Aktiengesellschaft.

1923. Max Friz creates the first BMW motorcycle, the R 32

Martin Stolle had started the development of the M 2 B 15 engine in 1921, finishing it while at Wilhelm Sedlbauer. While he managed to mount it on the Victoria KR II, Max Friz did not like the engine design. BMW technical staff delved into a deep analysis of the Helios chassis, but without spurring any ideas to improve it. In the meantime, however, Franz Josef Popp had changed his mind – the convincement that had forced Stolle to resign – realizing that the motorcycle industry had the potential to become an important area of commercial development for BMW. (The numbers would soon confirm his view given that, in the short span from 1922 to 1925, motorcycle circulation in Germany rose from 38,000 to over 162,000 units.) Max Friz began then designing the first motorcycle that would be made entirely by the company. After Victoria terminated its contract, BMW went "full steam ahead", officially

introducing the R 32 at the traditional Berlin Exhibition in 1923. It was an entirely new motorcycle that featured a boxer engine mounted crosswise on a twin-looped tubular frame. The transmission system transferred power to the wheel via a shaft with cardan joint, a construction principle that became a distinctive element of BMW motorcycles.

1923–24. Rudolf Schleicher arrives on the scene and BMW goes sporty with the R 37 and the single-cylinder R 39

In November 1922, **Rudolf Schleicher**, a young engineer with a deep passion for motorcycles and racing, joined BMW's team where he soon replaced Friz (who was busy in creating a new aircraft engine) at the helm of the motorcycle division. Convinced that the real hype for a motorcycle brand would come from victories in racing, Schleicher focused heavily on models designed to compete. On 18 May 1924, his efforts were rewarded when a BMW won its first official race, the Garmisch-Partenkirchen ADAC Winter Rallye. The R 37 was the first motorcycle entirely designed by Schleicher: he endowed the bike with a completely new engine with many sporty features, raced with it personally to win. Again in 1924, Schleicher presented the R 39, a 250cc sports motorcycle that launched BMW's single-cylinder tradition.

Rudolf Schleicher

Born in 1897, a member of the Bavarian Motor Vehicle Company during the First World War, the engineer and skilled rider Rudolf Schleicher was hired by BMW on 1 November 1922, just in time to participate – albeit only partially – in designing the company's first motorcycle, Friz's R 32. In 1924 he designed and built the first light-alloy head for the new R 37, with overhead valves completely enclosed and in an oil bath. A man of action rather than a desk person, Schleicher received his first accolades in his dual role of designer and rider in 1926: on his R 37, he won a gold medal at the International Six Days Trial in Buxton, England, bringing to BMW its first international honour. Schleicher left BMW in April 1927 because of budget cuts to the racing department, but he was urgently called back in August 1931 to give new momentum to the R&D department. He also took the helm of the racing

department, no longer able to win since he had left. It was a motorcycle of his design that won the Senior TT in 1939, as well as the engine design that allowed Henne to break the world record for speed in 1937. Schleicher stayed with BMW until 1942, when he was fired by Fritz Hille, about at the same time as Popp left the company. In 1945, with the BMW plants being dismantled, he bought several machines and started Schleicher GmbH, a small company specializing in repairing engines and manufacturing small spare parts. He then went back to work for BMW AG in the research and development department on 24 October 1956.

The legendary 750 Kompressor of 1929,
winner of the world speed record

1929. The fastest motorcycle in the world is a BMW

Thanks to Schleicher's input, BMW became convinced of the importance of racing as an unrivalled and indispensable advertising strategy. The prestigious motorcycle land-speed record became one of the company's main objectives, despite initial hesitation over the heavy financial investment it required. Thanks to the perseverance of the official rider, Ernst Jakob Henne, Popp understood the reputation BMW would have gained by succeeding in breaking the record, so he commissioned Friz and Hopf to build an ad-hoc motorcycle. The outcome was the phenomenal 750 Kompressor that, after several tests, was eventually taken on the Munich-Ingolstadt State Highway on 19 September 1929 for the "moment of truth". The land-speed record at the time was held by Herbert "Bert" le Vack on a Brough Superior 1000. Despite the 250cc gap, the Friz/Hopf motorcycle proved to be extremely fast, and allowed Henne to reach 216.750 km/h thus breaking the world record for the first time.

1930. The first motorcycles frames made of pressed steel

Until 1929, almost all motorcycles and bicycles in circulation were built with soldered tubes. The Bayerische Motoren Werke then introduced – from 1929 to 1934 – box-type frames made with pieces of torsion resistant pressed steel, connected by riveting and welding. These frames successfully equipped the new 750s, the R 11 and the R 16.

1931. The "people's bike"

The economic crisis that had gripped Germany as well as most of the developed world, due to the long period of post-war reconstruction and to the Wall Street crash of 1929, stimulated the BMW management to build motorcycles intended for everyday use and, above all, intended for social classes that could not afford the extraordinary, but expensive, 750cc. Moreover, in Germany motorcycles up to 200cc were tax exempted and did not require

Ernst Jakob Henne

BMW's official rider until 1926, and German champion in the 500cc class (1926) and 750cc class (1927), Ernst Jakob Henne tightly bond his name to the Munich brand. Both a rider and a dealer for BMW cars and motorcycles, Henne was able to beat the world record for motorcycle speed several times between 1929 and 1937, the year he reached the astonishing speed of 279.5 km/h with the streamliner designed by Schleicher. A true lover of challenges and champion of the development of new

vehicles through competitions, Henne took on four-wheel challenges as well and in 1936 he won the ADAC Eifelrennen at the Nürburgring complex, with a BMW 328, in the two-litre class. His courage and desire to exceed any limit are remembered to date. Among the major trophies Henne won throughout his racing career, he garnered the Targa Florio in 1928, at a record average speed.

Top, the R 2, the famous "people's bike";
right, the R 4

a driving license to be ridden. In this climate the R 2 was created; it became known as "people's bike", under the watchful eye of designer **Alfred Böning**. It was the first BMW in history to have in its name a reference to the engine displacement. It cost half the price of a two-cylinder motorcycle, but it maintained the same standard of quality. And the Germans immediately responded with enthusiasm to this new bike.

1933. BMW gears higher

On the wave of the R 2's success, which enjoyed the favour of the public and expanded the customer base for the Bayerische Motoren Werke, a new version of the 200cc motorcycle was released, based on a 400cc engine. It was indeed the R 4, a motorcycle that, after the first 100 produced units, was improved on with an unprecedented four gear transmission: one more than the usual three. It was an effective and winning solution that would become standard on all BMW motorcycles until 1973, when the five-geared R 90 S and the R 90/6 were released.

Alfred Böning

Born in Salerno, Italy, Alfred Böning started working at BMW at the end of 1930 at the age of 23. His first important task as a mechanical engineer came just a few days after his official start date: to develop the R 2, a strategic model in a phase of serious economic crisis. Later, thanks to his expertise in chassis and gearboxes, Böning made fundamental contributions (as director of the R&D department) to the R 12, the R 5 and the R 75 military motorcycle, as well as the flagship model, the R 7, which remained however a fantastic prototype. In 1943, Böning left the motorcycle development when the top management put him in charge of the aircraft engine production. He then returned to motorcycle design in May 1945, when the then-director Donath asked him to build the first post-war motorcycle, the R 24. He thereafter concentrated on the design of the BMW 501, giving the brand its signature features, which remained with it for years. Böning left BMW in October 1972 and retired two years later.

1935. BMW "invents" the telescopic fork

The year 1935 marked a watershed in the history of BMW and of motorcycle technology in general. Already in 1933 the Bavarian designers had begun focusing on the development of novel shock absorbers and suspension systems, in connection with research done on the celebrated R 7 flagship model, which unfortunately remained a prototype due to its high production costs and the lack of rigidity of the frame. Such new systems were developed to make the ride more comfortable, less dangerous on uneven roads and to ensure perfect adherence to the tarmac, thus offering better handling and greater safety. This work led to the first telescopic fork with hydraulic shock absorbers in the world, which debuted on the R 12 and the R 17. In the same year, Rudolf Schleicher introduced the new 500cc Kompressor on Berlin's AVUS racetrack, based on his previous experience with the 1929 record-breaking 750 Kompressor. It was a motorcycle that would finally be able to compete with English and Italian brands on every track in Europe.

1936. The return of the tubular frame and the debut of the foot-operated gear shift

On 15 February 1936, one of the main motorcycle attractions at the International Automobile and Motorcycle Exhibition in Berlin was the new R 5 sports model. It was built by the R&D department team headed by Alfred Böning. One of its most important innovations was the foot-operated gear shift (which replaced the traditional hand gear shift), a first for BMW, along with the return of the tubular frame. It only seemed to be a step back in comparison with the pressed steel frame, given that the technological evolution had made it possible to build extremely reliable and durable tubular frames, thanks to the new Arc-atom electrical welding which guaranteed a high level of resistance of the conical oval tubes of the chassis, welded in elliptical sections. This same frame was used for the R 5's big sister, the R 6.

1937. The BMW "bullet" breaks the world record

Thanks to a spectacular streamliner equipped with a 500cc engine, a full fairing and a Zoller compressor, Ernst Jakob Henne set the world record for motorcycle land speed at 279.503 km/h on the Frankfurt–Darmstadt highway. The record had previously been held by Piero Taruffi who had reached 274.181 km/h on the Italian, four-cylinder, Gilera Rondine. Henne's record was a legendary one, that lasted more than a decade and brought great fame to BMW, once again the "world's fastest motorcycle".

1938. BMW motorcycle no. 100,000 and the debut of rear suspension

On 24 November 1938, motorcycle no. 100,000 left the BMW plant. It was a historic achievement for the German brand, which had no intention of resting on its laurels but strived to advance in technology through several research studies, especially due at the time to the influence of **Alexander von Falkenhausen**. In his double role of rider and engineer, he had been directly inspired by Schleicher. One of his studies led to the development and debut of a new upright rear suspension (with telescopic tubes) for the R 61, resembling the front telescopic suspension. It was a solution that would provide the bike with better adherence to the road surface and consequently a greater safety. But 1938 was also the last year when a side valve engine was mounted by a BMW, namely the R 71. This engine was later retired to make way for the modern, overhead valve engine of the R 51.

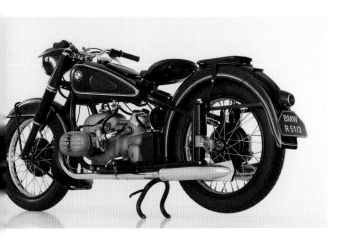

Alexander von Falkenhausen

Born in Munich, Baron Alexander von Falkenhausen joined the technical staff led by Schleicher in May 1934. He immediately focused on the design of new motorcycle models, while still making quick appearances at races, even on four wheels. When Böning was promoted in 1936, von Falkenhausen was put in charge of the "chassis and transmission" department. It was a position that allowed him to stimulate the development of BMW motorcycles towards a better comfort and a greater safety. It was this young engineer who designed the rear upright suspension for the R 61. After the Second World War, he temporarily left his post at BMW to start AFM (acronym for Alexander von Falkenhausen Munich), a small company that successfully competed in Formula 2 races culminating with the German championship title in the 1500cc category in 1948. He then joined the technical staff at BMW again in 1954 and was tasked with developing a new engine to replace the one of the R 69 S: the engine for the forthcoming "/5" series.

1939. BMW wins the Senior Tourist Trophy

If there ever was a race in Europe and the world that every rider and every brand wanted to win, it was the incredible Senior Tourist Trophy on the Isle of Man. An elimination race in the truest sense of the word, with one of the highest numbers of fatal accidents in history; a gruelling race for men and bikes, and therefore a main objective of BMW, which still vaunted Henne's 1937 fabulous world record and enjoyed the publicity that had ensued. Thus, Rudolf Schleicher further improved his racing masterpiece, the unrivalled 500 Kompressor that, following the victories at the 1938 European Championships, was entrusted to the official rider Georg "Schorsch" Meier for the 1939 Senior Tourist Trophy. Until then, no foreigner rider on a non-British motorcycle had been able to win this race. But the Kompressor's perfect synthesis between engine and chassis, combined with Meier's skills, did succeed in triumphing at the Senior TT, the "most famous race in the world".

1941. BMW enters the war

Beginning in 1933, the German government had ordered the rearming, part of which should be covered by military motorcycles with light engines and a sidecar. Later on, in November 1937, the Army published the basic requirements and specifications for each model intended for military use (the most important features were a gearbox with reverse gear, sidecar with lockable differential, and a hydraulic brake acting jointly on the rear wheel of the bike and on the sidecar). After some months of testing (partially conducted on the road by von Falkenhausen himself), the Army Armament Office finally approved and ordered a model that would later become an important protagonist of the war: the R 75. The huge success on field of the 750 with a sidecar forced BMW in 1941 to suspend civilian motorcycle production in favour of the Wehrmacht line.

Georg "Schorsch" Meier

Georg "Schorsch" Meier was born in 1910. A former police officer and off-road champion, he debuted on a BMW racing bike on 24 April 1938, winning his very first race. Meier's career continued with many other achievements. His 1939 win of the legendary Tourist Trophy on a BMW Kompressor 500 was the most famous, for he made history as the first foreign rider since 1907 to win the half-litre race. After the Second World War, Meier won several other trophies, always on BMW motorcycles.

In the early 1960s, Schorsch Meier designed the distinctive sports seat fitted on Bayerische Motoren Werke's new high-performance motorcycle, the R 69 S.

1945. It looks like the end for BMW

In October 1945, the US Army dismantled the BMW plants in Munich (reopened in 1949) and Allach (reopened even later, in 1955). As was the case with Popp at the end of the First World War, the new plant director, Kurt Donath found himself in a very difficult situation, as he needed to find a way to save BMW from what seemed to be a sure demise. He was hired as a consultant for overseeing the dismantling of the machinery installed in the two plants and for sending them around the world, to be used as spare parts for repairs in the war aftermath. It was a tough blow for BMW, which lost any power over its own assets. The end of the prestigious Munich manufacturer seemed inevitable. But thanks to Donath and several loyalists, the glimmer of hope did not die out: even overstepping the legal bounds, the former director managed to hide many pieces that would be essential to the recovery of BMW's business activities.

1948. BMW's rebirth has the signature R 24

In the spring of 1946, BMW was saved from bankruptcy (the Americans had put Bayerische Motoren Werke at the top of the list of German materiel plants, freezing the company operations in all its factories across Europe) thanks to the actions of the Deutsche Bank trustee directors. They managed to release the company assets that had been sequestered after the war. After collecting parts scattered among former dealers, hidden when the plants were dismantled or found in warehouses in Eastern Europe and even in abandoned mines, Donath asked the then independent Böning to develop a new model, the R 10. With a 120cc engine, it was the first BMW motorcycle to be built after the end of the war. Unfortunately, just like the R 7 from 1933, it remained a prototype. It would not be until 17 December 1948, the day the first R 24 was mounted, that the production re-launch of BMW could be celebrated.

Kurt Donath

There have been many people in the history of BMW who are not well known to BMW enthusiasts, but were of vital importance for Bayerische Motoren Werke. Berliner Kurt Donath is one of them. As the plant director, he was responsible for the survival of the Munich brand after the Second World War. A skilled strategist and a practical man, he was the beacon of hope giving BMW a direction in its darkest years: from agricultural vehicle repair to the manufacture of building equipment, mixers and aluminium cookware. It was also Donath's idea to gamble on the capacity limits imposed by the Allies after the war, preferring 250cc engines to those of inferior displacement. During his managerial career, Donath also greatly supported BMW's competition sports activities, until at least February 1957, when he retired and left the chair to the jurist Heinrich Richter-Brohm.

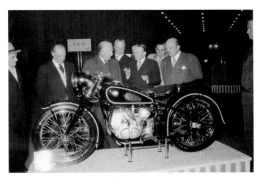

1950. The boxer makes a comeback

The limits imposed by the Allies on the 250cc cylinder capacity were finally dropped and at the beginning of 1950, the boxer BMWs were eventually back on the market. The new two-cylinder bike was called the R 51/2 and it was immediately christened "the best BMW of all time" by the motorcycle press. From 1951 on, it was followed by the R 51/3 and the 600cc series named R 67 (with the /2 and /3 variants), fitted with newly designed engines. On 29 November 1950, motorcycle no. 25,000 produced after the war was celebrated in the BMW plants: it was an R 51/2. For the occasion, an R25 was given away to one of the employees in a drawing.

1952. "The first 100 mph motorcycle"

Because of the commercial success of the R 51/3 and of the R67, BMW became convinced of the interest of launching a model that combined proven German reliability with their racers performance. Moreover, the racing team's wins on the tracks all over the world, led by the irresistible **Walter Zeller**, had to find their way into production as well. In the summer of 1952, the celebrated R 68 was released (only 1,452 were produced). It was the first mass-produced motorcycle to exceed 160 km/h (top speeds were recorded of over 164 km/h) and it made history as "the first 100 mph motorcycle". It was a record-breaking bike also because of its price tag: the list price was 3,950 marks, exactly double the list price of a Triumph 650. Even today, the R 68 is the most sought-after bike by collectors.

1953. BMW's best-selling motorcycle of all time

In October 1953, the updated version of the single-cylinder R 25/2 made its debut at the Frankfurt Motor Show and was christened R 25/3. With a production figure of 47,700 pieces until 1956, the R 25/3 became BMW's most built and sold motorcycle in history. It was so popular with the enthusiasts that it had to remain available even after the new single-cylinder R 26 was introduced. And to think that the company had originally intended to retire it!

Walter Zeller

Born in Ebersberg, near Munich, and active on the BMW racing team from the onset of the 1940s, Walter Zeller was one of BMW most famous riders along with Ernst Jakob Henne and Georg "Schorsch" Meier. German champion in the half-litre class in 1951, 1954 and 1955, second in the world championship to the legendary John Surtees in 1956 only by bad luck, Zeller triumphed across Europe until 1957, when he retired for family reasons (he took over his father's company). On 30 August 1952, he established the world record for land speed at the Grenzland Ring, when he clocked an amazing 290.2 km/h. To understand the importance of Zeller to Bayerische Motoren Werke's racing department, we can simply point to the "parting gift" his mechanics prepared for him: a "dream motorcycle" made by combining the 500 RS chassis with a compressor engine from the 600 sidecar. In other words – the first and only road Kompressor.

The BMW Isetta, a true revolution – and
not just in the automotive world

1955. BMW is seduced by the very Italian Isetta

On 5 March 1955, BMW presented to the press a revolutionary vehicle:
a crossbreed between a car and a motorcycle. It was the BMW Isetta, the
outcome of a partnership between the German manufacturer and Iso, a small
Italian company born in Bolzaneto, near Genoa, and later based in Bresso
(Milan), headed at the time by engineer Renzo Rivolta with great innovative
spirit. Launched the previous year at the automobile show in Geneva, the
Isetta was noticed there by C. A. Drenowatz, the BMW importer for
Switzerland, who talked about this vehicle to the top management in Munich,
garnering their interest. The German firm then dubbed the Isetta the "BMW
250" and produced it until 1962. In the nine years it was on the market,
it became the most widely sold single-cylinder vehicle in the world, with sales
of nearly 162,000.

1955. More comfort with the new Earles front fork

Although 1954 was the year of the first major drop in sales, BMW's top
management chose to foster a comeback, wagering everything on the
production of new two-cylinder models. The hope was to attract a growing
number of new buyers, winning over British brands thanks to technical
innovations. So the R 50, R 60 and R 69 were released, three models
that generated a wide interest thanks to the new frame equipped with a
Earles-type front swing arm and a long arm rear suspension. These solutions,
particularly the controversial Earles fork (unappealing to aesthetes because
of its imposing appearance), endowed the BMW motorcycles with
unprecedented stability.

1960. The last single-cylinder BMW

In September 1960, BMW introduced the R 27, an upgraded version of the
R26. Produced for six years, it made history as the last chapter in BMW's
glorious single-cylinder adventure. It is not a well-known tradition, especially
among youngsters; nevertheless, it allowed the company to survive until the
1970s thanks to the production of 228,875 units divided into 13 models, the
forerunner of whose was the R 39 of 1925.

1960. R 69 S, BMW's most powerful and prestigious machine

The persisting sales slump did not stop BMW from introducing two new, extremely sporty models at the Frankfurt IFMA of 1960. We're talking about the R 50 S and the R 69 S, the latter intended to conquer the American market. Each bike met a different fate: while the R 50 S was produced for only two years in just 1,634 pieces, the R 69 S remained on the market for a decade, establishing itself as a bike catering to a wealthy niche market. It was only for those that could afford the hefty price tag of 4,030 marks (a price unmatched on the market if we exclude the MV Agusta top four-cylinder model) and it was truly a "dream motorcycle". In fact, "dream motorcycle" was the nickname coined for the one-of-a-kind bike given to Walter Zeller by his racing squad mechanics in 1957, but the two motorcycles had a lot in common, from character to exclusivity. The press defined it "the most prestigious and powerful machine in the history of BMW".

1962. BMW sinks to its lowest point

While in 1954 the company produced 29,699 motorcycles, in 1962 the BMW output was limited to 4,302 only: an all-time low. This crisis almost led BMW to close its motorcycle division; however, it was saved by the intervention and perseverance of the (former) specialized journalist **Helmut Werner Bönsch**. In 1958 he was tapped to take over the reins of the division, and under his direction, BMW returned to five-figure production in 1970, when the motorcycle plants were transferred to Berlin-Spandau to cope with manufacturing the new "/5" series, produced in 12,287 units that year.

Helmut Werner Bönsch

A journalist and motorcycle enthusiast, Helmut Werner Bönsch helped to sell a large portion of the R 24 motorcycles thanks to a famous test article published in a 1949 issue of *Das Auto*. A contributor to the prestigious *Das Motorrad* magazine and a consummate professional for his entire career as a tester, also for the German Bicycle and Motorcycle Industry Association, Bönsch joined Bayerische Motoren Werke in the middle of 1958. He was called to Munich to take over as the director in charge of product planning, quality monitoring and marketing: an innovative position for an innovative man who led the company through a difficult time, introducing the R 50 S and the R 69 S sports models. He also admirably managed the raise of the motorcycle department, thanks to the "/5" series, which he championed from the beginning.

1969. BMW's comeback is fuelled by the "/5" series... sans sidecar!

First in autumn 1964, and then in August 1967, the motorcycle magazines published some photos of a BMW that was completely different from any previous Bavarian model. Initially developed using the R 69 S engine, this new bike was targeting to compete with English motorcycle brands. Engineer von der Marwitz clearly stated that he aimed to produce "a BMW that must ride like a Norton Manx". On 28 August 1969, Bönsch introduced the new "/5" series to journalists from all over the world whom he invited for the occasion at Hockenheim. He presented the first BMW 750cc since 1944 (the year the military R 75 was produced), the celebrated R 75/5, crucial to BMW success also on the American market, as well as the 500cc R 50/5 and the 600cc R 60/5. Sales started to take off again, which allowed BMW to emerge from the crisis once and for all.

1973. 500,000 BMW motorcycles, five-speed transmission and the first standard fairing

On 25 July 1973, fifty years after the birth of the first BMW, Friz's R 32, bike no. 500,000 left the assembly line of Bayerische Motoren Werke's Berlin-Spandau plant. At the same time, to meet the new market demands, the 750cc barrier was broken with the new R 90 S and the R 90/6, endowed with an unsurpassed 900cc engine. Several important new features were also added, such as the unprecedented five-speed transmission, a double-disc front brake and, for the first time ever, a cockpit fairing mounted as standard.

1976. The one-litre class

While in 1973 the 750cc capacity was reached, in 1976 it was the turn of the extremely powerful R 100/7, R 100 S and R 100 RS to amaze the market with their 1000cc engines that could reach well above 70 HP. In addition, the R 100 RS hit the world market as the first sports touring bike with a full fairing. Thanks to these models, in 1977 the BMW plants were able to exceed 30,000 models produced: 31,515 units.

Hans-Günther von der Marwitz

Hans-Günther von der Marwitz was hired by BMW in 1964 as an expert engine designer. With years of experience in companies like Porsche under his belt, engineer von der Marwitz linked his name to the "/5" series revolution, which he managed since the very beginning in his capacity as head of the design department. The decision to "free" the BMW motorcycle from the sidecar attachment made history: a choice that materialized with the "/5" series. He was also the one who promoted the new high-performance BMWs, first with the never-released R 90/5 and then with the legendary R 90 S. He left BMW in 1978 and was replaced by Richard Heydenreich.

Top, the first prototype of the R 80 G/S; above, the first official picture of the maxi enduro; right, Hubert Auriol with Fenouil and Neimer, stars of the 1981 Paris–Dakar

1980. BMW's first enduro race

There had never been a call to mass-produce off-road bikes at BMW. The bikes that were built for enduro races were always competition prototypes or test-bikes created to assess new features. But in 1980, with the world debut of the R 80 G/S, BMW invented a brand-new segment of the market: the big displacement off-road bikes that could be used away from the asphalt but were also great for long trips on road. The R 80 G/S, the first maxi-enduro in the world, stirred much interest because of its several unique technical elements, such as the single-sided swing arm of the rear wheel, the renowned BMW Monolever.

1981. The R 80 G/S wins the Paris–Dakar Rally and makes history

One year after the official launch of the R 80 G/S, BMW intertwined its history to the prestigious as well as backbreaking Paris–Dakar Rally, the toughest race in the world. In 1981 the Frenchman rider **Hubert Auriol** won the African marathon in the seat of an R 80 G/S prepared and enhanced by the German specialist HPN. It was only two years after BMW's first

participation in the famous race invented by Thierry Sabine, and this endeavour echoed across the world, marking an important part of BMW's history and offering "African dreams" to the owners of the innovative – and now winning – R 80 G/S.

Hubert Auriol

Born in Addis Ababa on 7 June 1952, Hubert Auriol moved almost immediately to France. He was one of the great stars in the African marathon races – particularly in the Paris–Dakar Rally – for over twenty years. Auriol's career in motorcycling set out in the early 1970s. He was especially active in motocross racing, which he left after many wins to follow his dream of winning the legendary race through the African desert, earning himself the nickname

"l'Africain". Auriol made his debut on the African terrain on the occasion of the 1979 Paris–Dakar Rally, and was soon able to win it twice (in 1981 and 1983), both times in the seat of a BMW. In 1985, he finished remarkably second on the outsider Cagiva, while in 1987 he was forced to a painful withdrawal at the start of the last leg while in the lead as he fractured both ankles. In 1988, Auriol moved from two to four wheels, first on a buggy and then shifting definitively

to cars in the following years. He won this category in 1992 with a Mitsubishi, becoming the first man to win on both a motorcycle and a car. Enamoured with the African races, Auriol created and organized new challenges, like the Heroes Legend (2007), an endurance race for historic bikes, and the Africa Race (2008).

1983. The new K series makes its debut with the revolutionary in-line flat engine

The front boxer engine has been a trademark feature of the BMW motorcycle for over sixty years. But in 1983, a new chapter began in BMW's history with the debut of the K series. It was a true revolution, in terms of technology and of looks. The layout of the cylinders was unprecedented: they were in line, but placed longitudinally to the motorcycle and laid on one side, in a horizontal position. This design choice marked the advent of the "in-line flat engine". The project came from the new R&D department intensely supported by Eberhardt C. Sarfert, the brisk and daring president of the BMW Motorrad GmbH group starting in 1979. The new engine was specifically developed by the engineer Joseph Fritzenwenger, who had already proposed it two years before, having taken the idea from the Briton Val Page. The latter had experimented it back in the 1930s for the English manufacturer Ariel, never taking it to production anyway; the top model of the new series, the K 100, was instead an immediate success and earned its place in the history of the motorcycle industry as the first mass-produced motorcycle to have electronic fuel injection.

1985. BMW manufactures and launches its first three-cylinder motorcycle on the market

Sixty-two years after the debut of the first BMW engine, the two-cylinder M 2 B 15 that equipped the R 32, the company introduced another first: a more affordable version of the K series, the K 75, which featured a three-cylinder engine, a configuration never seen before in the history of Bayerische Motoren Werke. The new model had many characteristics in common with its big sister, but was valued for its particularly low fuel consumption and surprising agility that did not compromise performance: the S version exceeded 210 km/h.

1987. The G/S gets bigger and loses the "slash"

After making some minor changes to the R 80 G/S series, BMW launched a genuine second series for the lucky and legendary enduro. The R 100 GS, without the previously used slash in its name, was released. The new Paralever rear suspension, an unprecedented parallelogram-type swing arm, with floating bevel gears that prevented "shaft jacking" in acceleration and release was by far the most important innovation, but the aerodynamic windscreen and the increased cylinder capacity were substantial improvements as well.

1988. ABS and the futuristic K 1

To forge ahead through innovation in motorcycles, equipment and design: BMW prepared for the transition into the 1990s with great care and the drive to innovate. It is in this context that some products absolutely brand new to the international motorcycle scene were introduced: the anti-lock braking system (ABS) and the astonishing K 1, which shocked the visitors at the 1988 IFMA. In addition to major engine features (including the four valves per cylinder, which brought along up to 100 HP and a top speed of almost 240 km/h), the K 1 was especially noted for the amazing aerodynamic efficiency of its integral fairing. Notably, the fairing even covered part of the front wheel.

1991. BMW produces its first "over 1000cc" and delivers its one-millionth motorcycle

In 1991, together with the 16-valve engine, BMW launched a super-tourer flagship model, the K 1100 LT. In addition to becoming the first motorcycle with over one litre engine (fifteen years after the first 1000 was released), it was the first of all the models in the line to show in full the capacity in its name. The same would subsequently be done for all forthcoming BMW models. With its radio, cassette player, ABS and assisted windscreen, the K 1100 LT was coveted by all long-range touring bikers. Again in 1991, the one-millionth BMW motorcycle left the company plant. It was a K 75 RT that was solemnly handed over to a representative of the German Ministry of Commerce and Technology, and later on used to raise money for the Red Cross.

1993. BMW brings back the single-cylinder thanks to the "Funduro"

Next to the launches of the new K series and of the R 1100 RS, BMW's biggest novelty of the 1990s was the F series, initially represented by the F650. A 360-degree enduro motorcycle, it was a return to BMW's past, given that the company had not developed and produced a single-cylinder engine since 1966. For this new run, BMW enlisted Italy's Aprilia (for the assembly) and the Austrian Rotax (for the engines).

1996. The latest two-valve boxer and the K 75 concludes its run

19 December 1996: a historic day for the Bayerische Motoren Werke. In the Berlin motorcycle plant, the last BMW bike with a two-valve-per-cylinder boxer engine was produced. It was an R 80 GS basic and it was the end of an important part in German motorcycle history, with almost 700,000 bikes produced from 1923 to 1996. In that very year, also the three cylinder K 75 production ended, after eleven seasons. It was a successful bike at 68,000 units sold and it is sought after by a number of collectors.

1997. A German "Easy Rider" with the R 1200 C

Straight from the Arizona State Highway, BMW introduced its first Cruiser in 1997. It was a really "German" interpretation and an up to date version of all the custom features favoured by the American public. The R 1200 C, which became an icon also thanks to a famous James Bond film, proved to be an impressive machine with innovative technology (digital engine electronics, ABS, Telelever) as well as an attractive shape and overall design, with plenty of chrome and "muscles".

1998. The R 1100 S becomes the dream motorcycle for BMW racing bike enthusiasts

Thanks to record figures (98 HP, the most powerful boxer of all time), the clever use of innovative materials (such as carbon fibre in fenders and magnesium in the head covers), and a novel and ergonomic shape, the R 1100 S ushered in the era of the "sports-tourer", motorcycles at ease on a track but also able to travel for many miles in total comfort.

1999. The century ends with a new record

The twentieth century closes with a new record for BMW: 65,186 motorcycles produced and delivered to Bayerische Motoren Werke clients all over the world. It is a success fuelled by new, interest-generating, innovative models like the maxi-touring R 1200 LT (weighing over 380 kg).

2000. "Small" BMW bikes enjoy the winners' circle at the first Dakar Rally that did not finish in Senegal and the launch of the C, the first BMW "scooter"

The first desert marathon of the new millennium started in Paris, in accordance with tradition, but ended in Cairo instead of the Senegalese beaches of Dakar. Four of the six BMW bikes lined up in Paris got the first places in the motorcycle category. Richard Sainct won with an F 650 RR for the second time in two years. And again in 2000, BMW launched its new city concept, an innovative scooter equipped with a roof, seatbelt, ABS and electronic engine management. We're talking about the revolutionary C1.

BMW 1923–2000

Buying a vintage motorcycle

You can step into the world of vintage collections in many ways. This is well known and probably the most fascinating and intriguing aspect. A relative gives you an old motorcycle he used when he was young; or a friend asks you to accompany him to some fair. And there you have it: you are captured. Or else your car dealer displays a beautiful 1950s or 1960s BMW and the minute you set your eyes on it you realize you cannot live without it.

A new world opens up to you; a new world that you must explore with a basic knowledge that will protect you from falling into avoidable mistakes. After all, not everyone has the technical background or the experience to tell at a glance whether a motorcycle is worth the expense or not. To be honest, we should say that there are no precise rules that can assure the perfectly safe buy. But one thing is certain: with a few simple tips the novice collector can step into this world with a little more ease. The next pages will not be about "commandments", but rather about useful guidelines you can follow while building up some experience. It is up to every would-be collector to follow them correctly and above all to understand whether the motorcycle is worth the price, also considering how much he or she wants that specific model.

What kind of collection do I want?

The first point to assess is what kind of collection you want to embark on. The significant money investment and the difficulty in finding the models require you to define the objective of your passion. The first important distinction is based on how you intend to use the motorcycle: if the aim of your collection is to ride the motorcycles, then the 1920s models probably won't be your choice. However, if your main objective is aesthetics, then the most exquisite and aristocratic models are

precisely those produced before the Second World War: this road will lead you to a high-end collection requiring lots of in-depth study, great finances and perseverance in the search for models on an international basis. Other collection themes can be defined by period (before-the-war, 1950s and 1960s, 1970s and 1980s), by model (overhead or side valve engines, Earles fork, leaf spring motorcycles, etc.), or by engine typology (single-cylinder, V-twin, 750cc, 1 litre, 500cc, etc.). But to start with, the easiest option will be to choose a model that for its aesthetics, value and general chemistry, attracts you the most.

Where to buy a motorcycle

Once you have identified the model you want to add to your collection, all you have to do is find it. In this respect, the Internet allows the matching of demand and offer beyond geographical boundaries. Nowadays, provided you are dealing with reliable contacts, the Internet gives you the opportunity to find and evaluate online the most interesting motorcycles, negotiate via phone or e-mail, and make your purchase with a simple bank transfer. But all this technology might dishearten those of you who are not at ease with these means, and in fact collectors often prefer to meet personally during exhibitions (such as those put up in Europe by Veterama, www.veterama.de)

Motorcycle auctions, such as the ones organized by Bonhams, offer excellent buying opportunities

Preserved or restored? Choosing a motorcycle is a very subjective matter

or to go to the ever more frequent auctions (such as those organized by the auction house Bonhams, www.bonhams.com). On these occasions, you can actually see and touch the motorcycle, evaluate the price and judge the reliability and the seriousness of the seller. A third possibility, generally the one chosen by novice collectors, is to rely on professionals who will guide you in the selection and the purchase of a motorcycle: "vintage motorcycle dealers" who combine their daily contemporary motorcycle business with vintage vehicles. A last option would be looking up insertions in specialized magazines or in classified advertisement newspapers. Today most of the paper magazines dedicated to motorcycles or trading in general feature a vintage motorcycle section. Sometimes the best deals are hidden in the few lines of a short insertion.

Choosing a motorcycle

An important factor to consider while choosing the model you want to buy is to assess the motorcycle's conditions in relation to your expectations. If you have no manual skills, if you have little time to dedicate to your passion or if your motoring expertise is limited, but nonetheless you want a spotless vehicle, we suggest going for a restored motorcycle. A restored motorcycle will cost more than a vehicle that is not in mint conditions but will avoid you a long series of touch-ups and checks to verify the originality of all its components.

Otherwise, if you think you can handle the restoration yourself, you need to be already in contact with the professional restorer who will take care of the motorcycle you have chosen. To look for one after having bought the motorcycle might lead to unpleasant surprises. A different case would be that of collectors who are prepared to turn a blind eye to certain aesthetic imperfections of the motorcycle in favour of the vehicle's history. In this case the choice will fall on a preserved motorcycle, always remaining in the range of a generally sufficient state of conservation, with no major signs of accidents or deterioration (rust spots in particular). The last important aspect to consider is the number of owners the motorcycle has had, which can be a generally reliable indicator of the level of care and use the vehicle has experienced during its lifetime. On the other hand, the number of kilometres the motorcycle has accumulated is not a crucial point while evaluating the purchase. This is because in the past, even more than today, the BMW motorcycles assured very high levels of mechanical longevity. Sometimes, even in cases of motorcycles that do not start, all you need is a small touch-up to have the vehicle back on track.

Preservation rules

When you decide to preserve your motorcycle you need to follow some rules that admit no exceptions: no small paint or plating touch-ups, no special protective transparent varnish coatings, no replacement of worn out pieces with other original but new components. The only admitted interventions are an accurate cleaning of the bodywork and of the mechanical components, removal of the rust patina with a careful oil cleanse, and minor interventions on the

Small imperfections are admissible on a preserved motorcycle

engine for a correct tune-up. Mechanical components should be replaced only with original parts, while every substitution of components subject to natural wear (such as brakes and tyres) must follow the preservation rules.

When restoration is necessary

A preserved motorcycle has undoubtedly a unique charm; we can almost breathe in its history while riding it. But there is a limit you cannot trespass, that is the irreversible wear of the components. A perfectly preserved motorcycle is a vehicle with all components in a state of usage that corresponds to its age, but that must allow the motorcycle to function correctly. A well-conserved motorcycle might have rust bubbles in its fuel tank or an exhaust taken from a different series or even from a different model. In these cases, restoration is necessary. The originality of a motorcycle is a concept regarding the bike as a whole, in all its components. If only one of these is not original then it must be replaced, because originality is not just a starting point but also a goal. This does not apply to the classic "signs of aging", such as minor dents, some opacity in the paintwork, or worn out grips or saddle. Those are the signs of the motorcycle's life and if you choose the road of conservation, you must be willing to turn a blind eye to these small imperfections, which bear witness to the originality of the piece.

The BMW Museum in Munich

Is there a way, other than reading books, to see all the motorcycles the Bayerische Motoren Werke produced over the years, to appreciate their beauty, and maybe to decide if that very model will be the next acquisition for your collection? Yes, there is: it is the BMW Museum. A sort of Disneyland for all you BMW bikers and lovers. Located on the edge of the Munich Olympic Park, the BMW Museum opened in 1973 and features a striking cup-shaped architecture that has become a symbol of the city's skyline. Thanks to the recent connection of the Museum to the adjacent flat roof building home to the BMW headquarters (the so-called Four Cylinder) the exposition area now covers 5,000

square metres, fully occupied by the history and the models that have made BMW famous all over the world. The BMW Museum takes you on a one-hundred-year journey from the first motorcycle, the R 32, to the legendary BMW 507 and 2002 models, including the Isetta micro-car, up to the recent days. The collection includes over 150 models in perfect conditions, and it is easy to get lost among such a variety of prototypes, production cars and motorcycles, and even the original models of the very cars and bikes that marked the history of the Bavarian company: the epic "no. 101" with which Gaston Rahier won the Paris–Dakar, the 1937 World Record "missile" driven by Henne, the Kompressor

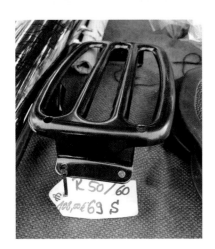

Economic evaluation of the restoration

Often you find yourself in front of a motorcycle you have long been looking for, but that appears to be in very bad conditions or clearly "out of order", with some pieces taken from other models. The price however is interesting, even inviting... but is it worth it? A most pertinent question, because what may appear as a good deal may transform itself into a boomerang leading to hard-to-find and extremely expensive repair parts and record price bodywork restoration interventions. So, before buying the motorcycle you must evaluate how much it will cost you to bring it back to its original state.

The missing parts can be found at small fairs and markets – here the cost range may vary, but it is generally medium-low; another option would be to go through the BMW Mobile Tradition division (for models from the R25/2 onwards), where the prices are generally medium-high. Or else, in case the pieces are not available from the producers, they will have to be reconstructed. In this case costs may vary, but they will surely be pretty high. Here are some practical tips: if the price asked for the motorcycle is 30 to 40% inferior to the lowest end of the price range indicated in our data sheets in the *Purchase guide*, even adding the cost for the single original components and the restoration, the final cost will surely fall within the price range we indicate, and your purchase will be in line with the market (setting aside the possibility of a hopeless absence of repair pieces, another rate included in the data sheet, in the *Spare parts availability* section). Instead, if the cost of the motorcycle falls within the price range, then the closer the price to the top, the fewer interventions should be required.

The motorcycle registration and papers

Buying a motorcycle with no papers does not mean buying a less valuable motorcycle. On the contrary. Very often the older models, the "flat tanks" for

500 that "Schorsch" Meier took to the first place at the Senior Tourist Trophy in 1939 and much else. During a visit to the Museum, you are led through the collection with a ramp-system connecting the 25 exhibition sections, distributed across 7 thematic areas. This system introduces visitors to the in-depth appreciation of a theme from a variety of angles. A central path guides you across space and time, while pointing out the various single exhibits. Visitors are free to enter the single rooms in whatever order they prefer, and can decide their own personal route through the Museum.

example, have no papers at all. But it is a fact that papers in order will save you from all the lengthy and fairly costly bureaucratic procedures to obtain a new registration number. Once you have checked the papers you need to compare the engine number and the bodywork number with those in the log book in order to verify the exact correspondence and thus the motorcycle's originality. This is because in the past, if there were no original repair pieces at hand, parts from similar but not identical motorcycles were used. This is particularly true for motorcycles produced soon before and shortly after the Second World War and especially for those coming from Eastern Europe (an exceptional treasure house of BMW motorcycles, currently still a point of reference for the importation of models dating before the 1960s). The same engine series might have been mounted on different models so that the progressive numeration of the engine does not always correspond to that on the bodywork.

Originality of the components

We have already discussed the subject of the originality of the mechanical and structural parts of the motorcycle. But to be "perfectly original", a vehicle must comply with some more criteria, ranging from the painting to the exhaust, from the saddle to the suspensions, from the brakes to the handlebar. And the list could go on and on. Even if nowadays a great deal of reference material on vintage BMWs is available, we must consider that the models advertised in magazines or catalogues of the time were not always true to the originals. In fact, in the past the manufacturers could often modify the features of the models without changing the photographs that were used for advertisement. Not to mention the fact that many parts subject to wear might have been replaced while the vehicle was in use. And sometimes, elements such as the fork, the fenders, the tank or the carburettor were also replaced to follow the changing fashion trends. So what should you do when you are face to face with a motorcycle that looks perfect, and that has already passed the bodywork and engine number check? You need to compare the most important components of the motorcycle with those you can identify in the photos published in the official catalogues or in the *Purchase guide*: fork, rear suspensions, exhaust, brakes, wheel rims, saddle, paint colour (paying attention to the size and the position of the pin stripes), headlights and taillights, tank, carburettors. Keep in mind that in the case of a total or partial restoration, many pieces such as lights and saddles can be replaced with original parts at a reasonable price. But original replacements for small components dating before the war, such as fuel taps, can be more expensive. So unless you are dealing with extremely valuable and rare models that will be difficult to ever find again, it might not be worth buying motorcycles with components that are not original. Spare parts can be expensive and hard to find, dramatically increasing the final cost of a motorcycle restored to its original state.

Different motorcycle conditions

While reading this book you will often encounter terms that collectors use to define the different conditions of a motorcycle. Here we offer a brief overview on the different conditions in which a vintage motorcycle can be found.

• **Incomplete:** motorcycles with seriously damaged engine and bodywork, that have never been repaired. Collectors use them as a source for original repair pieces.

• **Wrecked:** motorcycles in very bad conditions, usually covered in rust and dust, with many parts that need to be entirely replaced. Models in this state of repair do need a total restoration of the structure, of the paintwork, wheels, mechanical parts, etc. The purchase of such kind of motorcycle makes sense only if you stand before a very valuable piece or a motorcycle with all its papers in order, making registration a lot easier.

• **Poor conditions:** motorcycles needing medium level interventions (paintwork, replacement of some parts) to be restored to their original state.

• **Good conditions:** motorcycles that are complete but unkempt or not well running, in need of touch-ups but no replacement of parts except for those subject to wear.

• **Restored:** a motorcycle that has been brought back to its original state with interventions on the mechanics and the bodywork. The most sought after, and thus most expensive restored motorcycles are those carrying the Italian ASI (Automotoclub Storico Italiano) or equivalent certificate, carrying an evaluation of the motorcycle and of its restoration.

• **Excellent conditions:** the most sought after condition: a motorcycle that has never undergone any restorations but that is nevertheless in excellent general condition, with only some worn out parts due to the vehicle age (slightly opaque paintwork, worn-out grips, saddle with normal marks due to usage, etc.).

Bonhams: buying a BMW at an auction

Since the mid-1990s, a new way of purchasing BMW motorcycles has come about: auctions. Organized by illustrious, mainly British auction houses, these events have become increasingly popular among collectors from all over the world. They either personally attend the auction or participate via the Internet to buy prestigious motorcycles or just good bargains at reasonable prices. One of the most active organizations in this field is surely Bonhams (www.bonhams.com), one of the world's most ancient and respected auction houses. Founded back in 1793, it has resisted for four centuries and is today one of the most renowned auction houses, well known for its reliability and attention to the world of vintage cars and motorcycles. Bonhams

is internationally recognized in all sectors of art, but has become familiar to the BMW collectors since 2009 when it organized what has undoubtedly been the largest BMW auction ever.

On this occasion Bonhams sold all the 73 exclusive motorcycles that had belonged to Willy Neutkens's private collection, the most important in the world as Neutkens was listed in the Guinness World Records as the only person to own at least one model of all the BMW motorcycle production from 1923 to 1996. Thanks to the huge work of the Bonhams experts, the collectors battled for prestigious pieces such as a spotless R 32 (sold for 109,000 euros), or the beautiful R 63 (sold for 67,850 euros) and R 16 (sold at a hammer price of 57,500 euros). There was also space for some good bargains, such as an extraordinary and flawless R 90 S (sold at 6,000 euros) or a perfect R 100 GS (sold for 4,000

euros). A year later, once again on the prestigious premises of the BMW Museum in Munich, Bonhams set up another exceptional auction, again dedicated to the Bavarian house, entitled "The Power of BMW". Boats and cars of the Propeller Manufacturer were sold along with many BMW motorcycles, including a R 32 with white wheels (sold for 89,000 euros) and many sidecars (remarkable a beautiful R 69 S with Steib 501 C, hammer price 25,300 euros). To participate in an auction, like those organized by Bonhams, you need to register on the auction house website and, once having received notice of the event, enrol to receive the bidder number with which you place an offer during the auction, either in person or via Internet or phone (the bidder in this case will have to follow the event live on the Internet). Bonhams for example often organizes auctions in the BMW Museum that can also become an occasion to visit its collection. While considering whether to buy a motorcycle at an auction, you must remember that to the hammer price will be added the auction house commission: a few percentage points on that amount of money. One last recommendation is to figure out how to transport the motorcycle you might buy before the auction, especially if transportation will require an air flight: sometimes this cost can be decisive when evaluating whether or not to place a bid.

Bonhams 1793

Bonhams, established in 1793, is one of the world's largest auctioneers of fine arts and antiques. The current company was formed through the merger of Bonhams & Brooks and Phillips Son & Neale in November 2001. In August 2002, the company acquired Butterfields, the leading auction house on the West Coast of the United States. Today, Bonhams offers the largest number of objects and collections in the world, all of which through two large sales rooms in London, on New Bond Street and in Knightsbridge, plus three more in England and Scotland. Auctions are also held in San Francisco, Los Angeles, Carmel, New York and Connecticut for the United States, and in Germany, France, Monaco, Hong Kong and Australia. Bonhams has a worldwide network of offices and regional representatives in 25 countries, offering consultancy on sales and appraisal services in 60 specialized areas. For constant updates on auctions, visit www.bonhams.com.

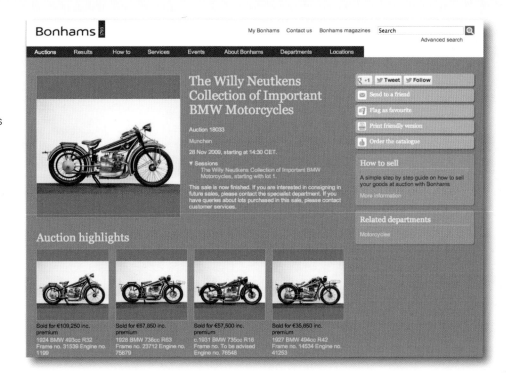

Suggestions for a correct maintenance of the vintage motorcycle

To keep a vintage motorcycle in order you do not need to be an expert mechanic or a skilful restorer. All you need to do is take care of your motorcycle with patience and follow a few important suggestions.

We often consider vintage motorcycles to be highly sophisticated or perhaps extremely delicate vehicles, and think that only a mechanic is capable of solving those small problems that a scarcely used vehicle can succumb to (such as a starting failure or the deterioration of some components). The truth is that all you need to do to keep your motorcycle in good repair is to carry out a series of minor interventions that are within any collector's reach, even of those that have no familiarity with mechanics. In fact, the "don'ts" are more than the "dos".

Choosing the storage place

The first crucial decision to make is where to store your motorcycle. If you don't have a dry indoor space to keep it, you might as well give up the idea of owning a vintage vehicle. Leaving it outdoors, at the mercy of the elements and temperature range, would mean ruining any motorcycle, even one in the best possible conditions. The ideal storage is a place with little or no humidity and a little air circulation. One of the most common mistakes is to cover the motorcycle with a plastic waterproof covering that is bound to create condensation and water stagnation. A much better option is to use an old bed sheet to simply protect the motorcycle from dust (1).

Starting and battery charge

Another mistake vintage motorcycle lovers often make is to start their motorcycle periodically without setting it in motion. Many think that turning the engine on and making it roar every now and then is a good way to keep the battery working and the motorcycle in order. This kind of operation can on the contrary cause much worse damage than a dead battery. If you want to keep the vehicle in order, what you should do is ride it for some fifty kilometres: only by doing so will you avoid condensation and allow the lubricant to warm up, reaching all the mechanical components. Every collector's dream would be to step into his garage, simply start his motorcycle and ride off to some motorcycle rally or to an occasional trip with his motorcycle club. But if you do not have the chance of using it at least once every two or three weeks, you should opt for a simple storage procedure: basically all you need to do is disconnect the battery through the fuse box (2) and maintain a high level of fuel in the tank (2, 3). Over the last few years, different solutions to keep the 6 Volt battery of vintage vehicles always charged have been put on the market: just keep the battery connected to the charger and you will avoid major problems (4).

5   6   7   8   9

Winter storage

Motorcycles, and especially vintage ones, are generally used more often in he warm season, from the beginning of spring up to the first cold days in autumn. If you decide not to use the motorcycle from October to February, you must arrange a winter storage. This implies a series of minor operations that clearly should be carried out whenever the vehicle is not used for a long period of time. The first thing to do is disconnect the battery through the fuse box: unscrew the connection and be careful to keep the two elements wide apart, preventing the fuse from falling (5). If the motorcycle is not going to be used for a long time, the best thing to do is remove the battery (2) in order to avoid any acid leaks that might damage or oxidize the bodywork coating – something that would lead to a costly restoration. Special attention must be paid to the fuel tank, one of the components that can be most affected by rust. To protect it from possible incrustations you should keep the tank full (3), leaving no space for air. Or else, you can empty it completely and leave it open with no cap nor tap. If you leave the motorcycle unused for a long period, it is a good rule to put some oil in the openings of the motorcycle spark plugs (6), moving the piston a few times in order to lubricate the cylinders. This simple operation is extremely effective in protecting the cast iron in the cylinder liners from oxidation. For carburettors, the best thing to do is to empty the float chambers completely (7) and then immediately add a coat of oil (8). As for the tyres, you need to keep them off the ground (9) and inflate them with a higher pressure to that indicated by the maker (10). This is the only way to avoid deterioration of the wheels' components and shape. As for aesthetic elements, should they be chromed or painted or in rubber, all you need to do is clean them thoroughly from all the dirt and then coat them with Vaseline or fuel oil (11). The "burdensome" silencers can be protected with specific plugs that have to be inserted at the extremities (12). In lack of these, you can alternatively insert pieces of old cloth soaked in oil into the terminal part of the exhaust (13).

10

11

12

13

Purchase guide

Acquiring a vintage BMW motorcycle is not difficult. The market for historic vehicles is constantly expanding, and opportunities to gain possession of a little piece of history are greater than ever. Moreover, the vintage-bike tradeshow market has expanded to include many authorized dealers, who now complement third-millennium models built by the Bayerische Motoren Werke with their prestigious historic counterparts. However, not every seemingly good deal turns out to be also a good investment for the collector. Hence the need for a guide that will help BMW fans carefully evaluate all pertinent criteria in judging vintage motorcycles before they make their purchase. Originality of pieces, faithfulness to the original characteristics of the model, critical details, availability of spare parts, frame and engine numbers are all vital statistics in the world of vintage motorcycles.

Purchase guide. As a perfect expression of the spirit with which we have written this book, we have chosen to give a clear and unequivocal title to this lengthy and fundamental section. Because the greatest difficulty in collecting vintage motorcycles made by the Bayerische Motoren Werke, one which is all too often underestimated, lays not in finding the bikes, but in buying them in the right way and at the right price. All too often imperfect, non-original bikes have been purchased at exorbitant prices by inexperienced buyers who lack information that would be useful in guiding negotiations. And conversely, there have also been practically perfect bikes sold as mere used machines rather than heritage pieces.

This *Purchase guide* is intended as an essential tool both for buyers and sellers. There are so many criteria to consider in assessing a vintage motorcycle – ranging from its state of conservation and the originality of its parts to its documentation and certification – that it is practically impossible to translate them all into a single number. No book, no piece of advice, no visual comparison between the actual bike and the official vintage photos can take the place of the sensations and desires of the collector. Like all passions, the love of historic motorcycles develops and grows in an absolutely personal manner. Something that is attractive to one collector may not be of interest to another. Anybody familiar with fairs, auctions and dealerships knows that no price is too high when you want a particular model at all costs, and that no price is low enough for a motorcycle that falls outside of the collector's sphere of interest.

This *Purchase guide* provides everything the potential buyer (or seller) needs to assess a motorcycle and appraise its market value and its value to the collector. Here is what you will find in the pages dedicated to the individual motorcycles, from the extraordinarily rare 1920s "flat-tank" to the bikes of the new century, which have been included even though in some cases just over ten years have passed since their production: in fact, the line between the markets for vintage and used motorcycles is a fading one. The technical data sheet lists all the essential information and is of great value for the proper assessment of a motorcycle.

The technical data sheet includes:

• The motorcycle production years
• The serial numbers of frames and engines
• The availability of spare parts
• The value as a collector's item
• The commercial value range

A caveat regarding the photos: the authors spent a great deal of time seeking motorcycles that are as close as possible, both aesthetically and in terms of components, to the original models as they emerged from the factory. This effort was relatively simple for motorcycles produced after the Second World War, yet much more complicated for those produced in the 1920s and 1930s. In certain cases, in lack of motorcycles truly conforming to the original models, the authors chose to use existing black and white photos from the Bayerische Motoren Werke historical archive in Munich, to ensure the most accurate representation of the vintage bikes. Since the visual comparison between the original machine and one that is to be bought or sold is of fundamental importance in determining the value of the vehicle, this kind of accuracy is essential. Especially noteworthy is the presence of motorcycles from historic collections, such as the huge, magnificent collection of Willy Neutkens, sold in 2009 at a Bonhams auction held in the BMW Museum of Munich.

The story behind the motorcycle

The text accompanying each page tells the story of the particular model and how it evolved over time, with a special focus on its main characteristics and technical innovations. The text includes the optionals and original colours that were available for the motorcycle during the years of its production, as well as presenting observations and considerations more strictly oriented to the collector.

Essential technical specs

There are a number of books on the market that include each and every possible technical specification for BMW motorcycles with maniacal precision. However, in truth, collectors are quite often attracted by factors that are more aesthetic and emotional in nature rather than technical. This is why the authors of this book have chosen to include only the essential technical data that uniquely characterize each motorcycle, from engine type and power rating to dimensions and frame design.

The identifying characteristics

A motorcycle conforming to the original photographs in terms of aesthetics may still not be faithful in terms of power plant and chassis. When buying or selling, you must also check the engine and frame numbers (motorcycles produced in the 1920s and 1930s have separate numbers for the frame and for the engine; from the 1940s onwards, the two numbers start to coincide) and make sure that they match both those on the vehicle registration and those in the data sheets provided in this book, that include the period of production and the number of vehicles manufactured as well. Starting in the mid-1980s, with the advent of the K series, frame numbers are no longer indicated, because the progressive numbering system had been abandoned in favour of a new system that encapsulates all the fundamental information. For example, the engine number 104EA 4383 3485 may be deciphered as follows: 104EA stands for an 8-valve engine of the K 100 series; 4383 specifies that it was built in the 44th week of 1983; and 3485 is the progressive production number for the engine.

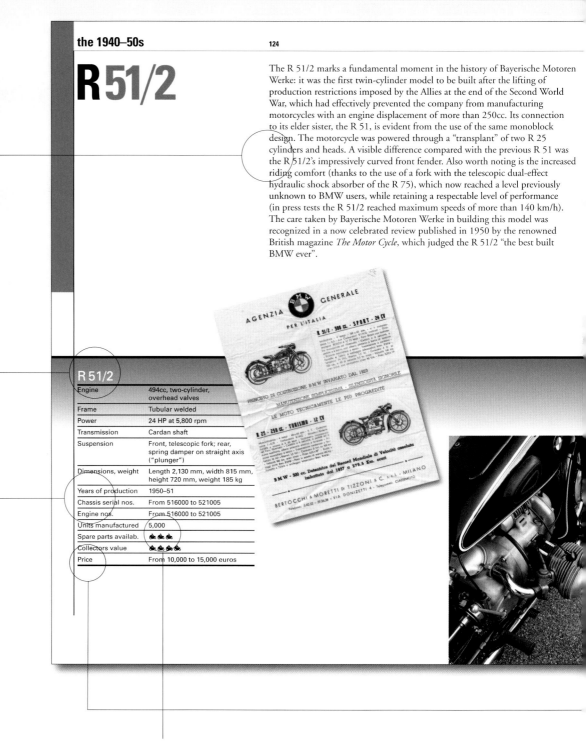

the 1940–50s 124

R 51/2

The R 51/2 marks a fundamental moment in the history of Bayerische Motoren Werke: it was the first twin-cylinder model to be built after the lifting of production restrictions imposed by the Allies at the end of the Second World War, which had effectively prevented the company from manufacturing motorcycles with an engine displacement of more than 250cc. Its connection to its elder sister, the R 51, is evident from the use of the same monoblock design. The motorcycle was powered through a "transplant" of two R 25 cylinders and heads. A visible difference compared with the previous R 51 was the R 51/2's impressively curved front fender. Also worth noting is the increased riding comfort (thanks to the use of a fork with the telescopic dual-effect hydraulic shock absorber of the R 75), which now reached a level previously unknown to BMW users, while retaining a respectable level of performance (in press tests the R 51/2 reached maximum speeds of more than 140 km/h). The care taken by Bayerische Motoren Werke in building this model was recognized in a now celebrated review published in 1950 by the renowned British magazine *The Motor Cycle*, which judged the R 51/2 "the best built BMW ever".

R 51/2

Engine	494cc, two-cylinder, overhead valves
Frame	Tubular welded
Power	24 HP at 5,800 rpm
Transmission	Cardan shaft
Suspension	Front, telescopic fork; rear, spring damper on straight axis ("plunger")
Dimensions, weight	Length 2,130 mm, width 815 mm, height 720 mm, weight 185 kg
Years of production	1950–51
Chassis serial nos.	From 516000 to 521005
Engine nos.	From 516000 to 521005
Units manufactured	5,000
Spare parts availab.	🏍🏍🏍
Collectors value	🏍🏍🏍🏍
Price	From 10,000 to 15,000 euros

Collectors criteria

One of the original characteristics of this book is the collector's criteria, novel indicators that the authors have chosen to include to provide motorcycle lovers with two pieces of information that are invaluable in guiding them in their buying or selling choices. One of these is *Spare parts availability*, which regards how difficult it is to obtain original replacement parts and how much they cost. For a given level of availability of parts, the higher their price, the lower the score. The other is *Collectors value*, which reflects the authors' evaluations of a mix of factors, presenting them in a unified graphic format: historic value of the motorcycle, technical innovations, availability on the market, demand by collectors, intrinsic value and commercial value. This mix explains why the first and extremely rare BMW, the R 32, has the same Collector's value (5) as motorcycles with a much lower commercial value,

COLLECTORS CORNER

The R 51/2 is a good addition to a collection, but is definitely not as sought after as its predecessor, the R 51, or its successor, the R 51/3. Even so, it commands a higher price than either, owing to the small number of units produced (5,000 in contrast to more than 18,000 of the R 51/3) and of the limited number of bikes on the market today, almost always in the hands of collectors and very well preserved. In perfect condition (an original motorcycle in excellent repair), an R 51/2 can fetch up to 15,000 euros. Models that require restoration or parts replacement should be purchased with caution, because official spare parts are in low supply and some are extremely difficult to find.

Collectors corner
A boxout is provided for each model, containing tips from the preeminent Italian experts on each specific period of production. The reader will find assessments of collectors value, occasional details of importance to collectors, and also information on critical factors. The configurations in greatest demand (spoke wheels, lateral brakes, tailpipe design, etc.) are also discussed, as well as possible peculiarities from a collector's standpoint.

A distinguishing feature of the R 51/2: they were single-finned (right)

such as the R 69 S or the R 90 S. Both *Spare parts availability* and *Collectors value* are represented by a maximum of five coloured symbols ranging from a minimum of 1 (spare parts virtually impossible to find; almost no value to the collector) to a maximum of 5 (full availability of spare parts; very high value to the collector).

Commercial value
It is always very difficult to assign a price to a vintage motorcycle. There are too many variables (originality, state of conservation, papers in order, etc.) that appear in the equation for determining its real commercial value. In order to account for this variability, after a painstaking assessment of the current market, the authors have specified not just a single value for each motorcycle, but rather a price range. The lower bond refers to

motorcycles in a poor state of conservation or with non-original parts, while the upper bond represents the maximum appraisal for a bike in excellent condition, with fully original components and all its papers in order. One point regarding motorcycles made in the 1920s and 1930s: the extreme rarity of certain models on the international market (especially the earliest BMWs) and the consequent scarcity of documentation regarding auctions and private sales

makes it impossible to objectively determine the price scale. In these cases, it must be considered entirely indicative, with actual selling prices varying widely at the moment of sale.

Bayerische Motoren Werke production figures, by year

(Data: Reichsverband der Automobilindustrie e.V. – Bayerische Motoren Werke AG.)

Production 1923–44

	1923	1924	1925	1926
200				
250			R 39	R 39
300				
350				
400				
500	R 32	R 32	R 32 R 37	R 32 R 37 R 42
600				
750				
Total	ND	c. 1,500	1,640	2,360

Production 1948–84

	1948	1949	1950	1951	1952	1953	1954	1955	1956	1957	1958	1959	1960	1961	1962	1963	1964	1965	1966	1967	1968
250	R 24	R 24	R 24 R 25	R 25 R 25/2	R 25/2	R 25/2 R 25/3	R 25/2 R 25/3	R 25/3	R 25/3 R 26	R 26	R 26	R 26	R 26 R 27	R 27	R 27	R 27	R 27	R 27	R 27		
450																					
500			R 51/2	R 51/2 R 51/3	R 51/3	R 51/3	R 51/3	R 50	R 50	R 50	R 50	R 50	R 50 R 50 S	R 50/2 R 50 S	R 50/2 R 50 S	R 50/2	R 50/2	R 50/2	R 50/2	R 50/2	R 50/2
600				R 67	R 67/2 R 68	R 67/2 R 68	R 67/2 R 68	R 67/3 R 69	R 67/3 R 69 R 60	R 69 R 60	R 69 R 60	R 69 R 60	R 69 R 60 R 69 S	R 60/2 R 69 S	R 60/2 R 69 S	R 60/2 R 69 S	R 60/2 R 69 S	R 60/2 R 69 S	R 60/2 R 69 S	R 60/2 R 69 S	R 60/2 R 69 S
650																					
750																						
800																						
900																						
1000																						
Total	59	9,400	17,061	25,101	28,310	27,704	29,699	23,531	15,500	5,29	7,156	8,412	9,473	9,460	4,302	6,043	9,043	7,118	9,071	7,896	5,074

1927	1928	1929	1930	1931	1932	1933	1934	1935	1936	1937	1938	1939	1940	1941	1942	1943	1944
				R 2	R 2	R 2	R 2	R 2	R 2	R 20	R 20						
											R 23	R 23	R 23				
									R 3								
											R 35	R 35	R 35	R 35			
					R 4	R 4	R 4	R 4	R 4	R 4							
R 42 R 47	R 42 R 47 R 52 R 57	R 57 R 52	R 57						R 5	R 5	R 51	R 51	R 51				
										R 6	R 66 R 61	R 66 R 61	R 66 R 61	R 66 R 61			
	R 62 R 63	R 62 R 63 R 11 R 16	R 11 R 16	R 11 R 16	R 11 R 16	R 11 R 16	R 11 R 16	R 12 R 17	R 12 R 17	R 12 R 17	R 12 R 17	R 12 R 71	R 12 R 71	R 12 R 71 R 75	R 12 R 75	R 75	R 75
3,397	4,932	5,680	c. 6,000	6,681	4,652	4,734	9,689	10,005	11,922	12,549	17,300	21,667	16,211	c. 10,250	c. 7,000	c. 7,000	c. 2,000

1969	1970	1971	1972	1973	1974	1975	1976	1977	1978	1979	1980	1981	1982	1983	1984
									R 45	R 45	R 45	R 45	R 45	R 45	R 45
R 50/2 R 50/5	R 50/5	R 50/5	R 50/5	R 50/5											
R 60/2 R 69 S R 60/5	R 60/5	R 60/5	R 60/5	R 60/5 R 60/6	R 60/6	R 60/6	R 60/6 R 60/7	R 60/7	R 60/7	R 60/7	R 60/7				
									R 65	R 65	R 65	R 65 R 65 LS	R 65 R 65 LS	R 65 R 65 LS	R 65 R 65 LS
R 75/5	R 75/5	R 75/5	R 75/5	R 75/5 R 75/6	R 75/6	R 75/6	R 75/6 R 75/7	R 75/7							
									R 80/7	R 80/7	R 80/7 R 80 G/S	R 80/7 R 80 G/S	R 80/7 R 80 G/S R 80 ST R 80 RT	R 80/7 R 80 G/S R 80 ST R 80 RT	R 80/7 R 80 G/S R 80 ST R 80 RT
			R 90/6 R 90 S	R 90/6 R 90 S	R 90/6 R 90 S	R 90/6 R 90 S									
							R 100/7 R 100 S R 100 RS	R 100/7 R 100 S R 100 RS	R 100/7 R 100 S R 100 RS R 100 RT R 100 T	R 100 RS R 100 RT R 100 T	R 100 RS R 100 RT R 100 T R 100 CS	R 100 RS R 100 RT R 100 T R 100 CS	R 100 RS R 100 RT R 100 T R 100 CS	R 100 RS R 100 RT R 100 T R 100 CS K 100 K 100 RS K 100 RT	R 100 RS R 100 T R 100 CS K 100 K 100 RS K 100 RT
4,701	12,287	18,772	21,122	15,078	23,160	25,566	28,209	31,515	29,580	24,415	29,260	33,120	30,559	28,048	34,001

Production 1985–2000 **

	1985	1986	1987	1988	1989	1990	1991	1992	1993	1994
450	R 45									
650	R 65 R 65 LS								F 650 ST Carb F 650 GS Carb	F 650 ST Carb F 650 GS Carb
750	K 75 K 75 S K 75 C	K 75 K 75 S K 75 C	K 75 K 75 S K 75 C	K 75 K 75 S K 75 C	K 75 K 75 S K 75 C K 75 RT	K 75 K 75 S K 75 C K 75 RT	K 75 K 75 S K 75 RT	K 75 K 75 S K 75 RT	K 75 K 75 S K 75 RT	K 75 K 75 S K 75 RT
800	R 80 G/S	R 80 G/S	R 80 G/S							
1000	K 100 K 100 RS K 100 RT	K 100 K 100 RS K 100 RT K 100 LT R 100 GS	K 100 K 100 RS K 100 RT K 100 LT R 100 GS	K 100 RS K 100 RT K 100 LT R 100 GS R 100 GS P D	K 100 RS K 100 LT R 100 GS R 100 GS PD K1 K 100 RS 16 V K 1100 LT	K 100 LT R 100 GS R 100 GS PD K1 K 100 RS 16 V K 1100 LT	K 100 LT R 100 GS R 100 GS PD K1 K 100 RS 16 V K 1100 LT R 1100 RS R 100 R	R 100 GS R 100 GS PD K1 K 100 RS 16 V K 1100 LT R 1100 RS R 100 R K 1100 RS	R 100 GS R 100 GS PD K1 K 100 RS 16 V K 1100 LT R 1100 RS R 100 R K 1100 RS R 1100 GS R 1100 R	R 100 GS R 100 GS PD K 1100 LT R 1100 RS R 100 R K 1100 RS R 1100 GS R 1100 R

** Yearly production figures are no longer provided by official sources.

1995	1996	1997	1998	1999	2000
F 650 ST Carb	F 650 ST Carb	F 650 ST Carb	F 650 ST Carb	F 650 ST Carb	F 650 ST Carb
F 650 GS Carb	F 650 GS Carb	F 650 GS Carb	F 650 GS Carb	F 650 GS Carb	F 650 GS Carb
				F 650 GS Dakar	F 650 GS Dakar
				F 650 GS	F 650 GS
K 75	K 75				
K 75 S					
K 75 RT	K 75 RT				
R 850 R	R 850 R	R 850 R	R 850 R	R 850 R	R 850 R
	R 850 GS	R 850 GS	R 850 GS	R 850 GS	R 850 GS
	R 80 GS Basic	R 80 GS Basic			
R 100 GS P D	R 100 GS P D				
K 1100 LT	K 1100 LT	K 1100 LT	K 1100 LT	K 1100 LT	
R 1100 RS	R 1100 RS	R 1100 RS	R 1100 RS	R 1100 RS	R 1100 RS
R 100 R					
K 1100 RS	K 1100 RS				
R 1100 GS	R 1100 GS	R 1100 GS	R 1100 GS	R 1100 GS	
R 1100 R	R 1100 R	R 1100 R	R 1100 R	R 1100 R	R 1100 R
	K 1200 RS	K 1200 RS	K 1200 RS	K 1200 RS	K 1200 RS
		R 1200 C	R 1200 C	R 1200 C	R 1200 C
			R 1100 S	R 1100 S	R 1100 S
				K 1200 LT	K 1200 LT
				R 1150 R	R 1150 R
				R 1150 GS	R 1150 GS
					R 1150 RS

the 1920s

After the experience gained building the Helios motorcycle, Bayerische Motoren Werke commissioned its chief designer, Max Friz, to draw up plans for the first-ever motorcycle with the BMW name. What emerged was the R 32, the progenitor of a whole generation of "flat-tank" bikes, beautiful and innovative, that were to become a distinctive symbol of the company. Along with the R 32, the magnificent but unattainable bike that collectors can only dream about, BMW enthusiasts can also admire the R 39, the first single-cylinder bike, and the R 62 of 1928, the first BMW motorcycle with a 750cc displacement.

R 32

The first motorcycle produced by Bayerische Motoren Werke was built by Max Friz in the peace and quiet of his house on Riesenfledstrasse. Friz, the chief designer at BMW, was responding to a specific request from the management. Teased by the company's experience with the Victoria KR I, a motorcycle equipped with the first-ever BMW-built "boxer" (opposed-twin) engine, namely the M 2 B 15 designed by Martin Stolle, and buoyed also by the success of the Helios motorcycle also fitted with a BMW-made engine, the management now believed the company could go for it alone and make a new market in the manufacture of bikes. The result, the R 32, was unveiled at the Paris Salon of 1923, and its technical features were an immediate hit. The boxer engine (for the design of which Max Friz drew his inspiration from the British Sopwith aircraft) was mounted transversely in a double tubular frame with the crankshaft positioned longitudinally to drag the gearbox, which was flanged directly onto the engine. The gearbox was three-speed, manually operated, with differentiated gearing, a sophisticated design that now requires special machinery to be replicated. The front fork had two friction dampers adjustable by means of a wing-nut. The torque was delivered to the rear wheel by means of a Cardan shaft, a solution that was to become a hallmark of BMW motorcycles. The R 32 was not a very fast machine (even if it could reach a top speed of 90 Km/h), but it stood out for its manoeuvrability, excellent road holding, low engine maintenance and silence. Sales took off at once, and, after three years, a remarkable 3,090 pieces had been sold. The success was in no small part due to the enthusiastic reaction of the press, an enthusiasm well placed indeed, for the R 32 was a small miracle of engineering replete with innovations. The heads

R 32

Engine	494cc, two-cylinder, side valves
Frame	Tubular twin cradle
Power	8.5 HP at 3,200 rpm
Transmission	Cardan shaft
Suspension	Front, leaf spring oscillating fork; rear, rigid
Dimensions, weight	Length 2,100 mm; width 800 mm; height 950 mm; weight 122 kg
Years of production	1923–26
Chassis serial nos.	From 1001 to 4100
Engine nos.	From 31000 to 34100
Units manufactured	3,090
Spare parts availab.	🏍
Collectors value	🏍 🏍 🏍 🏍 🏍
Price	From 65,000 to 105,000 euros

of the engine were monoblock, provided with two bronze screw caps from which it was possible to extract the valves; the bevel gears were housed in a large and robust box through which the frame tubes ran to strengthen the connection; the air for the combustion chamber was drawn in not through the carburettor, but from the flywheel chamber, then fed through a conveyor tube. For its engine and frame design, the R 32 was a small masterpiece, but it also had the looks to match. As a motorcycle, it was an object of beauty, with plenty of chrome details, a rich assortment of levers on the handlebar (seven) and a Bosch lighting system, which in those days was sold as an optional. With the R 32, BMW introduced the practice of including an identification plate on the steering column giving the details of the motorcycle and including the word "Rad". Although in German *Rad* means wheel, in this case it was short for *Kraftrad*, which refers specifically to a motorized two-wheeled vehicle. This is the reason for the use of the letter R, which features in all the names of all BMW models until the K series started in 1983. During its three years of life (it was available for sale until 1926, when it was replaced by R 42), the R 32 underwent several stylistic and equipment enhancements. The new cosmetic touches included the addition of broad white stripes on the tank (replaced in 1924 by the traditional "pinstripe" edging). A passenger saddle was added as an accessory in 1925, along with passenger foot pegs. Other new features included a trumpet-style horn, a speedometer, which was an optional extra (in the original 1923 version it was fitted as standard). The mushroom-shaped protective shield for the cylinders disappeared from the engine in 1925. The braking system merits its own special mention. The original version of 1923

had no front brake; the rear wheel was equipped with an annular brake with a wooden block, and was operated by a foot pedal. Later, a 150-mm central drum brake was added to the front, and, for the rear wheel, a block brake mechanism that acted on the drum of the drive shaft via a heel-operated pedal.

COLLECTORS CORNER

The R 32 is the founder of the species of all BMW motorcycles, so it is only natural that it should be the forbidden fruit for all BMW collectors. Sadly, the surviving examples are very few, and some of these are in a very poor state of preservation, often lacking many pieces of the frame as well as engine parts. Restoring a motorcycle such as the R 32 is an extremely difficult and demanding task. Hunting for the very expensive original spare parts may take several years and necessitate many visits to markets all over the world. Equally expensive, especially in Germany, is the option of having some parts remade by hand. As for those models that are still in good condition or have been restored,

the records indicate that they are in the hands of major collectors, who would scarcely be willing to part with so valuable a treasure, even for much higher offers than the official price given in the data sheet below. Sometimes we hear reports of individual auctions of BMW motorcycles from the 1920s, but even the starting prices would not look out of place at the sale of works by a renowned artist. The huge demand for original pieces should also be borne in mind. We therefore recommend collectors to seize any opportunity to purchase R 32 parts, unless they are priced exorbitantly, and, indeed, spare parts belonging to any of the many other flat-tank models.

R 37

The quality of the materials used by BMW for the construction of the R 32 and the innovative mechanical solutions of Max Friz formed the basis for the excellent reputation that BMW managed to acquire within just two years of its first official attempt to build a motorcycle. In 1924, then, thanks mainly to the addition to the design team of Rudolf Schleicher, an engineer and passionate rider who had won several official races, BMW became persuaded of the need to build a motorcycle with a marked sporty feel and look. Delighted with the chance to design his first bike, Schleicher decided to get the most out of the R 32 frame, completely re-designing the engine to improve its performance; he then personally rode the machine to racing success. Soon the R 37 was born, which BMW unveiled at the end of 1924 at the Berlin Motor Show. It was the first Bayerische Motoren Werke motorcycle to make use of the overhead-valve configuration. It was a competition jewel, aesthetically notable for its large aluminium cylinder heads with valves inclined at 90° and its cylinder fins set parallel to the direction of travel (rather than perpendicular as in the R 32): a solution that was very beneficial to engine cooling. The innovative intake process benefited from suction taking place in a quiet zone located in the clutch compartment. With regard to its frame, the R 37 was little changed from the R 32, if we exclude the modifications to the fork, which now featured a pair of friction dampers, and the inclusion of a drum brake for the front wheel. An interesting technical detail was the single-block carburettor with three-piece telescopic valves (two for the fuel and one for the air). Compared to the R 32, the R 37 was mainly produced for racing, where its 16 HP at 4,000 rpm

R 37

Engine	494cc, two-cylinder, overhead valves
Frame	Tubular twin cradle
Power	16 HP at 4,000 rpm
Transmission	Cardan shaft
Suspension	Front, leaf spring oscillating fork; rear, rigid
Dimensions, weight	Length 2,100 mm, width 800 mm, height 950 mm, weight 134 kg
Years of production	1925–26
Chassis serial nos.	From 100 to 275
Engine nos.	From 35001 to 35175
Units manufactured	152
Spare parts availab.	🏍
Collectors value	🏍 🏍 🏍 🏍 🏍
Price	From 30,000 to 60,000 euros

(twice as many as the 1923 bike) could push the machine to a top speed just a shade below 125 km/h. The commercial, non-racing, version of the R 37 also won plaudits; indeed, it is fair to say that it was this version that met with most success among critics and fans. A side note: in the R 37 Rudolf Schleicher managed to combine his twin passions of engine design and competitive racing. In 1926, the young German engineer drove the R 37 to victory at the extremely tough Buxton Six Days Race, in England.

COLLECTORS CORNER

From the collectors' perspective, the R 32 and R 37 have much in common. Whereas for the R 32 (more than 3,000 of which were made) one might at least rely on the direct experience of collectors who have bought and restored one, for the R 37 there are no official references apart from some starting bid prices from auctions in the United States. Built mainly for racing, many of them were cannibalized in their own day to provide spare parts for the offi-

cial racing machines ridden by champions such as Friz Roth and Sepp Stelzer. If we consider that just 152 R 37s rolled out of BMW factory, then we get some idea of the absolute rarity of this bike. For the reasons just mentioned, the spare parts situation is decidedly difficult, and the commercial values shown in the data sheet below are therefore purely indicative, since obtaining ownership of a complete R 37 is in practice an impossible undertaking.

R 39

At the Berlin Motor Show of 1924, BMW not only introduced the R 37 – the sports version of the R 32, as it were – but also an innovative single-cylinder 250cc motorcycle, the R 39. This, too, was built for racing, but with an eye also on its potential for mass production. The price tag of 2,900 Reichmarks for the R 37 was extremely high for the time; it was the most expensive bike on the German market and out of the financial reach of almost all fans. With a view to expanding its customer base, BMW resolved to make the R 39 available for sale at the much more affordable price of 1,870 Reichmarks, without any reduction in the quality of materials or in the level of technological research. Indeed, this first single-cylinder motorcycle from the Munich house had many elements in common with its predecessors: the cradle frame, an engine with overhead valves operated by pushrods and rockers, the crankshaft positioned longitudinally, a three-speed gearbox in a single assembly with the Cardan shaft. The R 39 was even equipped with an innovative braking system. In lieu of the brake-block solution that had been used for the rear wheel, a brake clamp with external brake shoes was mounted on a special drum positioned at the front end of the driveshaft. Between 1925 and 1927, 855 units of the R 39 were manufactured. The motorcycle won many racing events, thanks also to the masterful driving of Sepp Stelzer, who rode this single-cylinder bike to victory in the 1925 German Championship. Thanks to these successes, customer demand rose sharply, in spite of some hidden costs that elevated the actual purchase price. While the initial list price might have seemed competitive, it was in fact mandatory to equip the bikes with two "optional" extras, namely the Bosch lights and the speedometer, which brought the final

R 39

Engine	247cc, single-cylinder, overhead valves
Frame	Tubular twin cradle
Power	6.5 HP at 4,000 rpm
Transmission	Cardan shaft
Suspension	Front, leaf spring oscillating fork; rear, rigid
Dimensions, weight	Length 2,050 mm, width 800 mm, height 950 mm, weight 110 kg
Years of production	1925–27
Chassis serial nos.	From 8000 to 8900
Engine nos.	From 36000 to 36900
Units manufactured	855
Spare parts availab.	🏍
Collectors value	🏍 🏍 🏍 🏍 🏍
Price	From 15,000 to 31,000 euros

price of the machine to 2,150 Reichmarks, almost as much as the 500cc R 32. Unfortunately, a few months after its launch the R 39 ran into technical problems, including premature wear and tear of the cylinders, which hugely increased oil consumption. The Bayerische Motoren Werke technical department was forced to make repairs to models already sold. For the motorcycles under production, the resistance of the steel cylinder liners was increased, but this was not enough to solve the problem permanently.

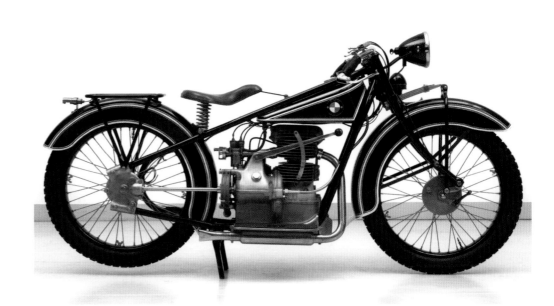

COLLECTORS CORNER

As far as collectors are concerned, the R 39 is the most expensive single-cylinder BMW ever made, and this is maybe one reason for it is not the most sought for. Moreover, the fact that it represents the first of the rare technical failures of Bayerische Motoren Werke has made it of limited interest to major collectors, and only the most avid flat-tank BMW aficionados would consider the R 39 as a pivotal part of their collection. The limited production run (855 units) and the difficulty of finding spare parts make this bike very much of a niche speciality. Commercially, the R 39 is not comparable to the R 32 and R 37, although there are reports of sales of some specimens practically unused since manufacture going for very high prices in Germany (the reason being that, since production was suspended in 1927, many new units have remained sitting unsold in BMW warehouses and dealerships, so that they survived to the present day in practically mint condition). As with the other flat-tank models, you would be well advised to pick up any R 39 parts, whatever their condition, but only if you are truly convinced you can and want to spend a lot of money and time on reassembling and restoring this ancestor of the BMW single-cylinder family.

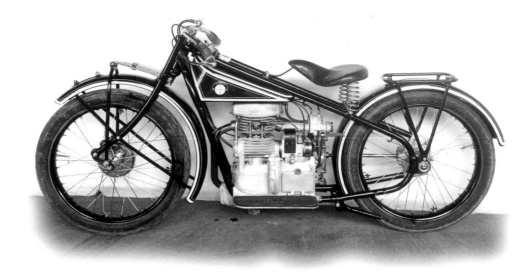

R42
R47

In parallel with the official competitions, which bestowed prestige on the brand and therefore boosted sales, in the mid-1920s BMW began to think about offering a new touring rather than sports motorcycle, one that would inherit the mantle of the glorious R 32. Given the commercial success of the R 32 and the soundness of the technical solutions used, BMW chose the path of "evolution rather than revolution". Thus, having worked on tweaking the details, in November 1925 it presented the R 42 at the Berlin Motor Show. Among the most important changes with respect to the R 32 were new cylinders, now with a more rational arrangement of the fins (in the direction of travel) and capped with aluminium alloy heads that could be disassembled on two planes: innovations that significantly improved ventilation and engine cooling. Some small changes were made to the carburettor (adding an extra 3.5 horsepower compared to the R 32), and to the transmission system, involving the reinforcement of the single-plate dry clutch between the engine and the gearbox. Another notable addition was a cast eyelet on the transmission housing, to attach there the sidecar. Other changes were made to the frame, the most important of which involved a move from curved to straight front tubes. The engine was shifted farther back to improve weight distribution, and the frame tube at seat height was curved downwards to the rear of the bike. Borrowing from the R 39, the R 42 made use of the new brake with external brake shoes and a novel tachometer driven by the gearbox rather than by a front wheel belt. As regards appearance, the bike had newly designed fenders with a shallower groove and shortened at the bottom, which lent the R 42 a sportier appearance than its progenitor, the R 32. At the same time as they continued

R 42

Engine	494cc, two-cylinder, side valves
Frame	Tubular twin cradle
Power	12 HP at 3,400 rpm
Transmission	Cardan shaft
Suspension	Front, leaf spring oscillating fork; rear, rigid
Dimensions, weight	Length 2,100 mm, width 800 mm, height 950 mm, weight 126 kg
Years of production	1926–28
Chassis serial nos.	From 10001 to 16999
Engine nos.	From 40001 to 46999
Units manufactured	6,502
Spare parts availab.	🏍
Collectors value	🏍🏍🏍🏍🏍
Price	From 20,000 to 35,000 euros

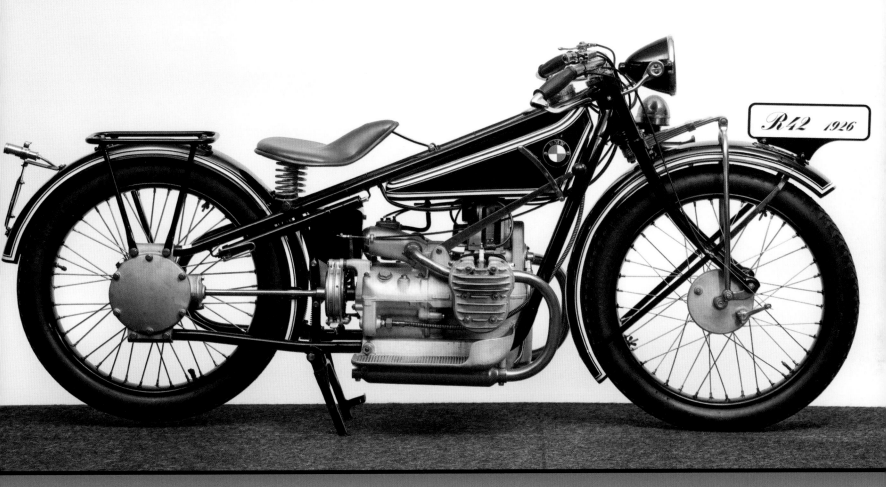

R42 1926

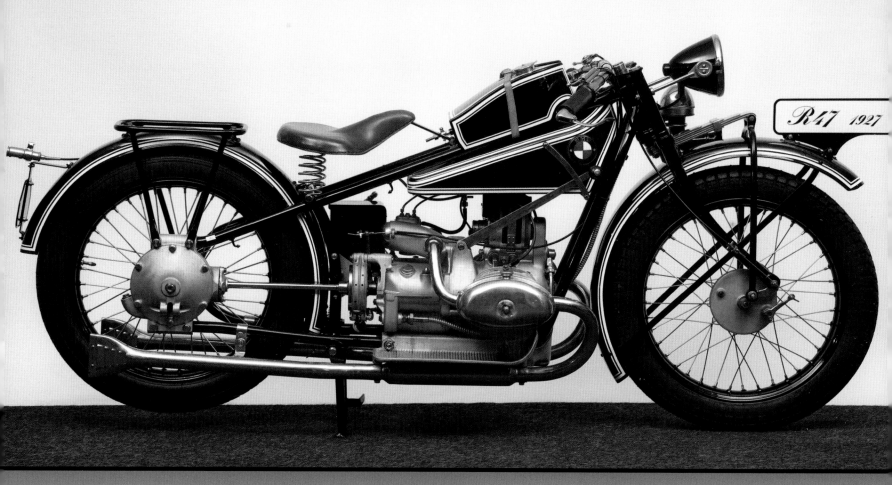

R 47

Engine	494cc, two-cylinder, overhead valves
Frame	Tubular twin cradle
Power	18 HP at 4,000 rpm
Transmission	Cardan shaft
Suspension	Front, leaf spring oscillating fork; rear, rigid
Dimensions, weight	Length 2,100 mm, width 800 mm, height 950 mm, weight 130 kg
Years of production	1927–28
Chassis serial nos.	From 4201 to 5999
Engine nos.	From 34201 to 35999
Units manufactured	1,720
Spare parts availab.	🏍
Collectors value	🏍 🏍 🏍 🏍 🏍
Price	From 25,000 to 39,000 euros

to develop push-rod engines with side valves, BMW's engineers were also working hard on giving a successor to the R 37 with a flathead, overhead-valve engine, even though customers were still heavily demanding the old R 37. So exactly one year after the R 42, the company unveiled the R 47, which pretty much followed the "evolution-not-revolution" philosophy that had guided the design of the R 42. The new half-litre motorcycle was offered to the public at the relatively low price of 1,850 Reichmarks thanks to the achievement of production efficiencies for many of its components. The engine had cast iron instead of steel cylinders, in spite of an increase in the output of two horsepower. Both the R 42 and the R 47 were equipped with a leaf spring mechanism on the front fork.

COLLECTORS CORNER

The R 42 and R 47 were produced in similar numbers, but from the collectors' point of view they have a markedly different appeal. To begin with, fans of flat-tank motorcycles prefer the founding R 32 to its successor, the R 42, for while the two are very similar with respect to the build of the frame, the former has far greater historical value. The different degree of difficulty of finding the two bikes also counts. Just over 3,000 units of the 1923 model were produced compared with more than 6,500 units of the later R 42. The overhead valve engine R 47 is more keenly sought after by collectors than the flathead R42; therefore the commercial value of an R 47 is practically double than that of an R 42. A limiting factor for both models is the difficulty of finding spare parts, even in poor repair. Be advised that examples of the R 42 and R 47 are to be found in some South American countries, especially Argentina, as well as in South Africa and the United States, the first non-European nations to import BMW bikes.

R 52
R 57

The year 1928 brought an unexpected revolution in the sales catalogue of Bayerische Motoren Werke, with the debut of no fewer than four new models. These included evolutions of the flathead touring R 42 motorcycle and the push-rod sportsbike R 47 which, in keeping with tradition, were respectively named the R 52 and R 57. These new half-litre motorcycles came with the same suspension and frame as their previous models, but included a brand-new, more robust and effective front braking system, where the internal brake shoes were replaced with a large 200mm drum. The new features of the R 52 and R 57 also included a completely re-designed engine, with the gear-shift lever in a different position with respect to the 1927 models. In other changes, the connecting rods were attached to a single-piece crankshaft via split double rows of roller bearings, the kick-start lever was placed transversely, and a new type of carburettor with two sliding valves was installed. All these important modifications, however, added more than 20 kilograms of weight to the machine. The exhaust system was also improved, with silencers bearing now a sportier fish tail shape, while the three-speed gearbox was strengthened, and motor oil now replaced grease as its lubricant. With respectively 4,377 and 1,006 units built, the R 52 and R 57 enhanced the reputation of BMW for making motorcycles that were reliable, high performing (the sports version of the overhead-valve model could reach 115 km/h) and indestructible, as suitable for use in the city as for a challenging mountain terrain. (In a famous report on the prestigious *Das Motorrad* magazine, a reader who successfully crossed the Alps on an R 52 with sidecar boasted that no mountain pass had caused his motorcycle

R 52

Engine	487cc, two-cylinder, side valves
Frame	Tubular twin cradle
Power	12 HP at 3,400 rpm
Transmission	Cardan shaft
Suspension	Front, leaf spring oscillating fork; rear, rigid
Dimensions, weight	Length 2,100 mm, width 800 mm, height 950 mm, weight 152 kg
Years of production	1928–29
Chassis serial nos.	From 20000 to 30600
Engine nos.	From 47001 to 51383
Units manufactured	4,377
Spare parts availab.	🏍
Collectors value	🏍 🏍 🏍 🏍 🏍
Price	From 20,000 to 29,000 euros

any difficulty.) With the new models of 1928, BMW finally adopted deep-groove wheel rims. Repeating a past practice, the Bosch lights were mounted on almost every model, even if the sales catalogue still listed them as optional.

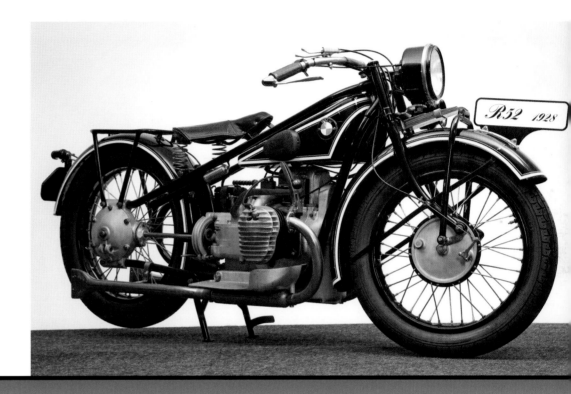

R 57

Engine	494cc, two-cylinder, overhead valves
Frame	Tubular twin cradle
Power	18 HP at 4,000 rpm
Transmission	Cardan shaft
Suspension	Front, leaf spring oscillating fork; rear, rigid
Dimensions, weight	Length 2,100 mm, width 800 mm, height 950 mm, weight 150 kg
Years of production	1928–30
Chassis serial nos.	From 20000 to 30600
Engine nos.	From 70001 to 71012
Units manufactured	1,006
Spare parts availab.	🏍
Collectors value	🏍 🏍 🏍 🏍 🏍
Price	From 25,000 to 33,000 euros

COLLECTORS CORNER

Much easier to find and more commonplace than the previous R 42 and R 47 models, the R 52 and R 57 are, along with their 750cc siblings, the last flat-tank motorcycles produced by Bayerische Motoren Werke. For this historical reason and thanks to the relatively large number of units produced, which has kept the price from rising exponentially, these are the two most collectible models from the 1920s. As with the R 42 and R 47, a considerable price difference exists between the side-valve R 52 and the overhead-valve R 57, particularly as a result of the far lower production numbers caused by the exorbitant cost of the R 57, whose sales price made it the most expensive half-litre motorcycle on the German market, only 250 Reichmarks shy of the price of the more performing 750cc R 63. While the greater availability of spare parts compared to the earlier models makes the task of restoration somewhat easier, it has also led to some non-original assemblies. Before entering into the purchase of a motorcycle, it is therefore a good idea to check that the chassis and engine numbers match the BMW factory numbers.

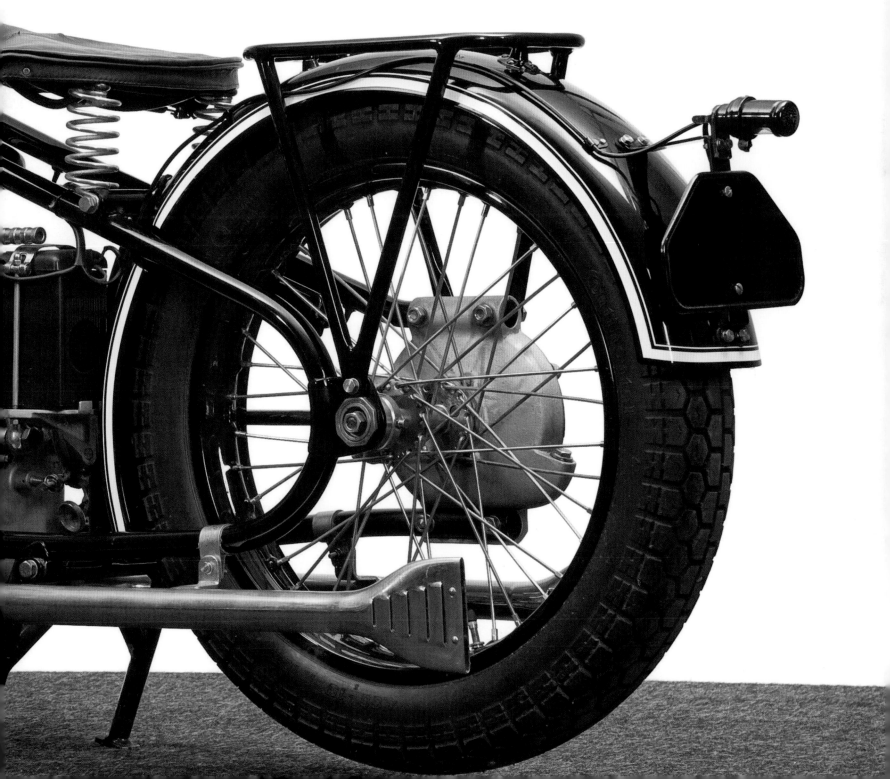

R 62
R 63

The new range presented by Bayerische Motoren Werke in 1928 included advances on the two half-litre models plus two important new departures that marked the entry of the BMW into the 750cc class. These were the R 62 and R 63 with, respectively, a side-valve and overhead-valve engine. It had by now become something of a BMW tradition to develop the two types of engine in parallel, a choice that had proven commercially successful. BMW marketed the R 62 as a classy touring motorcycle, perfect for long-range journeys, and the R 63 as a super-sports bike, designed for competition. Both were aimed at highly exigent customers, who could afford the 2,100-Reichmark official price tag plus, if they were buying the R 62, an extra 250 Reichmarks for the "mandatory optionals" consisting of a trumpet horn and the Bosch lighting system. In terms of power, the R 62 had the same HP rating as the R 57 (18), but at a lower rpm (3,400 versus 4,000), while the R 63 produced 24 HP and a maximum speed of over 120 km/h, which was enough to satisfy customers but still was not enough to compete with the powerful British and Italian motorcycles on European circuits. In any case, the new engines were full of innovative solutions, some so good that, in the case of R 62 side-valve engine, characterized by an excellent elasticity, the setup was retained on BMW motorcycles for more than thirteen years. Among the main features of the new 750cc motorcycles that excited great interest was a three-speed gearbox based on an entirely innovative technical design that did away with grease as a lubricant. The new and powerful 200-mm drum brake replaced the previous internal brake shoe one at the front wheel (at the rear, the external brake shoes were replaced by a shaft brake); the new slide-valve carburettors were fitted with

R 62

Engine	745cc, two-cylinder, side valves
Frame	Tubular twin cradle
Power	18 HP at 3,400 rpm
Transmission	Cardan shaft
Suspension	Front, leaf spring oscillating fork; rear, rigid
Dimensions, weight	Length 2,100 mm, width 800 mm, height 950 mm, weight 155 kg
Years of production	1928–29
Chassis serial nos.	From 20000 to 30600
Engine nos.	From 60001 to 65000
Units manufactured	4,355
Spare parts availab.	🏍
Collectors value	🏍 🏍 🏍 🏍 🏍
Price	From 25,000 to 37,000 euros

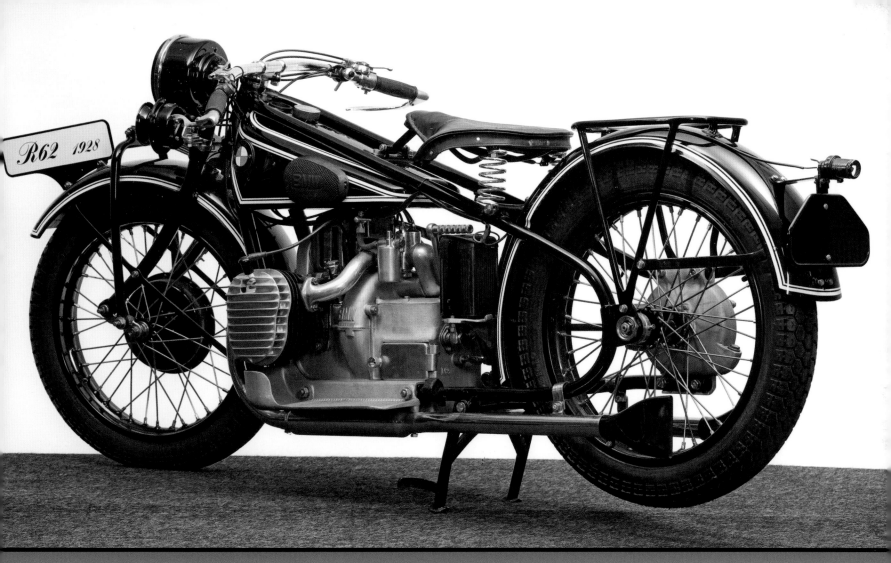

an air intake to recycle motor oil vapours. Another new element was the double plate clutch, which became standard on all models in 1929. The beginning of the new year also saw an important new development for the 750cc category. As an alternative to the traditional tubular steel cradle, BMW started offering a new type of frame made by welding together pieces of pressed steel. This new welded frame gave superior rigidity, and became the production standard for the later R 11 and R 16 motorcycles.

R 63

Engine	735cc, two cylinder, overhead valves
Frame	Tubular twin cradle
Power	24 HP at 4,000 rpm
Transmission	Cardan shaft
Suspension	Front, leaf spring oscillating fork; rear, rigid
Dimensions, weight	Length 2,100 mm, width 800 mm, height 950 mm, weight 152 kg
Years of production	1928–29
Chassis serial nos.	From 20000 to 30600
Engine nos.	From 75001 to 76000
Units manufactured	794
Spare parts availab.	🏍
Collectors value	🏍 🏍 🏍 🏍 🏍
Price	From 55,000 to 70,000 euros

COLLECTORS CORNER

The first Bayerische Motoren Werke 750cc motor-cycles are, of course, among the most sought-after items for collectors specializing in the BMW flat-tank range. Like all motorcycles from the 1920s, considering the relatively low production numbers (just over 4,000 units of R 62 and less than 800 of the R 63 were made) and the disappearance of most specimens with the passing of time, it comes as no surprise that they are so difficult to find on the market, and the remaining ones tend to be in the hands of private collectors. As with previous models, the overhead-valve version is the favourite and most wanted, and is therefore valued significantly higher than the side-valve version. The availability of spare parts is very low, and, in any case, original pieces command very high prices; also because dealers in spare parts almost never put on sale a complete piece, but sell it bit by bit to maximize their earnings.

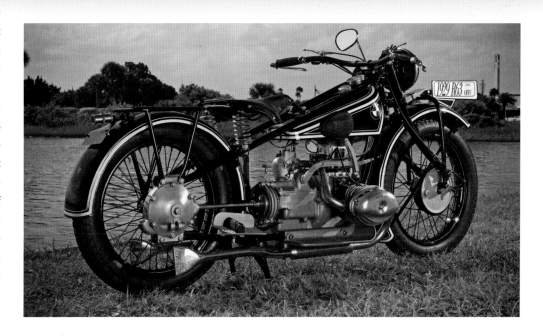

R 11
R 16

At the beginning of 1929, BMW surprised the customers with the introduction of new pressed-steel frames that could be mounted on the R 62 and R 63 instead of the traditional welded-pipe configuration. This innovative design became the most characteristic feature of the new side-valve R 11 and overhead-valve R 16 motorcycles, both with a displacement of 750cc. Such construction made for a sturdier frame and the better handling of forces and weights. The new frames, which looked massive and were especially well suited for sidecar use, were constructed from sections of pressed torsion-resistant riveted and welded steel. There were many more firsts to be found in the R 11 and R 16. The new 750cc engine marked in fact for BMW the end of the flat-tank era, with the characteristic triangular fuel tanks attached to the frame, now replaced by those mounted outside the chassis, in front of the saddle. The decision to adopt the new frame was partly the result of BMW's entry into the automotive industry, and the consequent optimization of the production with steel presses at its Eisenach automotive plant; but mostly it was a response to the many problems of frame breakage that had occurred to models with sidecar attached. The modification of the frame did not lead, at least not at first, to any change of the front fork, which remained the same as on the R 62 and R 63 models. Only after numerous complaints from customers did BMW create a more comfortable version by lengthening the cantilever springs and adding a new type of pressed-steel bracket. During the five years of production, these motorcycles underwent repeated updates that, for ease of identification, the company divided into five series. The main changes regarded the gears spacing, the lengthening of the driveshaft brake, the clutch and, from the third series

R 11

Engine	745cc, two-cylinder, side valves
Frame	Double-cradle pressed steel
Power	18 HP at 3,400 rpm, 20 HP at 4,000 rpm (fifth series)
Transmission	Cardan shaft
Suspension	Front, oscillating fork, pressed-steel leaf spring; rear, rigid
Dimensions, weight	Length 2,100 mm, width 890 mm, height 950 mm, weight 162 kg
Years of production	1929–34
Chassis serial nos.	From P 101 to P 9893
Engine nos.	From 60001 to 73984
Units manufactured	7,500
Spare parts availab.	🏍️ 🏍️
Collectors value	🏍️ 🏍️ 🏍️ 🏍️ 🏍️
Price	From 20,000 to 30,000 euros

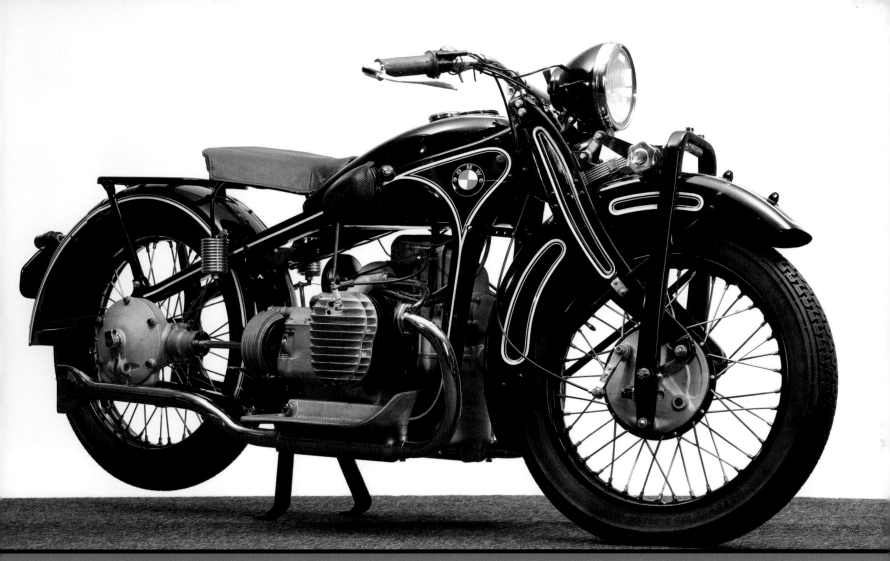

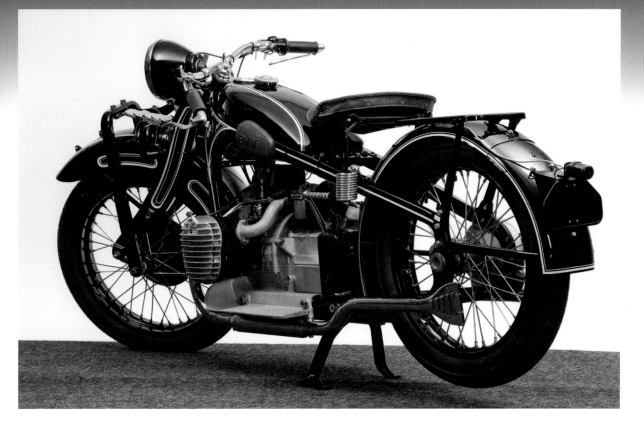

R 16

Engine	735cc, two-cylinder, overhead valves
Frame	Double cradle pressed steel
Power	25 HP at 4,000 rpm, 33 HP at 4,000 rpm (third series)
Transmission	Cardan shaft
Suspension	Front, oscillating fork, pressed-steel leaf spring; rear, rigid
Dimensions, weight	Length 2,100 mm, width 890 mm, height 950 mm, weight 165 kg
Years of production	1929–34
Chassis serial nos.	From P 101 to P 9893
Engine nos.	From 75001 to 76956
Units manufactured	1,106
Spare parts availab.	🏍🏍
Collectors value	🏍🏍🏍🏍🏍
Price	From 45,000 to 60,000 euros

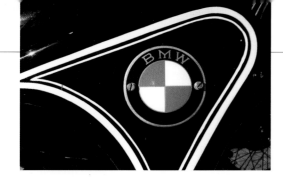

in 1932 on, the adoption of a friction damper in the spring assembly in place of the traditional leaf spring. In detail, the main changes for the R 11 were: first series (1929–30), electrics included in the price; second series (1930–31), change in the thrust bearing on the clutch and enlargement of the driveshaft-mounted brake; third series (1931–32), adoption of an inverted double barrel, three jet, Sum carburettor; fourth series (1933–34), new saddle with tension spring, replacement of ball bearings on connecting rod with single-row roller bearings, driveshaft turning on double ball bearings at the extremity of the transmission, new hand-operated gear stick attached to tank; fifth series (1934), adoption of two single Amal pump carburettors, new-look headlamp, exhaust pipe with slash-cut silencers, pipe for the preheating of the intake manifold, optional battery. The following are the most important changes made over the years to the R 16: first series (1929–30) and second series (1930–32), new-look headlamp, enlargement of the driveshaft brake; third series (1932), double Amal carburettor; fourth series (1933), new gear lever attached to the tank, replacement of ball bearings on connecting rod with single-row roller bearings; fifth series (1934), optional battery, exhaust pipe with slash-cut silencers.
A big improvement was made to both models with the fifth series in 1934, which added a timing belt instead of spur gears for driving the camshaft and the ignition system.

COLLECTORS CORNER

The R 11 and R 16 are the last motorcycles made by Bayerische Motoren Werke in the 1920s, as well as the first to abandon the flat-tank configuration, using instead a new frame of pressed steel with the tank positioned in front of the saddle. These features are sufficient in themselves to explain the great interest collectors have in these two models. There is also a good availability of spare parts, particularly in Germany, where it is still possible to find some R 11s in fair condition (the R 16 less so). The existence of five series for both models leaves much room for subjective evaluation both from an aesthetic and from a technical perspective, though the models with the two Amal carburettors are rarities and much sought after by fans. The R 11 and R 16 bring us into a decade that is slightly less distant from the present, and restoration can be performed with greater peace of mind, even if the economic value of the two bikes is in any case very high, and finding spare parts is pretty challenging.

data sheet | 1920s

Model	Cylinders	cc	Production years	Units made	Spare parts availability	Collectors value	Price (euros)	Chassis	Engine
R 32	2	494	1923–26	3,090	🏍	🏍🏍🏍🏍🏍	65,000–105,000	From 1001 to 4100	From 31000 to 34100
R 37	2	494	1925–26	152	🏍	🏍🏍🏍🏍🏍	30,000–60,000	From 100 to 275	From 35001 to 35175
R 39	1	247	1925–27	855	🏍	🏍🏍🏍🏍🏍	15,000–31,000	From 8000 to 8900	From 36000 to 36900
R 42	2	494	1926–28	6,502	🏍	🏍🏍🏍🏍🏍	20,000–35,000	From 10001 to 16999	From 40001 to 46999
R 47	2	494	1927–28	1,720	🏍	🏍🏍🏍🏍🏍	25,000–39,000	From 4201 to 5999	From 34201 to 35999
R 52	2	487	1928–29	4,377	🏍	🏍🏍🏍🏍🏍	20,000–29,000	From 20000 to 30600	From 47001 to 51383
R 57	2	494	1928–30	1,006	🏍	🏍🏍🏍🏍	25,000–33,000	From 20000 to 30600	From 70001 to 71012
R 62	2	745	1928–29	4,355	🏍	🏍🏍🏍🏍	25,000–37,000	From 20000 to 30600	From 60001 to 65000
R 63	2	735	1928–29	794	🏍	🏍🏍🏍🏍🏍	55,000–70,000	From 20000 to 30600	From 75001 to 76000
R 11	2	745	1929–34	7,500	🏍🏍	🏍🏍🏍🏍🏍	20,000–30,000	From P 101 to P 9893	From 60001 to 73984
R 16	2	735	1929–34	1,106	🏍🏍	🏍🏍🏍🏍🏍	45,000–60,000	From P 101 to P 9893	From 75001 to 76956

the 1930s

The economic crisis that followed the Black October of 1929 had a devastating effect on the habits of Europeans. As banks went bust, the lines of the unemployed grew longer and longer. In the midst of this, the new National Socialist Party of Adolf Hitler notched up electoral success in Germany. Once in government, the Nazi Party did in fact manage to bring about a slight boost to industrial production, but it was also leading the world towards war. In spite of the circumstances and under the wise direction of its management, BMW continued with its mission, and was to create some of the most beautiful and sophisticated machines in its history, from the R 2, the "people's bike" to the extraordinary R 51 and the glorious and innovative R 5 and R 61.

R 2

In 1931, six years after the ill-fated R 39, the first and so far only single-cylinder machine to leave the factories of Bayerische Motoren Werke, the company directors recognized the need for a motorcycle designed for people who were not affluent enough to buy one of the powerful and expensive 750cc models. Thus, under the watchful management of chief designer Rudolf Schleicher, BMW developed the R 2, the "people's bike" as it was called (and the first BMW to use the engine displacement, 200cc, as the basis for the name of the motorcycle). The minds behind the project were essentially aiming to make the most of the German government's decision in 1928 to exempt from the requirement of a driving licence and from road tax motorcycles of up to 200cc. The R 2 was built with high-quality materials, but also made use of solutions that were appropriate to the difficult times (one of these was to leave the overhead valves uncovered, in order to reduce production costs, for the first series). The general public was immediately enthusiastic about the new bike, which made a deliberate appeal also to female users. The R 2 was built using a smaller and lighter version of the pressed-steel frame of the R 11. The crankshaft was longitudinal, the gearbox was directly flange-connected, the transmission housing was set inside the frame cradle, and the rear Cardan shaft brake was abandoned for a new drum brake. For the first time, a coil ignition with battery was used. The front suspension was a trailing link setup that included a manually adjustable damper. As with the R 11 and R 16, improvements were made during the six years of production of the R 2, which can be divided into five different series: first series (1931); second series, (1932–33), cylinder head now

R 2

Engine	198cc, single-cylinder, overhead valves
Frame	Double-cradle pressed steel
Power	6 HP at 3,500 rpm, 8 HP at 4,500 rpm (third series, 1934)
Transmission	Cardan shaft
Suspension	Front, pressed-steel oscillating fork with leaf spring; rear, rigid
Dimensions, weight	Length 1,950 mm, width 850 mm, height 950 mm, weight 130 kg
Years of production	1931–36
Chassis serial nos.	From P 15000 to P 19260
Engine nos.	From 101 to 15402, from P 80001 to P 97700
Units manufactured	15,288
Spare parts availab.	🏍 🏍
Collectors value	🏍 🏍 🏍 🏍 🏍
Price	From 5,000 to 10,000 euros

Wirtschaftlichkeit bedeutet Geldersparnis

A 1930s brochure

with cover for valve springs, pipe added for delivery of pressurized oil supply; third series (1934), forced lubrication, Sum carburettor replaced by an Amal one, power increased from 6 to 8 HP; fourth series (1935), a new-design, longer and flatter fuel tank with blue top finishing, dampers included in front fork, new look headlamp; fifth series (1936), changes made to shaft drive, longer fender over rear wheel.

COLLECTORS CORNER

Collectors love the single-cylinder R 2 because, along with the R 4 and R 3, it combines the thrill of owning a 1920s-style motorcycle with a machine whose frame and technical solutions make it easier to ride it on the road. The high production numbers mean that finding an R 2 is a difficult but not a hopeless undertaking. As regards spare parts, including original pieces that have survived as warehouse stock or pieces from disused motorcycles, the availability is better than for the models of the previous decade. Like the R 11 and R 16, the R 2 registers no particular price differences between one series and the next (for whose, unfortunately, the engine and frame serial numbers cannot be accurately given); the fourth series, thanks to its special two-tone fuel tank, is however regarded as a precious gem.

R4
R3

The sales success of the R 2, which found favour with the less affluent public and enlarged the customer base of the company, persuaded BMW management to persist with the design and production of low priced single-cylinder models. So it was that in 1932, only one year after the launch of the famous "people's bike", BMW rolled out an updated version of the R 2 with the engine displacement expanded to 400cc. This was the R 4, which in appearance differed from the R 2 only for a larger engine, a bigger front fender borrowed from the BMW two-cylinder range, a muffler closer to the rear wheel, and a speedometer moved from the tank to the headlamp. Designed by Rudolf Schleicher (who had left BMW in 1927 only to return in 1931), the R 4 went down in BMW history as the first to adopt a four-speed gearbox, a solution that was to feature on BMW motorcycles until the R 90 S of 1973. (The solution was reached after a pre-series production of 100 models with a three-speed gearbox.) The decision to increase the engine displacement with respect to the R 2 was also driven by increasing market demand for models that could easily handle the added weight of a sidecar, a means of family transport that was very popular at the time. In the case of the R 4, the bullet-shaped sidecar was shipped directly by BMW, even though it was not manufactured by the company. Once again, Bayerische Motoren Werke's commercial instincts were spot on, and over 15,000 units were shipped, thanks also to the large number ordered by the Army, which used the R 4 with increasing frequency until the Second World War. The motorcycle gained a reputation for indestructability and agility – its massive frame and 140 kilograms-plus weight notwithstanding – and justified this reputation by repeated victories in enduro European race

R 4

Engine	398cc, single-cylinder, overhead valves
Frame	Double-cradle pressed steel
Power	12 HP at 3,500 rpm, 14 HP at 4,200 rpm (third series, 1934)
Transmission	Cardan shaft
Suspension	Front, pressed-steel oscillating fork with leaf spring; rear, rigid
Dimensions, weight	Length 1,950 mm, width 850 mm, height 950 mm, weight 137–48 kg
Years of production	1932–37
Chassis serial nos.	From P 80001 to P 97700 and from P 1001 to P 10437
Engine nos.	From 80001 to 95280
Units manufactured	15,193
Spare parts availab.	🏍 🏍
Collectors value	🏍 🏍 🏍 🏍 🏍
Price	From 3,500 to 8,000 euros

R 3

Engine	305cc, single-cylinder, overhead valves
Frame	Double-cradle pressed steel
Power	11 HP at 4,200 rpm
Transmission	Cardan shaft
Suspension	Front, pressed-steel oscillating fork with leaf spring; rear, rigid
Dimensions, weight	Length 1,950 mm, width 850 mm, height 950 mm, weight 149 kg
Years of production	1936
Chassis serial nos.	From P 1001 to P 1740
Engine nos.	From 20001 to 20740
Units manufactured	740
Spare parts availab.	🏍 🏍
Collectors value	🏍 🏍 🏍 🏍
Price	From 3,000 to 7,500 euros

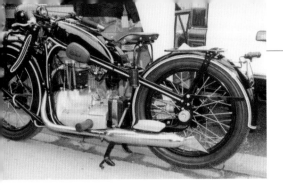

meets. In common with all motorcycles manufactured in the early 1930s, the R 4 underwent continuous improvements, resulting in five different series: first series (1932), as of June a friction damper was introduced into the front fork; second series (1933), four-speed gearbox, alterations made to manual shift lever, head with forced lubrication, kick-starter repositioned longitudinally and no more transversely; third series (1934), output raised to 14 HP, new larger fuel tank, adoption of a second chain to drive the dynamo, gear lever attached to the fuel tank; fourth series (1935), new design of headlamp, changes to the aluminium crankcase, crank shifted to the right to align the drive shaft with the rear wheel, V-belt to drive the dynamo; fifth series (1936–37), unified four-speed gearbox with new housing, repositioning of the oil cap. In 1936, an intermediate version between the R 2 and R 4 with a 300cc displacement engine was created and, following the new praxis of naming with reference to engine size, it was baptized the R 3. Unlike its more fortunate siblings, the R 3 found favour neither with the public, which continued to prefer the larger displacement version, nor with the Army, which likewise continued to order the R 4.

COLLECTORS CORNER

The resistant and virtually indestructible R 4 is without a doubt one of the most reliable and successful single-cylinder BMW motorcycles ever built. More than 15,000 specimens of this bike were manufactured, many as part of the motorization of the Army, but many also for the civilian population. This is why at certain market-shows and in collector circles, it is relatively easy to find some of these machines for sale. In terms of spare parts, the most important components are available only at very high prices, but restoring an R 4 or R 3 is not an impossible task. With regard to preferences among the five variants, the highest demand is for the third series of 1934, which has the (four-speed) gear lever mounted on the (larger) tank, and 2 extra HP of power. Fewer in number and almost impossible to find are the R 3s, which were available for sale for just one year and of which just 740 were made. Even so, since almost all of the R 3 parts are the same as those for the R 2 and R 4, it is possible to restore an R 3, even starting out from one in poor condition.

R 12
R 17

Between 1933 and 1934, thanks to the sales of the single-cylinder R 2, R 3 and R 4 to both private clients and the Army, BMW enjoyed a period of such strong economic growth that it could afford to start thinking of renewing its top-range models, which were still the 750cc R 11 and R 16. The development department, directed by engineer Alfred Böning, was therefore assigned the task of building a new flagship that might compete with the powerful four-cylinder 800cc motorcycle being produced by rivals Zündapp. This was the background to the birth of the "beautiful but impossible" R 7, which boasted a novel 750cc overhead-valve engine enclosed in a distinctive sheet-metal chassis. Fairings almost entirely incorporated the fuel tank and engine in a single shell. Indeed, so ambitious was the R 7 project that it never got beyond the prototype stage. The production costs were excessive and, worst of all, the frame was not rigid enough. It was, however, an important project that produced technical innovations that would soon become a milestone in the history of BMW. In fact, the design of the R 7 had forced Alfred Böning's department to develop a new system of shock absorbers and suspension to replace the by then obsolete leaf-spring system; the result was a significant increase in driving comfort and grip that enabled the motorcycles to ride safely over uneven road surfaces. The breakthrough came with the world's first telescopic fork with an inbuilt hydraulic shock absorber (i.e. a "hydraulic fork"), which marked a real revolution in the world of two-wheeled transport. The new hydraulic fork made its debut as a standard fitting in 1935 with the new 750cc R 12 and R 17, with respectively side-valve and overhead-valve engines. The latter, a sports bike and heir of the R 63 and R 16, immediately caught the attention of the lay public

R 12

Engine	745cc, two-cylinder, side valves
Frame	Double-cradle pressed steel
Power	18 HP at 3,400 rpm, 20 HP at 4,000 rpm (in the version with two carburettors)
Transmission	Cardan shaft
Suspension	Front, telescopic fork; rear, rigid
Dimensions, weight	Length 2,100 mm, width 900 mm, height 940 mm, weight 185 kg
Years of production	1935–42
Chassis serial nos.	From P 501 to P 24149 and from P 25001 to P 37161
Engine nos.	From 501 to 24149 and from 25001 to 37161
Units manufactured	36,008
Spare parts availab.	🏍 🏍
Collectors value	🏍 🏍 🏍 🏍
Price	From 12,000 to 25,000 euros

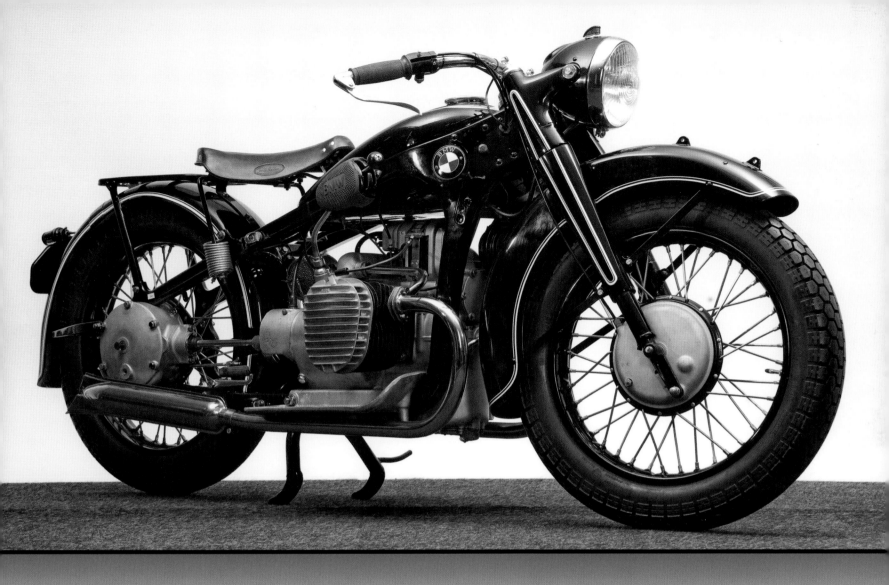

and professionals alike as the most powerful and fastest motorcycle of the day. The debut of the telescopic fork put all the other innovations of the R 12 and R 17 in the shade, though they included completely interchangeable 19-inch wheels, battery ignition, a rear drum brake and a reinforced crankshaft. The four-speed gearbox was confirmed, while the horsepower remained unchanged with respect to the previous 750cc models. The motorcycle with the side-valve engine was also available in a single carburettor version with a magneto ignition that delivered 18 HP, two HP less than the double carburettor version. This less powerful version of the R 12 won large orders from the Army, especially when combined with the sidecar (the first batch came with the sidecar attachment connected directly to the bevel gear, though this was later replaced by a more resistant screwed coupling head). The difference between the civilian and military versions of the R 12 is essentially one of appearance. The military version was different in colour (monochrome without any pinstripes). It also showed differences with respect to the front fender, the stiffeners on the side of the fuel tank, the colour of the speedometer and the air intake of the carburettor. Neither the R 12 nor the R 17 underwent substantial changes during their production. A few minor touches were made, including in the design of the front fender, which in 1936 was given an elegant terminal curve.

COLLECTORS CORNER

The R 12 and R 17 are two of the most popular motorcycles from the 1930s among collectors, especially those who have focused on the pre-war period. In terms of market availability, however, the two models could hardly be more different. On the one hand, thanks to a production run of more than 36,000 units, it is not at all that difficult to find a reasonably priced R 12 mounted with a side-valve engine, whether in the more sought-after civil, more powerful version, or in the military version; those equipped with original Royal sidecar, though, cost almost twice as much as those without. On the other hand, it is almost impossible to buy an R 17 that has not been restored by collectors, and whose sale price is sure to be exorbitant. With a production run of just 434, the R 17 is second only to R 37 of 1925 (production run, 152) for the shortest production run of a BMW motorcycle. As for its spare parts, those for the engine are substantially the same as for the R 11 and R 16.

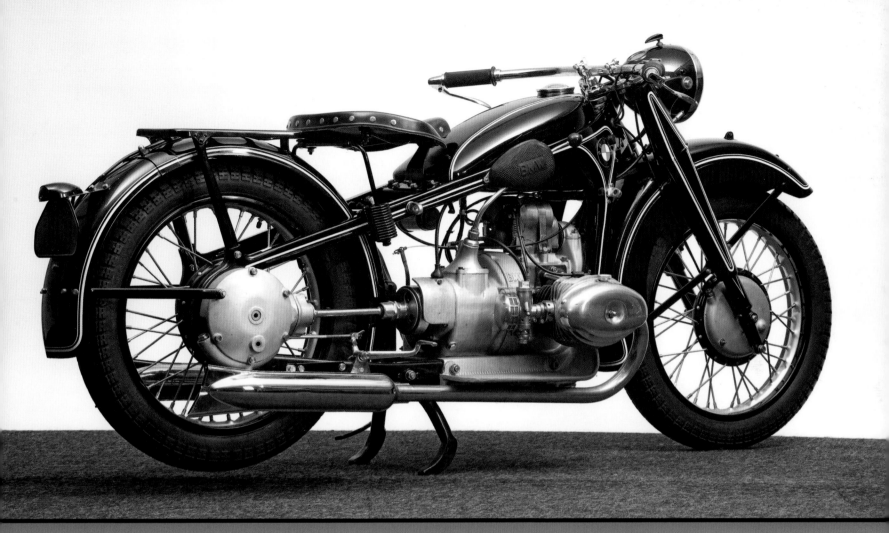

R 17

Engine	735cc, two cylinder, overhead valves
Frame	Double-cradle pressed steel
Power	33 HP at 5,000 rpm
Transmission	Cardan shaft
Suspension	Front, telescopic fork; rear, rigid
Dimensions, weight	Length 2,100 mm, width 900 mm, height 940 mm, weight 165 kg
Years of production	1935–37
Chassis serial nos.	From P 501 to P 24728
Engine nos.	From 77001 to 77436
Units manufactured	434
Spare parts availab.	🏍️🏍️
Collectors value	🏍️🏍️🏍️🏍️
Price	From 20,000 to 26,000 euros

R5
R6

In a recent survey, leading BMW collectors crowned the sporty R 5 as the most beautiful motorcycle made by Bayerische Motoren Werke in all its ninety years of production. Such is the reputation of the sports motorcycle that we are about to consider here, a bike that is the ultimate and impossible dream of BMW aficionados. The R 5 made its official debut on 15 February 1936 at the International Motor Show of Berlin and immediately bewitched the general public and the experts alike. The machine was a masterwork that marked the return of the half-litre boxer engine as well as of the tubular frame, which had been replaced in 1929 owing to problems with the welding of parts. The issue was finally solved by the innovative process of welding called Arcatron, which guaranteed extraordinary strength in the tapered oval tubes of the frame with their conic cross-sections. The novelties included in the R 5 did not stop with this. The bike also introduced an epoch-making change to the gearbox. After thirteen years of honourable service, the hand shift was finally retired to be replaced by a new foot-operated shift, a solution that has lasted to the present day. On the R 5, it already came equipped with a special mechanism that returned the lever to its original position after each shifting. The R 5 also included a secondary, hand-operated shift lever, even though it is decidedly premature to speak in terms of a combined gear shift. Moreover, the R 5 perfected the telescopic fork that had first appeared on the R 12 and R 17: it now included a tie rod used to calibrate the damping effect. The engine was a totally new monoblock type, enclosed in a sturdy tunnel casing instead of the traditional construction with separated blocks, divided by a horizontal plane. With its 24 horsepower and top speed of over 140

R 5

Engine	494cc, two-cylinder, overhead valves
Frame	Tubular twin cradle
Power	24 HP at 5,500 rpm
Transmission	Cardan shaft
Suspension	Front, telescopic fork; rear, rigid
Dimensions, weight	Length 2,130 mm, width 800 mm, height 950 mm, weight 165 kg
Years of production	1936–37
Chassis serial nos.	From 8001 to 9504 and from 500001 to 503085
Engine nos.	From 8001 to 9504 and from 500001 to 502786
Units manufactured	2,652
Spare parts availab.	🏍 🏍
Collectors value	🏍 🏍 🏍 🏍 🏍
Price	From 22,000 to 25,000 euros

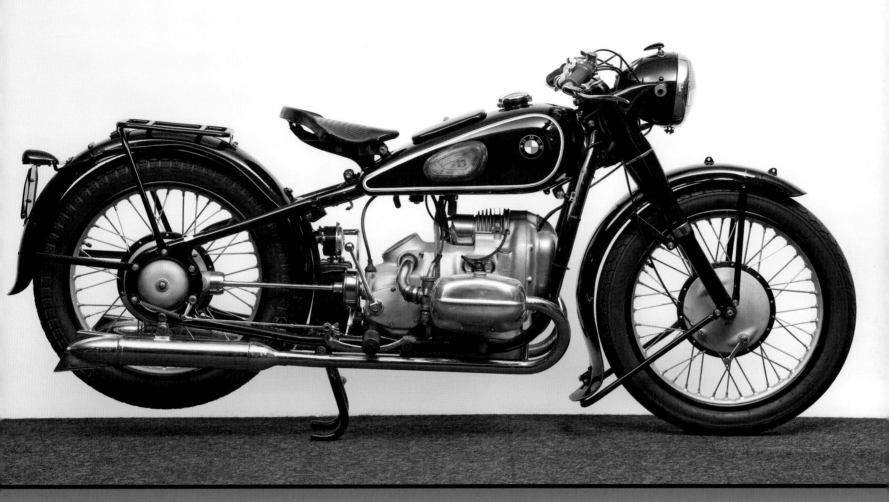

Left, a very rare R 5 engine, characterized
by the gear train to drive the camshaft

R 6

Engine	596cc, two-cylinder, side valves
Frame	Tubular twin cradle
Power	18 HP to 4,500 rpm
Transmission	Cardan shaft
Suspension	Front, telescopic fork; rear, rigid
Dimensions, weight	Length 2,130 mm, width 800 mm, height 950 mm, weight 175 kg
Years of production	1937
Chassis serial nos.	From 500001 to 503085
Engine nos.	From 600001 to 601850
Units manufactured	1,850
Spare parts availab.	🏍🏍
Collectors value	🏍🏍🏍🏍🏍
Price	From 10,000 to 18,000 euros

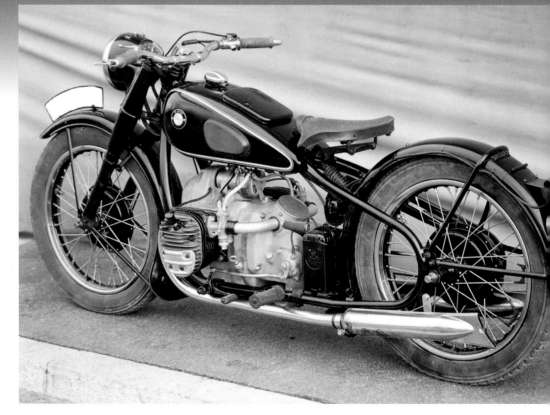

km/h, the R 5 was marketed as a motorcycle combining a touring attitude (the telescopic fork guaranteed a sufficiently comfortable ride) and a sport capability, so successfully that it was even exported to England, home of decidedly tough competition in this area. In 1937, problems caused by water getting into the two Amal carburettors during use on wet roads led to the installation of a single filter in the upper part of the gear assembly, which was connected to the carburettors by way of two metal pipes with a chrome finish. Another alteration concerned the placement of the dynamo on the collar, to give a tighter fit. 1937 was also the year the 600cc side-valve R 6 came out. This was intended for a public keener on acquiring a touring motorcycle than one with a pronounced sporty character such as the R 5. For obvious reasons of cost rationalization, the two machines had much in common, from the frame and suspension to the wheels, brakes, drive train, gear assembly (excluding the external housing) and electrics. The engine on the R 6 was also new, and came with two Amal carburettors and a single camshaft, now positioned above the crankshaft and regulated by two mating gears. As on the R 5, the dynamo was positioned on the upper section of the engine block.

COLLECTORS CORNER

The R 5 and R 6 are among the most difficult BMW to find of the post flat-tank generation. The production run was quite low (2,652 of the R 5 and 1,850 of the R 6), with many of the overhead-valve R 5 being acquired for race use. The keen interest of collectors since the early 1960s has soaked up the specimens then available, practically removing these models from the market. The importance of these bikes, especially of R 5, is such as to justify buying any spare parts that can be found (not that there are many), even if in poor condition. Given that the supply has dried up anyhow, it is pointless making any value distinctions between the 1936 R 5 and the improved 1937 version. The major collectors who have these bikes in their possession are going to hold fast on to them, even if their restoration requires years of hunting for parts and a considerable outlay of money.

R20
R23

1936 was the last year of production for the R 2, the "people's bike", an important chapter in the history of BMW that with this model had made its debut in the 200cc class. Once the remaining warehouse stock had been sold on, the management of Bayerische Motoren Werke ordered the development department to create a bike able to replace the R 2. This led to the creation in 1937 of the R 20, a brand new model that had very little in common with the previous 200cc motorcycle, but was much more alike the new generation of two-cylinder engines. That's the case of the frame, which abandoned the pressed-steel technology to make use of new tubular forms, now bolted rather than welded; of the telescopic front fork derived from that of the R 35; of the new foot-operated gearbox, which had made its debut on the R 5. The engine was completely overhauled to improve its efficiency and reduce noise, with a different cylinder bore, compression ratio and arrangement of the components (for example, the battery was placed under the seat, the ignition moved forward to the front cover). More graceful and less massive than the R 2, the R 20 immediately won plaudits, helped by a sales price that was even lower than the latest variants of the R 2 and by extremely low fuel consumption: the magazines of the day estimated it could do 35–40 kilometres on one litre of petrol. In 1938, however, the R 20 was replaced in the catalogue by the R 23, a move that was almost dictated by the amendments to the highway code introduced by the government. The new provisions abolished the right to ride motorcycles of up to 200cc without a license (the limit was dropped to 98cc). A decision was thus made to redeploy the basic frame and engine of the R 20 to create a more powerful motorcycle with a 250cc displacement (the second with

R 20

Engine	192cc, single-cylinder, overhead valves
Frame	Tube frame held fast by screws
Power	8 HP at 5,400 rpm
Transmission	Cardan shaft
Suspension	Front, telescopic fork; rear, rigid
Dimensions, weight	Length 2,000 mm, width 800 mm, height 920 mm, weight 130 kg
Years of production	1937–38
Chassis serial nos.	From 100001 to 105029
Engine nos.	From 100001 to 105004
Units manufactured	5,000
Spare parts availab.	🏍️ 🏍️
Collectors value	🏍️ 🏍️ 🏍️
Price	From 3,000 to 8,000 euros

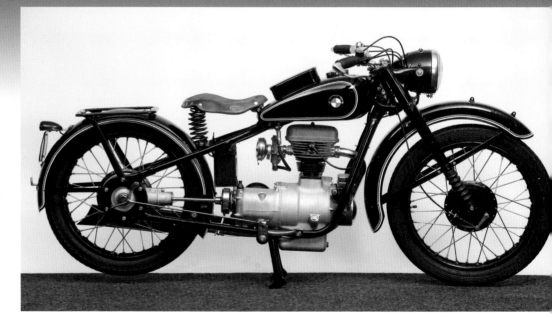

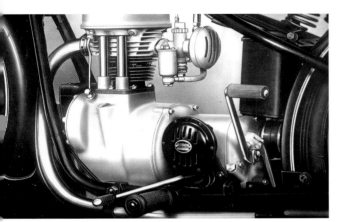

such a displacement after the R 39 of 1925). The upshot was the R 23, essentially an R 20 with two extra horsepower and a shorter range caused by the shift of the storage compartment to the back of the fuel tank, the capacity of which had to be reduced from 12 to only 9.6 litres. Both models used a three-speed gearbox (as on the R 2) in place of the four-speed gearbox that had been in use on BMW motorcycles since 1932.

R 23

Engine	247cc, single-cylinder, overhead valves
Frame	Tube frame held fast by screws
Power	10 HP at 5,400 rpm
Transmission	Cardan shaft
Suspension	Front, telescopic fork; rear, rigid
Dimensions, weight	Length 2,000 mm, width 800 mm, height 920 mm, weight 135 kg
Years of production	1938–40
Chassis serial nos.	From 106001 to 114203
Engine nos.	From 106001 to 114021
Units manufactured	8,021
Spare parts availab.	🏍 🏍
Collectors value	🏍 🏍 🏍
Price	From 3,000 to 8,000 euros

COLLECTORS CORNER

The R 20 and R 23 bikes are of little collectible value as a result of weak demand from aficionados who prefer either the earlier, more priced models, such as the R 2 or R 35, or the later, more evolved ones such as the R 25 and R 25/2. No great price difference separates the 200cc and the 250cc models, though a slight preference for the latter is evident. It is hard to find examples in good or excellent condition, and the cost of a total restoration is almost never going to make economic sense: the parts are few and expensive, especially if set beside the relatively low price that you would fetch for a restored version of the R 20.

R 51
R 66

On 24 November 1938, the directors, engineers, designers and all the workers of Bayerische Motoren Werke celebrated the manufacture of the 100,000th motorcycle, a historic achievement for a company that at the time held a market share of just 10%, and was only a minor force in German industry. Under the indefatigable guidance of Rudolf Schleicher, the design and development division had produced a large number of technical innovations over recent years, such as the pedal shifter, a renewed version of the tubular frame and the telescopic fork. The arrival in the department of a young pilot and engineer called Alexander von Falkenhausen was to bring about a shift of research focus, and BMW's priority now became to compete with English and Italian motorcycles in terms of both safety and comfort. Bearing in mind the race experiences of brands such as Norton and Moto Guzzi, von Falkenhausen became convinced of the need to equip the chassis of the new models with a rear suspension. His idea was very simple: to refashion the tubular frame of the R 5, eliminating the support for the transmission housing and the rear arch of the frame, and reinforcing the whole with a tube placed vertically in front of the arms of the new suspension, which became known as a "plunger" suspension. Backed by Schleicher, von Falkenhausen built prototypes and personally drove one of them to its debut in 1937 at the International Six Days Trial. The result was remarkable. The new plunger suspension offered better road grip and rider comfort, and the top management was persuaded to take it in production models which, in the following year 1938, were to include both new overhead-valve models (the R 51 and R 66) and side-valve models (the R 61 and R 71). The R 51 was the direct heir of the R 5,

R 51

Engine	494cc, two-cylinder, overhead valves
Frame	Tubular twin cradle
Power	24 HP at 5,600 rpm
Transmission	Cardan shaft
Suspension	Front, telescopic fork; rear, spring damper on straight axis ("plunger")
Dimensions, weight	Length 2,130 mm, width 815 mm, height 960 mm, weight 182 kg
Years of production	1938–40
Chassis serial nos.	From 505001 to 515164
Engine nos.	From 503001 to 506172
Units manufactured	3,775
Spare parts availab.	🏍 🏍
Collectors value	🏍 🏍 🏍 🏍 🏍
Price	From 12,000 to 18,000 euros

A white R 51; this non-original colour scheme may be found in restored versions

A racing version of the R 51

R 66

Engine	597cc, two-cylinder, overhead valves
Frame	Tubular twin cradle
Power	30 HP at 5,300 rpm
Transmission	Cardan shaft
Suspension	Front, telescopic fork; rear, spring damper on straight axis ("plunger")
Dimensions, weight	Length 2,130 mm, width 815 mm, height 960 mm, weight 187 kg
Years of production	1938–41
Chassis serial nos.	From 505001 to 515164 and from 662001 to 662039
Engine nos.	From 660001 to 661629 and from 662001 to 662039
Units manufactured	1,669
Spare parts availab.	🏍 🏍
Collectors value	🏍 🏍 🏍
Price	From 15,000 to 22,000 euros

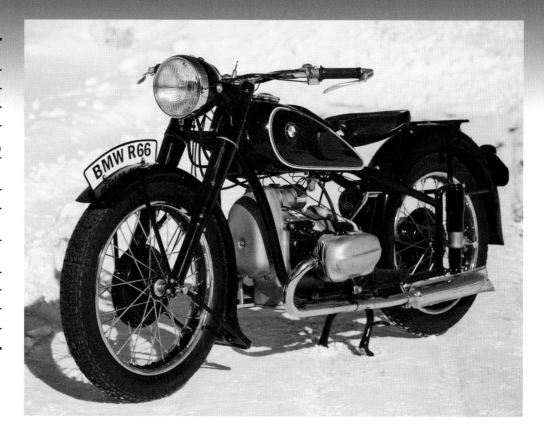

and from a technical perspective remained virtually unchanged from its predecessor, with the same rating power of 24 HP, the same two Amal carburettors, the same braking system and the same double-cradle frame. Unlike their ancestors, R 5 and R 6, the R 51 and R 66 had the foot lever directly on the gearbox cover, thus eliminating the old connecting rod. As an optional, the manufacturer could mount a traditional manual gear lever, positioned on the right side of the fuel tank at the height of the knee protector. On the R 66 only, and only if requested, the gear ratios could be shortened for an owner planning to attach a sidecar. The R 51 (which provided the basis for the development of the "super-sport" versions, the R 51 RS and R 51 SS, the latter equipped with engine compressor and return shafts) achieved moderate sales. The R 66, on the other hand, turned out to be an excellent product thanks to some of the tweaks made in it, which have led some to consider it the best among the pre-war series. The engine, which was also mounted on the R 51, was notable for its "porcupine cylinders" (a name it acquired in reference to the layout of the cooling fins to improve heat dispersion) and the tilted-forward cylinder heads based on the R 6 design with its side-valve engine and a single central camshaft. The qualities of reliability and rating (30 horsepower for a top speed of 150 km/h) allowed the R 66 to acquire the commercial nickname "Sidecar Sport".

COLLECTORS CORNER

The R 51 and R 66 share a common destiny with the previous R 5 and R 6, and their commercial value is almost identical to that of R 6. This is because the introduction of the plunger rear suspension, although causing a great impression at the time and favouring the sales of new models, is now seen as marking the dividing line that separates the second-generation BMW motorcycles (i.e. from the end of the flat-tank models until the Second World War) from the motorcycles of the post-war period. Many collectors are keener on the frames with no rear suspension, and others are mainly interested in post-war models, and prefer bikes with rear dampers. In any case, being able to find original motorcycles in good condition is a difficult task, especially because the most of them were modified for racing purposes. You may find it easier to look for motorcycles that have been completely restored, in which case the asking price will be huge; or for bikes in very poor condition and hunt for missing parts. The traditional German markets are the best place to find these.

R 61
R 71

The fortunes of the R 61 and R 71, the last side-valve motorcycles in the history of Bayerische Motoren Werke, are inextricably bound up with the fate of its two overhead-valve counterparts, the R 51 and R 6. All four models were launched in the same year, 1938, and marked the adoption for all models of the new rear suspension with telescopic dampers enclosed in tubes (the "plungers"), a solution designed and developed by Baron Alexander von Falkenhausen. The new system brought several benefits, ranging from the comfort of the rider to better road adherence and increased safety. Parallel to the development of the frame, the design department set to work on creating a new 750cc engine to replace the one in use since 1928. As for the 600cc, the idea was to base it on the tried and tested R 6. It was therefore the R 61 that supplanted the R 6 in the sales catalogue, at a price that was 178 Reichmarks less than what was being asked for the more powerful R 51 and R 71. It was not a trivial cost saving considering the particular socio-political context of Germany at the time. When ordering the R 61, R 51 and R 66, buyers could, for a substantial extra charge, request to have a manual shift lever on the right side of the tank; however, very few customers actually opted for this rather dated solution. The R 71 was built to replace the R 12 of 1935 and went on sale for 35 Reichmarks less than the older model, while production of the military version of the R 12 continued even later on. The new 750cc motorcycle was well received by the Wehrmacht, who ordered a large number of them. Given that the R 71 could be used with a sidecar, owners could ask to have the final drive ratios made shorter. The manufacture of the R 61 and R 71 was abruptly interrupted in 1941, even though they had

R 61

Engine	600cc, two-cylinder, side valves
Frame	Tubular twin cradle
Power	18 HP at 4,800 rpm
Transmission	Cardan shaft
Suspension	Front, telescopic fork; rear, spring damper on straight axis ("plunger")
Dimensions, weight	Length 2,130 mm, width 815 mm, height 960 mm, weight 184 kg
Years of production	1938–41
Chassis serial nos.	From 505001 to 515164 and from 607001 to 607340
Engine nos.	From 603001 to 606080
Units manufactured	3,747
Spare parts availab.	🏍️ 🏍️
Collectors value	🏍️ 🏍️ 🏍️ 🏍️
Price	From 8,000 to 15,000 euros

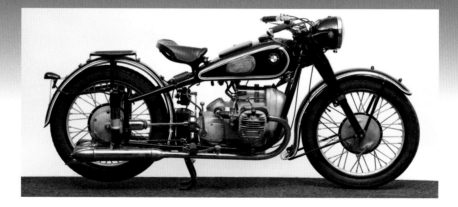

been both selling well (3,747 units of the former and 3,458 of the latter). BMW's hand was forced in this respect, since it had been called upon to focus solely on production of the new military version of the R 75 with a sidecar specially designed for use on various fronts of the Second World War. As we observed above, after the Second World War BMW stopped making any motorcycles with side-valve engine. The R 61 and R 71 became then the last survivors of a long series of models that were particularly important to the fortunes of the company down through the years.

R 71

Engine	746cc, two-cylinder, side valves
Frame	Tubular twin cradle
Power	22 HP at 4,600 rpm
Transmission	Cardan shaft
Suspension	Front, telescopic fork; rear, spring damper on straight axis ("plunger")
Dimensions, weight	Length 2,130 mm, width 815 mm, height 960 mm, weight 187 kg
Years of production	1938–41
Chassis serial nos.	From 505001 to 515164 and from 703001 to 703511
Engine nos.	From 700001 to 702200 and from 703001 to 703511
Units manufactured	3,458
Spare parts availab.	🏍️🏍️
Collectors value	🏍️🏍️🏍️
Price	From 10,000 to 15,000 euros

COLLECTORS CORNER

The collectible value of the R 61 and R 71 is conditioned by the value of the coeval R 5 and R 51, which have won the battle for the hearts of BMW aficionados. Nevertheless, their quotations remain quite interesting, for an obvious reason: nostalgia for the last two side-valve motorcycles made by BMW. The R 71, however, is worth considerably less, a reflection of the low level of market demand for it. Compared with other earlier models, the R 61 and R 71 have the advantage of having been produced in good quantity (over 7,000 units) and of counting on a slightly higher stock of spare parts. Of the two models, the main source of market interest is unquestionably the military version of the R 71 with sidecar. Also much desired is the version of the R 61 made for the German Post Office (Reichspost), with its distinctive red fuel tank.

R 35

In the first half of the 1930s, the single-cylinder motorcycle was the mainstay of BMW's production, with particular regard to the R 2 and R 4. Both were reliable, very well put together, and popular with both the general public and the military. In 1936 BMW had also created a model with an intermediate displacement engine, the R 3, but it soon proved a commercial flop. Convinced of the validity of the R 3 project but also well aware of its failure, the designers at Bayerische Motoren Werke developed a new bike to replace both the R 3 and the R 4. In 1937, it brought out the R 35, whose frame was based on the tried and tested pressed-steel configuration (the new tubular frame of the 750cc and 500cc was not used). The engine and gearbox (operated manually, not by foot pedal as on the two-cylinder R 5) were taken from the fifth series of the R 4, along with the new telescopic fork – an incomplete innovation since for cost reasons the hydraulic damper included in the R 5 fork was not included. The R 35 was a commercial success, thanks also to the usual large order book from the German Army.

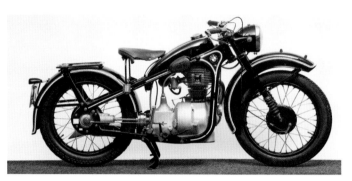

R 35

Engine	342cc, single-cylinder, overhead valves
Frame	Double-cradle pressed steel
Power	14 HP at 3,500 rpm
Transmission	Cardan shaft
Suspension	Front, telescopic fork; rear, rigid
Dimensions, weight	Length 2,000 mm, width 800 mm, height 950 mm, weight 155 kg
Years of production	1937–40
Chassis serial nos.	From 300001 to 315654
Engine nos.	From 300001 to 315387
Units manufactured	15,386
Spare parts availab.	🏍 🏍
Collectors value	🏍 🏍 🏍 🏍
Price	From 3,000 to 7,000 euros

COLLECTORS CORNER

The R 35 is the last bike of the single-cylinder with pressed steel frame generation manufactured by BMW. It was one of the best-selling BMW motorcycles in the 1930s, which explains the decent availability of the model in collectors' circles and at major exhibition-markets. Given the lack of substantial technical differences between the models for civilian use and those for the motorization of the military corps, there are few price differences between the two versions. Recently, price estimates of the R 35 have been rising; it is still considered less valuable than an R 2 or R 4, but is now on equal footing with the R 20 and R 23.

1930s

data sheet

Model	Cylinders	displacement cc	Production years	Units made	Spare parts availability	Collectors value	Price (euros)	Chassis	Engine
R 2	1	198	1931–36	15,288	🏍🏍 (2)	🏍🏍🏍🏍🏍 (5)	5,000–10,000	From P 15000 to P 19260	From 101 to 15402, P 80001 to P 97700
R 4	1	398	1932–37	15,193	🏍🏍 (2)	🏍🏍🏍🏍🏍 (5)	3,500–8,000	From P 80001 to P 97700, 1001 to P 10437	From 80001 to 95280
R 3	1	305	1936	740	🏍🏍 (2)	🏍🏍🏍🏍 (4)	3,000–7,500	From P 1001 to P 1740	From 20001 to 20740
R 12	2	745	1935–42	36,008	🏍🏍 (2)	🏍🏍🏍🏍 (4)	12,000–25,000	From P 501 to 24149, 25001 to 37161	From 501 to 24149, 25001 to 37161
R 17	2	735	1935–37	434	🏍🏍 (2)	🏍🏍🏍🏍🏍 (5)	20,000–26,000	From P 501 to P 24728	From 77001 to 77436
R 5	2	494	1936–37	2,652	🏍🏍 (2)	🏍🏍🏍🏍🏍 (5)	22,000–25,000	From 8001 to 9504, 500001 to 503085	From 8001 to 9504, 500001 to 502786
R 6	2	600	1937	1,850	🏍🏍 (2)	🏍🏍🏍🏍🏍 (5)	10,000–18,000	From 500001 to 503085	From 600001 to 601850
R 20	1	192	1937–38	5,000	🏍🏍 (2)	🏍🏍🏍 (3)	3,000–8,000	From 100001 to 105029	From 100001 to 105004
R 23	1	247	1938–40	8,021	🏍🏍 (2)	🏍🏍🏍 (3)	3,000–8,000	From 106001 to 114203	From 106001 to 114021
R 51	2	494	1938–40	3,775	🏍🏍 (2)	🏍🏍🏍🏍🏍 (5)	12,000–18,000	From 505001 to 515164	From 503001 to 506172
R 66	2	597	1938–41	1,669	🏍🏍 (2)	🏍🏍🏍🏍 (4)	15,000–22,000	From 505001 to 515164, 662001 to 662039	From 660001 to 661629, 662001 to 662039
R 61	2	600	1938–41	3,747	🏍🏍 (2)	🏍🏍🏍🏍 (4)	8,000–15,000	From 505001 to 515164, 607001 to 607340	From 603001 to 606080
R 71	2	746	1938–41	3,458	🏍🏍 (2)	🏍🏍🏍 (3)	10,000–15,000	From 505001 to 515164, 703001 to 703511	From 700001 to 702200, 703001 to 703511
R 35	1	342	1937–40	15,386	🏍🏍 (2)	🏍🏍🏍🏍 (4)	3,000–7,000	From 300001 to 315654	From 300001 to 315387

the 1940—50s

For BMW, the 1940s were inevitably buffeted by the winds of war during which Germany threw all its industrial strength into a fierce arms race ordered by Adolf Hitler. Only two motorcycles were produced in a decade that was notable for the effort made to design and build the legendary R 75, the motorcycle with sidecar for the German Army, a stalwart that saw action in Africa as well as in Europe. It was not until the end of the war that BMW returned to civilian production with the single-cylinder R 24, a renewed version of the R 23. The 1950s marked the return of the powerful boxer engines, any work on which had been put on hold in the previous decade as a result of the restrictions imposed by the Allies at the end of the war. Along with the two-cylinder models that were to become part of BMW history such as the prestigious R 51/3 or the R 68 "fireball", or the new R 50, R 60 and R 69 with their completely new oscillating frame and Earles forks, BMW manufactured its last-ever single-cylinder models including the R 25/3, the best-selling bike that BMW ever made.

R 75

In the autumn of 1933, the electoral victory of Adolf Hitler marked a turning point for BMW, as well as for German industry at large. From that moment until the outbreak of the Second World War, almost the only purpose of industrial production was rearmament. The expansionist ambitions of the Führer had repercussions on all the major industrial firms of Germany, including Bayerische Motoren Werke: hence the need to replace the functional but outdated R 12s supplied to the Army with a more versatile, sturdier and faster vehicle. The Army was clear about its requisites. They wanted a motorcycle with sidecar that would guarantee high performance on any terrain (from desert sands to muddy forests and even ice), a handling far superior to that of military automobiles, high performance but also the ability to go long distances at a reduced speed without problems. BMW entered into direct competition with the Nuremberg-based Zündapp company, but this was eventually to turn into collaboration (the armaments office of the Army ordered BMW and Zündapp to standardize some components in their respective sidecars, so they could swap around spare parts when the need arose). The BMW engineers led by Alexander von Falkenhausen created the R 75, which the Army renamed the "Ultra Heavy Motorcycle of the Wehrmacht". The machine proved its excellence from the first test, thanks also to a sophisticated gearbox that allowed drivers to choose between four gears for road use and three for off-road use. The reverse gear drove both the motorcycle and the sidecar, a necessary solution given that fully loaded with driver, passenger and arms, the whole thing weighed some 650 kilos. In June 1940, the final go-ahead was given for production, which the German military

R 75

Engine	745cc, two-cylinder, overhead valves
Frame	Tubular bolted
Power	26 HP at 4,000 rpm
Transmission	Driveshaft to lockable differential, driven sidecar wheel
Suspension	Front, telescopic fork; rear, rigid, with side leaf springs
Dimensions, weight	Length 2,400 mm (with sidecar), width 1,730 mm (with sidecar), height 1,000 mm (with sidecar), weight 420 kg (with sidecar)
Years of production	1941–44
Chassis serial nos.	From 750001 to more than 768000
Engine nos.	From 750001 to more than 768000
Units manufactured	18,000
Spare parts availab.	🏍 🏍 🏍
Collectors value	🏍 🏍 🏍 🏍 🏍
Price	From 18,000 to 33,000 euros

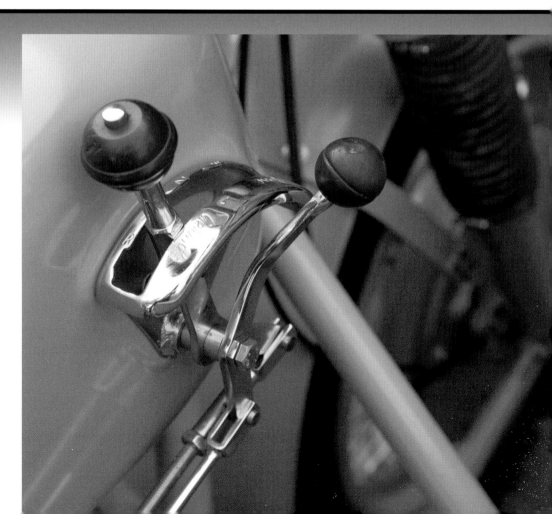

machine supported with no expense spared. Thus was born a small masterpiece of engineering, a versatile war machine with clever features, such as a bolted tubular frame, that made for quick and easy maintenance. The bike was so perfect that it was adopted with the relevant customizations by the Army, the Air Force and the Afrikakorps. The R 75 is still a cult object, even outside the universe of BMW, admired at exhibitions and gatherings where it speaks of the myth of German invincibility.

COLLECTORS CORNER

First a note of caution: this bike was designed to be used exclusively with a sidecar and was intended for military use. Finding an R 75 on the market without a sidecar is decidedly difficult, and if it is not an impossible undertaking, it is hardly a worthwhile one either: if you are buying one, you should make sure it comes with a sidecar. Bear in mind that the detached motorcycle, in addition to being virtually unrideable, may also not be homologated. To avoid unwanted surprises when purchasing a military R 75, and to avoid ending up with something that has been "cobbled together", it is best to opt for one of the specimens present in Western Europe before the fall of the Berlin Wall (1989). This is because the versions of the motorcycle used in Eastern Europe were often used as mules for agricultural work and transport, and were often patched up using parts of dubious origin and poor quality. Another important element to watch out for is the provenance of the sidecar, which, to be a valid collector's item, must be marked with the "Steib" logo, which was BMW's preferred brand. The weakness of the bike is the transmission, which is extremely complex and sophisticated and therefore involves huge repair costs. The main colours of the original motorcycle, which should be given priority consideration when buying, are: dark grey (produced until 1942 for the Army), dark beige (produced from 1941 to 1942 for the Afrikakorps), beige (produced from the end of 1942 for the Army), grey (produced from 1941 to 1945 for the Air Force).

R 24

The end of the Second World War was accompanied by several strict prohibitions, which curtailed industrial recovery in Germany. One of these referred to the manufacture of motorcycles. This lasted until 1947, when the Allies allowed BMW to build a very limited number of specimens (approximately 100) of the old R 23, which were assembled from spare parts stored in warehouses. This was the first step towards lifting the ban (removed in the following year) on the construction of motorcycles, provided that their capacity did not exceed 250cc. Without funds to design a completely new bike, BMW's managers decided to restart activities by building an updated version of the R 23, to which several changes were made in respect of the gears (which went from three to four) and the shape of the head (based on the experience gained with the R 75). Thus was born the R 24, officially presented in March 1948 and quickly ordered in large numbers (BMW almost immediately received orders for 3,000 units, thanks also to a very positive road test by motoring journalist Helmut Werner Bönsch for the prestigious publication *Das Auto*). The production of the R 24 began on 17 December 1948 (the event marked by a ceremony involving all the employees of BMW and the raffle of a bike) and was stopped just a year and a half later, after a significant production of more than 12,000 units. Like the military R 75, the R 24 was the only BMW with a bolted cradle frame for easy maintenance. One special feature of the R 24 was the addition of a spring element and a cush drive to mitigate the rigidity of transmission.

R 24

Engine	247cc, single cylinder, overhead valve
Frame	Tubular bolted
Power	12 HP at 5,600 rpm
Transmission	Cardan shaft
Suspension	Front, telescopic fork; rear, rigid
Dimensions, weight	Length 2,020 mm, width 750 mm, height 710 mm (to seat), weight 130 kg
Years of production	1948–50
Chassis serial nos.	from 200001 to 212007
Engine nos.	From 200001 to 212007
Units manufactured	12,020
Spare parts availab.	🏍️ 🏍️
Collectors value	🏍️ 🏍️
Price	From 3,000 to 8,000 euros

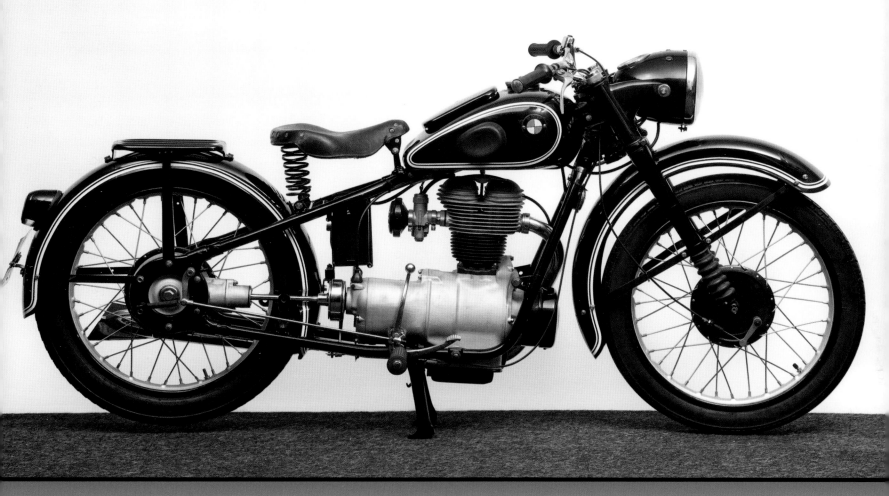

COLLECTORS CORNER

Currently it is quite difficult to find a complete R 24 with all its parts, even one in need of restoration. For this reason, the motorcycle has a value on par with that of the R 23 (even though fewer of the latter were made) and of the later models (R 25/2 and R 25/3, which are much more important from a collector's point of view). Complete but non-original versions of the model also exist. At markets and fairs in Europe, you might find fully-assembled R 24s made from spare parts belonging to earlier or later models. While the purchase price may be very tempting, it will be difficult and costly to carry out the restoration work, owing to the poor availability of original spare parts.

R 25
R 25/2

During the production of the R 24, made difficult by the aftermath of the war, BMW set about restructuring, expanding its plants and retooling. The designers, meanwhile, came up with a new motorcycle with a completely different frame (welded rather than bolted), with strengthened mechanical features (a new single-piece crankshaft in place of the former five-sectioned one) and a plunger suspension for the rear wheel, which gave a far more comfortable ride than the R 24. The R 25 made its debut in September 1950, both as a stand-alone and with a sidecar (the Steib LS 200 was the most used). A year later, it was replaced by the R 25/2, which remained in production until 1954 reaching the remarkable figure of 23,400 units. Reading the newspapers of the day reminds us of how the new version of the R 25 series immediately got rave reviews, and the bike was popularly called the "unbeatable single-cylinder". Few aesthetic differences divide the R 25 from the R 25/2. The changes that were made regarded: the saddle (vertical springs on the R 25, horizontal springs on the R 25/2), the light switch (mechanical on the R 25, electric on the R 25/2), the opening of the storage box (side-mounted on the R 25 and behind the tank on the R 25/2), the rims (all-black on the R 25 and two-tone black outside and grey inside on the R 25/2) and the front fender (less voluminous on the R 25/2). On the road, the bike performed extremely well by the standards of the day, with the R 25/2 capable of more than 100 km/h, a perfectly decent speed that makes it still suitable for short-range tourism journeys even today. The R 25 series, ended with the R 25/3 of 1953, with nearly 110,000 units produced remains to this day the most successful BMW series of all time.

R 25

Engine	247cc, single-cylinder, overhead valves
Frame	Tubular welded
Power	12 HP at 5,600 rpm
Transmission	Cardan shaft
Suspension	Front, telescopic fork; rear, rigid
Dimensions, weight	Length 2,073 mm, width 750 mm, height 710 mm, weight 140 kg
Years of production	1950–51
Chassis serial nos.	From 220001 to 243410
Engine nos.	From 220001 to 243410
Units manufactured	23,400
Spare parts availab.	🏍 🏍 🏍 🏍
Collectors value	🏍 🏍 🏍 🏍
Price	From 3,000 to 8,000 euros

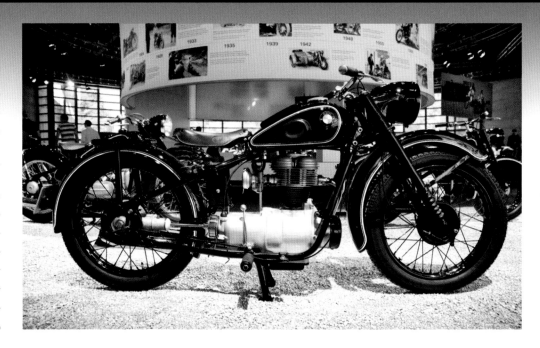

R 25/2

Engine	247cc, single-cylinder, overhead valves
Frame	Tubular welded
Power	12 HP at 5,600 rpm
Transmission	Cardan shaft
Suspension	Front, telescopic fork; rear, rigid
Dimensions, weight	Length 2,020 mm, width 790 mm, height 730 mm (to seat), weight 142 kg
Years of production	1951–54
Chassis serial nos.	From 245000 to 283650
Engine nos.	From 245000 to 283650
Units manufactured	38,651
Spare parts availab.	🏍️🏍️🏍️🏍️🏍️
Collectors value	🏍️🏍️🏍️🏍️
Price	From 3,000 to 8,000 euros

COLLECTORS CORNER

Aesthetically, the R 25 and R 25/2 are among the most elegant motorcycle produced by Bayerische Motoren Werke, thanks to the special "teardrop" design tank, which makes them aesthetically superior to the later R 25/3, which may have been better mechanically but was not as pleasing to the eye. The R 25 and R 25/2 are the most sought-after postwar single-cylinder motorcycles, a fact that has helped to keep up their value despite the huge production and wide distribution. The R 25 has a major advantage with respect to the previous R 24, in that spare parts are easy to come by. A caveat regarding models with a sidecar: it is hard to find examples in fair condition with the original Steib sidecar, unless you are prepared to pay a very steep price indeed. A stand-alone R 25 or R 25/2, however, is both a much wanted and historically important machine.

R 51/2

The R 51/2 marks a fundamental moment in the history of Bayerische Motoren Werke: it was the first twin-cylinder model to be built after the lifting of production restrictions imposed by the Allies at the end of the Second World War, which had effectively prevented the company from manufacturing motorcycles with an engine displacement of more than 250cc. Its connection to its elder sister, the R 51, is evident from the use of the same monoblock design. The motorcycle was powered through a "transplant" of two R 25 cylinders and heads. A visible difference compared with the previous R 51 was the R 51/2's impressively curved front fender. Also worth noting is the increased riding comfort (thanks to the use of a fork with the telescopic dual-effect hydraulic shock absorber of the R 75), which now reached a level previously unknown to BMW users, while retaining a respectable level of performance (in press tests the R 51/2 reached maximum speeds of more than 140 km/h). The care taken by Bayerische Motoren Werke in building this model was recognized in a now celebrated review published in 1950 by the renowned British magazine *The Motor Cycle*, which judged the R 51/2 "the best built BMW ever".

R 51/2

Engine	494cc, two-cylinder, overhead valves
Frame	Tubular welded
Power	24 HP at 5,800 rpm
Transmission	Cardan shaft
Suspension	Front, telescopic fork; rear, spring damper on straight axis ("plunger")
Dimensions, weight	Length 2,130 mm, width 815 mm, height 720 mm, weight 185 kg
Years of production	1950–51
Chassis serial nos.	From 516000 to 521005
Engine nos.	From 516000 to 521005
Units manufactured	5,000
Spare parts availab.	🏍 🏍 🏍
Collectors value	🏍 🏍 🏍 🏍
Price	From 10,000 to 15,000 euros

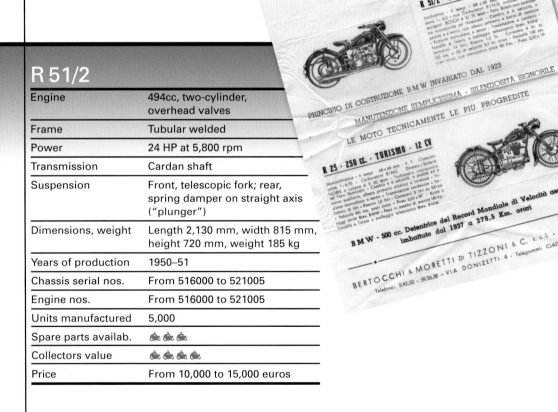

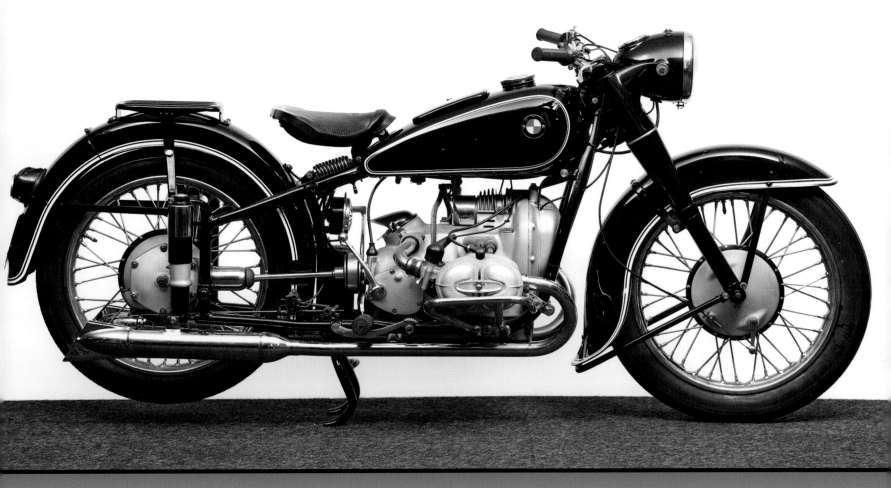

COLLECTORS CORNER

The R 51/2 is a good addition to a collection, but is definitely not as sought after as its predecessor, the R 51, or its successor, the R 51/3. Even so, it commands a higher price than either, owing to the small number of units produced (5,000 in contrast to more than 18,000 of the R 51/3) and of the limited number of bikes on the market today, almost always in the hands of collectors and very well preserved. In perfect condition (an original motorcycle in excellent repair), an R 51/2 can fetch up to 15,000 euros. Models that require restoration or parts replacement should be purchased with caution, because official spare parts are in low supply and some are extremely difficult to find.

A distinguishing feature of the R 51/2: they were single-finned (right)

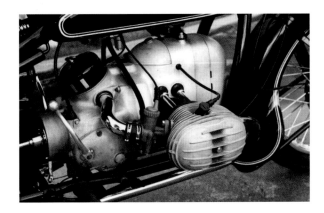

R 51/3

Only a year after the launch of the R 51/2, the new R 51/3 was unveiled at the Amsterdam Motor Show in 1951. The bike, very similar to the previous in the look, was indeed characterized by an extremely quiet engine and surprisingly good road handling, even with the sidecar (Steib TR 500 as the official choice). Also the R 51/3 was manufactured in three different series over the years, so that its already excellent performance was improved over time. The first series was equipped with full metal fork legs, side drum and exhaust pipes aligned with the muffler. The second series was distinct for its fork housed in rubber boots, raised silencers to increase ground clearance, and for the use of Duplex brakes on the front wheel. On the third and final series, made in 1954, the wheels were no longer iron but aluminium with a central drum, a sportier shaped exhaust silencer (called the "torpedo") and a headlight assembly of innovative design that survived until 1969. The R 51/3 entered the history of BMW as its engine would equip all the 500cc to 600cc models until the R 69 S. The gear driven valvetrain, automatic ignition timing and a camshaft operating both cylinder heads were features destined to last for more than a decade. All three series used a dual-effect hydraulic fork (dampening both in the compression and in the extension strokes). The R 51/3 set the paradigm for later large-displacement BMW motorcycles: the R 67, R 67/2 and the R 67/3. Finally, a distinguishing feature of the R 51/3: unlike the R 51/2, the pinstripes on the front fender are no more along the edge but raised higher.

R 51/3

Engine	494cc, two-cylinder overhead valves
Frame	Tubular welded
Power	24 HP at 5,800 rpm
Transmission	Cardan shaft
Suspension	Front, telescopic fork; rear, "plunger"
Dimensions, weight	Length 2,130 mm, width 790 mm, height 720 mm (to seat), weight 190 kg
Years of production	1951–54
Chassis serial nos.	From 522001 to 540950
Engine nos.	From 522001 to 540950
Units manufactured	18,420
Spare parts availab.	🏍🏍🏍🏍🏍
Collectors value	🏍🏍🏍🏍🏍
Price	From 10,000 to 12,000 euros

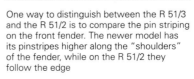

One way to distinguish between the R 51/3 and the R 51/2 is to compare the pin striping on the front fender. The newer model has its pinstripes higher along the "shoulders" of the fender, while on the R 51/2 they follow the edge

COLLECTORS CORNER

From a collector's point of view, the R 51/3 is without a doubt the most representative BMW motorcycle of the 1950s that is still affordable – it costs less, for example, than its predecessor the R 51/2, mainly due to its widespread availability. The good availability of spare parts makes even R 51/3 in bad repair worth buying. Its engine, used on all the bikes made by Bayerische Motoren Werke until 1969, makes it a must-have for any BMW collector. Not much separates the three series of the R 51/3 in terms of price, but fans tend to prefer the first two series with side drums, which are much more aesthetically pleasing than the full-width brakes that came afterward. On this page, a beautiful R 51/3 with the wrong pin striping on the front fender.

R 25/3

The final moment of the evolution of the R 25 series came in 1953. Although the R 25/2 was still in production, the R 25/3, created for military use, turned out to be very popular among civilians. With over 47,000 units produced, the R 25/3 is the most manufactured and highest-selling BMW ever. The main differences compared with the previous R 25/2 regarded the new full-width brakes and the addition of the first-ever BMW-manufactured hydraulic fork without the rubber bellows, which gave a more advanced and elegant look. These forks were superior to their predecessors and offered a considerably higher level of riding comfort on uneven surfaces. It also featured a modified tank, abandoning the classic teardrop design that had characterized the R 25 and the R 25/2 in favour of a more generous-sized, if less aesthetically pleasing, one. The Bayerische Motoren Werke Research and Development department suggested that the cylinder be painted all-black to better dissipate heat. The model also had an innovative air intake system with a pipe passing through the fuel tank to reach the carburettor. Absent, with respect to the R 25/2, was the small knob attached to the carburettor and the auxiliary gear lever located on the right of the engine that enabled neutral to be found more easily. The R 25/3 was also the first BMW equipped with 18-inch wheels, giving greater stability.

R 25/3

Engine	247cc, single-cylinder, overhead valves
Frame	Tubular welded
Power	13 HP at 5,800 rpm
Transmission	Cardan shaft
Suspension	With hydraulic dampers
Dimensions, weight	Length 2,065 mm, width 760 mm, height 730 mm (to seat), weight 150 kg
Years of production	1953–56
Chassis serial nos.	From 284001 to 331705
Engine nos.	From 284001 to 331705
Units manufactured	47,700
Spare parts availab.	🏍 🏍 🏍 🏍 🏍
Collectors value	🏍 🏍
Price	From 3,000 to 7,000 euros

COLLECTORS CORNER

The R 25/3 is one of the most easily found bikes of the 1950s, at both exhibitions and markets. Naturally, being the BMW motorcycle produced in the largest-ever numbers counts for a lot. When purchasing this model the most important thing to check is the integrity of the frame, given the heavy use to which these bikes were subjected. Few or no problems in sourcing spare parts since, as with the R 25/2, they are available directly from the BMW Mobile Tradition department. This model has a slightly lower value than the previous R 25 and R 25/2 because of the preference amongst enthusiasts for the older single-cylinder models. But in truth, if you plan to use it for touring and bike meets, the R 25/3 is to be preferred over the other models of the series for its relative higher levels of comfort and safety.

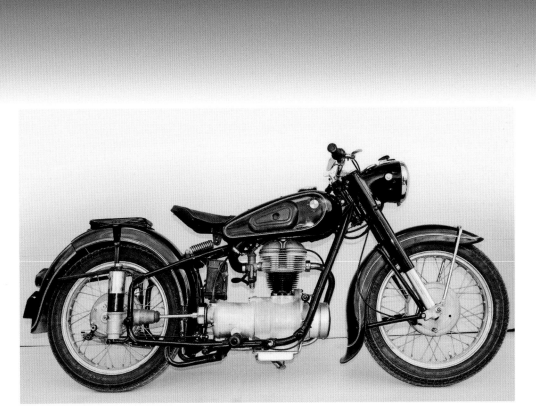

R 67
R 67/2
R 67/3

A few months after marketing the first post-war 500cc and thirteen years after the R 66, BMW launched a new 600cc bike. It was substantially an R 51/3 with a larger engine. Given its low production numbers (only 1,470 units) and short life-span of a few months (beginning and ending in the same year) the R 67 can be considered a sort of pre-series model that was followed in 1952 by the updated R 67/2 and later, between 1955 and 1956, by the R 67/3. The latter, of which only 700 units were produced (almost all for the German domestic market, even though production of the R 60 and the R 50 had already begun), was simply an updated version adopting the new features of the 1954 R 51: a full-width drum braking system, alloy rims and a change from "fish tail" to "torpedo" mufflers. The reference model of this series is thus the R 67/2, created primarily for use with a sidecar (in particular, the Spezial model with a swinging axis that BMW manufactured directly in close collaboration with Steib of Nuremberg, which came with a hydraulic brake and, upon request, a telescopic damper), as well as for use by the police. In the version adapted for use by public authorities, the R 67/2 sidecar was fitted with radio equipment and off-road style tires and exhaust; the front fender was simple in design and followed the curve of the tyres, and the brackets holding the silencer were angled in a way that afforded protection for the engine.

Engine	594cc, two-cylinder, overhead valves
Frame	Tubular welded
Power	26 HP at 5,500 rpm (R 67/2 & R 67/3 28 HP at 5,600 rpm)
Transmission	Cardan shaft
Suspension	Front, telescopic fork; rear, "plunger"
Dimensions, weight	Length 2,130 mm, width 790 mm, height 720 mm (to seat), weight 192 kg
Years of production	R 67 1951, R 67/2 1952–54, R 67/3 1955–56
Chassis serial nos.	R 67 from 610001 to 611449, R 67/2 from 612001 to 616261, R 67/3 from 617001 to 617700
Engine nos.	R 67 from 610001 to 611449, R 67/2 from 612001 to 616261, R 67/3 from 617001 to 617700
Units manufactured	R 67 1,470, R 67/2 4,234, R 67/3 700
Spare parts availab.	🏍️🏍️🏍️🏍️
Collectors value	🏍️🏍️🏍️🏍️

Price	From 10,000 to 13,000 euros (R 67), from 10,000 to 12,000 euros (R 67/2), from 12,000 to 16,000 euros (R 67/3), from 12,500 to 14,000 euros (R 67/2 with sidecar)

A gorgeous off-road R 67
with high tailpipes

COLLECTORS CORNER

Unlike the military R 75, used exclusively with a sidecar, the R 67 series was also used as a motorcycle, and for this reason it is easier to find legitimate models on the market without a sidecar. While there are no particular aesthetic or mechanical differences between the 500cc R 51/3 and the R 67, the latter is more hotly coveted by collectors due to the fact that fewer were made. Nevertheless, they both sell for a similar price, with the sole exception of the off-road makes characterized by high-rise exhausts, which may fetch an extra 5,000 euros with respect to their standard counterparts. Within the series itself, the lower production numbers of the R 67 and the R 67/3 have hiked up their price by about 2,000 euros. The R 67/3 is particularly hard to find.

R 68

If the R 69 S is the most popular BMW motorcycle for post-war collectors, the R 68 is without a doubt the most desired model among enthusiasts. This sports bike, produced exclusively for off-road competition (its official debut taking place in mid-1952 at the Alpine International), carried a price tag twice that of a Triumph 650. The R 68 became famous as the first "100 miles bike" when it appeared on the market in 1952, and was the first production bike to exceed 100 mph (160 km/h). Its sports character is further evidenced by the unusual choice (for Bayerische Motoren Werke) not to equip it with attachments for a sidecar. As with the R 51/3, and despite the low number produced – only 1,452 pieces – the R 68 came in three series with only minor differences in detail between them: the rubber housing on the front fork (the middle series had none), the positioning of the brake drums on the hubs (the 1954 version had full-width central brakes and aluminium wheels), the design of the silencer (a "fish tail" in the 1952–53 series, a "torpedo" in the third series), the roller rockers and a more efficient hydraulic damper on the swingarm (the latter modifications appeared after the production of the first 300 bikes). The R 68 was the first bike to have as standard a "2 in 1" high-mounted exhaust, with no difference in price to a conventional low-mounted exhaust, giving it a distinctively sporty aspect. From 1953 the high-mounted exhaust became optional. The historic firsts of the BMW R 68 did not stop there, and included new valve covers with transverse fins (which were to feature on all the R 50 S and R 69 S sports models) and the famous *Rennbrötchen* ("bread loaf") saddle, which was not actually a second saddle but rather an appendage located above the rear wheel to help the rider lay down

R 68

Engine	594cc, two-cylinder, overhead valves
Frame	Tubular welded
Power	35 HP at 7,000 rpm
Transmission	Cardan shaft
Suspension	Front, telescopic fork; rear, "plunger"
Dimensions, weight	Length 2,150 mm, width 790 mm, height 725 mm (to seat), weight 193 kg
Years of production	1952–54
Chassis serial nos.	From 650001 to 651453
Engine nos.	From 650001 to 651453
Units manufactured	1,452
Spare parts availab.	🏍 🏍 🏍 🏍 🏍
Collectors value	🏍 🏍 🏍 🏍 🏍
Price	From 15,000 to 32,000 euros

The Belgian journalist Marianne Weber test rides the R 68 for the French magazine *Motorcycle*, 1952

A rare Italian R 68 outfitted for use with a sidecar (in this case a Steib LS 200)

during races to improve aerodynamics. The success – especially from an aesthetic perspective – of the *Rennbrötchen* meant that, though fashioned for sport competitions, it entered everyday bikes, and became a standard fixture, as on the R 69. Another important feature was the hand pump mounted near the rear suspension for the off-road versions of the bike.

COLLECTORS CORNER

The R 68 is undoubtedly the most popular and sought after model by collectors, despite enjoying less visibility and publicity than bikes such as the R 69 S and the R 51/3. In part this is due to its "glorious sporting past" and to its unique appearance, which marks it out from other BMW bikes. It is no coincidence, therefore, that the R 68 is the BMW bike with the highest commercial value, with the exception, of course, of the early flat-tanks and racing bikes. Given the importance of this model, the low production numbers (of the 1,452 produced many have been "cannibalized" over the years for competition use) and the ease of finding spare parts, you would do well to buy one, even if it is in a poor state of repair. Although a matter of taste, the models with a high-mounted exhaust are more sought after than the ones with the traditional low-slung silencer. High prices are required also for the very few models homologated for sidecar use, especially if Steib.

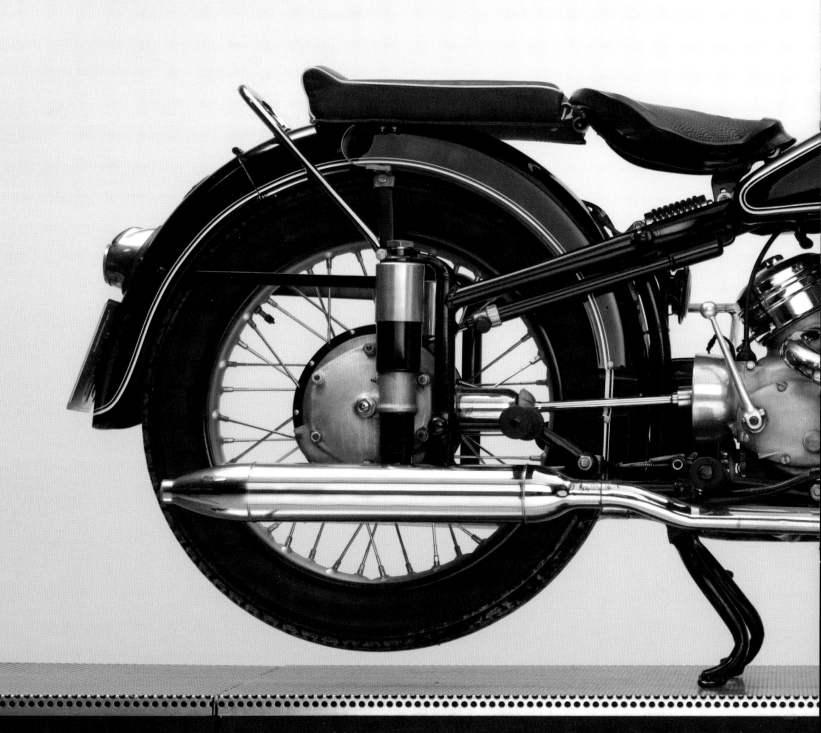

The controversial Earles forks

One of the watershed moments in the production of motorcycles by Bayerische Motoren Werke after the Second World War was the advent of the famous and controversial Earles forks, which in 1955 replaced the telehydraulic forks that BMW, in a pioneering move, had adopted in 1935.

Invented by the British engineer, Ernie Earles, the Earles fork was strongly favoured by the then director of the BMW Motorcycle division, Helmut Werner Bönsch who, as a great racing fan, decided to adopt the design as standard. At the time, the Earles fork was used on the most famous racing machines, from MV Agusta to BMW itself (as of 1952). This decision brought about the new "swinging frame" models of 1955; later on, the Earles fork appeared on the sports "S" versions and also on the R 26 and the R 27, on the grounds that it brought several advantages:
• a greater torsional and bending stiffness, which guaranteed a better wheel alignment, especially when cornering with a sidecar;
• a better dynamic behaviour of the bike, thanks to the reduced trail variation during the compression stroke;
• the almost complete disappearance of the undesirable "pendulum" effect during braking, and consequently a better distribution of braking power on the two wheels;
• little variation in the motorcycle geometry both when accelerating and when braking;
• the same shock absorbers could be used both for the front fork and for the rear suspension;
• the possibility of adjusting the trail and the shock absorbers preloading in case of attachment of a sidecar;
• a simpler and sturdier construction.

These were the benefits. But the Earles fork, apart from having a rather heavy visual impact, also had disadvantages:
• the wobble, a "trembling" effect that happens in acceleration (this issue was resolved with the addition of a steering damper in the sports models);
• the fork was very heavy and most of the weight was concentrated low down and behind the wheel, far from the steering axis, which made for poor control;
• when braking, especially with the bike even slightly inclined, the fork tended to stiffen and to lift up the front, causing loss of control;
• the length of the oscillating arms required the rider to make considerable effort when carrying out certain manoeuvres, especially when making a sharp change of direction.

Massimo Bonsignori (co-author of this book), wrote the following in the Italian magazine *Motociclismo d'Epoca*: "BMW customers did not like the Earles because it did not match with the otherwise streamlined profile of the bike. It was welcomed by sidecar users because it allowed adjustment of the trail and handled lateral stresses better than the telescopic fork. Maintenance of the Earles was relatively simple because the shock absorber had an easily replaceable sealed cartridge.

The only problem was the steering axle, which used ball bearing type such as those for bicycles: an unfit solution for this kind of motorcycle. I usually replace them with adjustable tapered bearings that also make the machine more stable. On the road, the Earles fork needed some practice by the rider, especially when cornering and braking, when the forks reacted poorly and reduced manoeuvrability."

BMW retired the Earles fork in 1969, when the new "/ 5" series adopted telescopic forks. Seven models produced from 1955 to 1969 used the Earles forks (R 50, R 50/2, R 60, R 60/2, R 69, R 50 S, R 69 S, R 26, R 27) amounting to a total of 114,889 motorcycles.

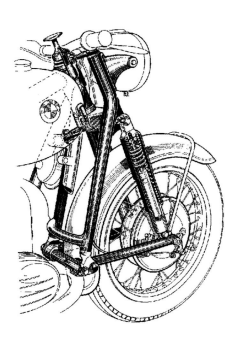

R 50
R 50/2
R 60
R 60/2

The period between the 1950s and 1960s was one of the darkest in BMW history, when a drop in sales seriously threatened to put an end to production (output fell from 29,699 units in 1954 to just 4,302 in 1962). For this reason, nobody in the motorcycle sector expected any other than updated versions of the R 51/3 or the R 68. Instead, the company defied all expectations by releasing two completely new bikes, which made huge headway in terms of chassis and handling. For the first time the designers focused on fun and comfort, while retaining performance. Many saw this change in design philosophy as a response to the inroads being made by British manufacturers (BSA, Triumph and Norton above all), whose models better met the sporting whims of bike enthusiasts. This is how the R 50 and the R 60 were born, the latter of which was to become, starting in 1957, the reference model in the BMW range for use with a sidecar. These, along with the R 69, pushed BMW out of its crisis, and were to nurture its legendary status as a manufacturer of "powerful, quiet, reliable and comfortable" motorcycles. With respect to the R 51/3 and the R 67/3, there were no changes to the engine, and innovation was focused rather on the gearbox and the frame (which became "fully swinging" thanks to the new rear suspension and front Earles fork). The gearbox gained a third shaft that reduced the typical "crunch" when shifting. Despite BMW's pioneering use of the telescopic fork (which "America" models kept from 1957), the much-discussed Earles fork (allowing to adjust the trail and the shock absorbers preload for use with a sidecar) was chosen instead. This decision immediately divided opinion among fans; but when on road, the Earles fork, although

R 50 · R 50/2

Engine	494cc, two-cylinder, overhead valves
Frame	Tubular welded
Power	26 HP at 5,800 rpm
Transmission	Cardan shaft
Suspension	Front and rear long swingarms with Earles spring assembly/damper
Dimensions, weight	Length 2,125 mm, width 660 mm, height 725 mm (to seat), weight 195 kg
Years of production	R 50 1955–60, R 50/2 1960–69
Chassis serial nos.	R 50 from 550001 to 563515, R 50/2 from 630001 to 649037
Engine nos.	R 50 from 550001 to 563515, R 50/2 from 630001 to 649037
Units manufactured	R 50 13,510, R 50/2 19,036
Spare parts availab.	🏍️🏍️🏍️🏍️🏍️
Collectors value	🏍️🏍️🏍️🏍️
Price	From 8,000 to 10,000 euros (15,500 euros R 50 with sidecar)

R 60 • R 60/2

Engine	594cc, two-cylinder, overhead valves
Frame	Tubular welded
Power	28 HP ay 5,600 rpm (R 60/2 30 HP at 5,800 rpm)
Transmission	Cardan shaft
Suspension	Front and rear long swingarms with Earles spring assembly/damper
Dimensions, weight	Length 2,125 mm, width 660 mm, height 725 mm (to seat), weight 195 kg
Years of production	R 60 1956–60, R 60/2 1961–69
Chassis serial nos.	R 60 from 618001 to 621530, R 60/2 from 622001 to 630000 and from 1810001 to 1819307
Engine nos.	R 60 from 618001 to 621530, R 60/2 from 622001 to 630000 and from 1810001 to 1819307
Units manufactured	R 60 3,530, R 60/2 17,306
Spare parts availab.	🏍️🏍️🏍️🏍️🏍️
Collectors value	🏍️🏍️🏍️🏍️
Price	from 8,000 to 12,000 euros (15,500 euros R 60 with sidecar)

undoubtedly "oversized" in appearance, gave a superior level of ride comfort than any other system on the market. Other innovations were made to the rear shock absorbers (a swingarm replaced the "plunger" suspension), the transmission shaft (now inside the swingarm) and new tapered roller bearings on the wheels and arms to allow for preload adjustment. Of note on models produced from 1957 is the addition of a generous-sized casing to house the brake light. In 1960, a second series of both models was launched with small modifications to the crankshaft, the camshaft (which was strengthened) and to the engine. The updated engine components of the R 60/2 added two HP to the previous R 60. Finally, from 1962, the bikes were equipped with two turn signals at the end of the handlebar. It is worth observing here that two "America" versions of the R 50 and R 60 were produced specifically for the US market from 1967 with production runs of, respectively, 401 and 1,879. These differed from the European models by only a few details such as the telescopic fork rather than the Earles fork, higher handlebar (as preferred by American riders), a longer saddle for improved comfort on long trips and a front fender bracket of different design, which no longer radiated from the centre of the wheel to the upper section of the fender, but rather framed the fender, starting from the rubber bellows covering the telehydraulic suspension.

COLLECTORS CORNER

Together with the celebrated R 69 S and the R 69, the R 50 and the R 60 are an important watershed in BMW history, and are thus of importance to collectors. They also have the distinction of combining a classic design with technical innovations (above all, the introduction of the Earles fork). Even today, these two models provide a good level of reliability for medium-range touring. There is no substantial difference in the collector value of the R 50 and the R 60, nor between the following "/ 2" series. However, the R 60 with a Steib sidecar (model TR 500) is venerated by many collectors, as is reflected by its higher value. With regard to the "America" versions, the judgement is merely a matter of taste rather than collectible or commercial value. Very few original "America" models survive, although it is possible to refit a European version to the "America" specifications.

R 69

The R 51/3 and R 67/3 were replaced in 1955 and 1956 respectively by the R 50 and R 60 with swinging frame; in the same months, a modern version of the historic R 68 was launched. This was the R 69, a high-end model presented to the public as a combination of the sporting soul (the engine) of the R 68, and the frame (swinging) of the R 60. Although triumphantly heralded as "the super sport bike for everyday use", the R 69 unfortunately failed to achieve the success of the R 68, mainly because it was heavier and less sporty in appearance than its predecessor, the first "100 mph bike". Such look problems came of course from the use of the Earles fork, which ensured excellent road performance but, for sports bike enthusiasts, looked bulky and cumbersome. The R 69 was produced for five years (1955 to 1960) with little commercial success (production never exceeded 3,000 units, compared with 32,000 and 20,000 of the R 50 and R 60); and from a racing point of view, it was also short-lived.

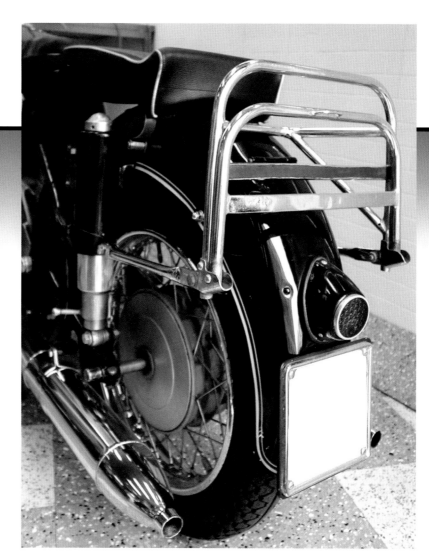

R 69

Engine	594cc, two-cylinder, overhead valves
Frame	Tubular welded
Power	35 HP at 6,800 rpm
Transmission	Cardan shaft
Suspension	Front and rear long swingarms with Earles spring assembly/damper
Dimensions, weight	Length 2,125 mm, width 660 mm, height 725 mm (to seat), weight 202 kg
Years of production	1955–60
Chassis serial nos.	From 652001 to 654955
Engine nos.	From 652001 to 654955
Units manufactured	2,956
Spare parts availab.	🏍 🏍 🏍 🏍 🏍
Collectors value	🏍 🏍 🏍
Price	From 12,000 to 15,000 euros

COLLECTORS CORNER

Despite having a slightly lower collectible value than the R 50 and R 60 (due to a general lack of market knowledge and because it is overshadowed by the R 69 S), the R 69 commands a decent price by virtue of its small production run. A pleasant bike to ride, but difficult to find fully working especially if outside the circles of major collectors. If buying one, pay at- tention to details such as the original colour (all-black and not also white, as in the case of the R 69 S); a sin- gle seat combined with, at most, a Rennbrötchen- style extension (the longer seat is exclusively found on the R 69 S); and the rear light (smaller for models manufactured in 1955 and 1956, with a larger brake light added in 1957).

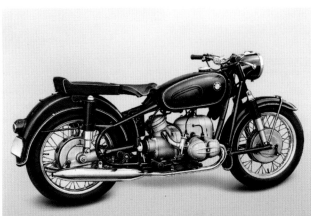

R 26
R 27

One year after the launch of the new R 50 and R 60, BMW updated its by then obsolete R 25/3, and built a new single-cylinder machine with the same characteristics as the last twin-cylinder motorcycles, starting with the "swinging frame" and the controversial but effective Earles forks. On the new R 26, the surface of the cylinder head cooling fins was increased by 50%, which rendered unnecessary the black cylinder painting of the R 25/3. The upgraded engine delivered two more HP than the 1956 model, though this compromised ride comfort and the very structure of the bike. The sturdiness of the new small BMW model was not only apparent, but was clearly demonstrated in practice as it was often to be seen in use with a sidecar. During production the technicians made various tweaks, the most important involving the replacement of bearing-free aluminium connecting rod with a tried and tested ball bearing mount. After four years of production and despite an enduring crisis in the motorcycle market, Bayerische Motoren Werke launched an updated single-cylinder, the R 27, designed to address the problems with the previous frame. The new bike did not differ greatly in appearance from the R 26, but it finally had the engine and gearbox elastically mounted on silent blocs, which improved ride comfort but above all preserved the structure of the bike. Some changes were also made inside the engine, notably adding a tensioner to the timing belt. The innovation proved to be a double edged sword: the elastic mount compromised the stability of the carburettor, and the engine was unable to sustain idling. As on the twin-cylinders from 1957 on, a new casing to house a rear brake light was added and from 1962 turn indicators were mounted at the end of the handlebar. Production of the R 27

R 26

Engine	247cc, single-cylinder, overhead valves
Frame	Tubular welded
Power	15 HP ta 6,400 rpm
Transmission	Cardan shaft
Suspension	Front and rear long swingarms with Earles spring assembly/damper
Dimensions, weight	Length 2,090 mm, width 660 mm, height 770 mm (to seat), weight 158 kg
Years of production	1956–60
Chassis serial nos.	From 340001 to 370242
Engine nos.	From 340001 to 370242
Units manufactured	30,236
Spare parts availab.	🏍 🏍 🏍 🏍 🏍
Collectors value	🏍 🏍 🏍
Price	From 3,000 to 7,000 euros

ceased in 1966, and it remains the last small single-cylinder bike manufactured by Bayerische Motoren Werke. In the early 1970s three prototypes were built: the R 28 (with the telescopic fork of the R 25/3), the R 28 b (with a shorter swing arm) and the R 28 c (with the fork used on the /5 series). These had been intended for the Army of the German Federal Republic, but did not make it past testing stage.

The prototype of the R 28, which was never produced but did serve as a source of inspiration for the R 26 and R 27

COLLECTORS CORNER

Given that there is not great demand for the R 26 and, especially, in light of the practical impossibility of finding specimens with the frame intact (repairs to frames damaged by vibrations were a matter of course in the 1950s), the motorcycles of the period 1955–60 are not of high value to collectors. There is a higher demand for the R 27, because it is more comfortable and can still be used for medium-range touring. Although almost all spare parts are available for both models, you should be careful when buying a bike that needs to be fixed up. For, while the cost of restoration will not be substantially different from the cost of restoring a boxer model, the resale value of the resulting bike will be much lower. No price can be given for the prototype R 28: the few surviving examples were never added to the official market for vintage motorcycles.

R 27

Engine	247cc, single-cylinder, overhead valves
Frame	Tubular welded
Power	18 HP at 7,400 rpm
Transmission	Cardan shaft
Suspension	Front and rear long swingarms with Earles spring assembly/damper
Dimensions, weight	Length 2,090 mm, width 660 mm, height 770 mm (to seat), weight 162 kg
Years of production	1960–66
Chassis serial nos.	From 372001 to 387566
Engine nos.	From 372001 to 387566
Units manufactured	15,364
Spare parts availab.	🏍 🏍 🏍 🏍 🏍
Collectors value	🏍 🏍 🏍
Price	From 3,000 to 8,000 euros

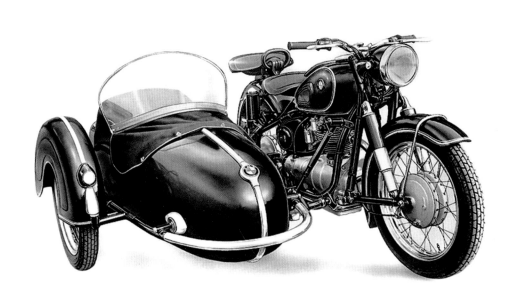

1940–50s

data sheet

Model	Cylinders	cc	Production years	Units made	Spare parts availability	Collectors value	Price (euros)	Chassis	Engine
R 75	2	745	1941–44	18,000	🏍️×3	🏍️×5	18,000–33,000	From 750001 to 768000	From 750001 to 768000
R 24	1	247	1948–50	12,020	🏍️×2	🏍️×2	3,000–8,000	From 200001 to 212007	From 200001 to 212007
R 25	1	247	1950–51	23,400	🏍️×5	🏍️×5	3,000–8,000	From 220001 to 243410	From 220001 to 243410
R 25/2	1	247	1951–54	38,651	🏍️×5	🏍️×4	3,000–8,000	From 245000 to 283650	From 245000 to 283650
R 51/2	2	494	1950–51	5,000	🏍️×4	🏍️×4	10,000–15,000	From 516000 to 521005	From 516000 to 521005
R 51/3	2	494	1951–54	18,420	🏍️×5	🏍️×6	10,000–12,000	From 522001 to 540950	From 522001 to 540950
R 25/3	1	247	1953–56	47,700	🏍️×5	🏍️×2	3,000–7,000	From 284001 to 331705	From 284001 to 331705
R 67	2	594	1951	1,470	🏍️×4	🏍️×4	10,000–13,000	From 610001 to 611449	From 610001 to 611449
R 67/2	2	594	1952–54	4,234	🏍️×4	🏍️×4	10,000–12,000	From 612001 to 616261	From 612001 to 616261
R 67/3	2	594	1955–56	700	🏍️×4	🏍️×4	12,000–16,000	From 617001 to 617700	From 617001 to 617700
R 68	2	594	1952–54	1,452	🏍️×6	🏍️×6	15,000–32,000	From 650001 to 651453	From 650001 to 651453
R 50	2	494	1955–60	13,510	🏍️×5	🏍️×5	8,000–10,000	From 550001 to 563515	From 550001 to 563515
R 60	2	594	1956–60	3,530	🏍️×5	🏍️×6	8,000–12,000	From 618001 to 621530	From 618001 to 621530
R 69	2	594	1955-1960	2,956	🏍️×5	🏍️×4	12,000–15,000	From 652001 to 654955	From 652001 to 654955
R 26	1	247	1956–60	30,236	🏍️×5	🏍️×4	3,000–7,000	From 340001 to 370242	From 340001 to 370242
R 27	1	247	1960–66	15,364	🏍️×6	🏍️×4	3,000–8,000	From 372001 to 387566	From 372001 to 387566

the |1960s

For Bayerische Motoren Werke, the 1960s were a fruitful decade in terms of quality that saw the production of historical sports bikes such as the R 50 S and R 69 S. From a commercial perspective, however, the decade was not quite such a success. Indeed, so bad was the crisis in the industry that the company was on the verge of making the very painful decision to wind up its motorcycle division. The numbers painted a very bleak picture, and, indeed, this was to be the decade with the lowest sales in the history of BMW. Happily, the fortunes of the company were revived with the roll-out of new "Slash Five" (/5) series, which became the jewel in the BMW crown.

R50 S

With the arrival at the head of the BMW motorcycle division of former journalist Helmut Werner Bönsch, a keen road-tester and always alert to bike performance, and with the victories of BMW bikes at racing circuits throughout Europe (direct orders from management had moreover arrived to fight with the much better-performing English bikes and eat away at their market), at the beginning of 1960 BMW introduced two new high-performance sports models, the R 50 S and R 69 S. Both drew directly on the experience the company had acquired in competitive racing. In particular, the R 50 S claimed the glorious legacy of the prestigious R 5 and R 51 and, with its 35 HP engine, could rival the fantastic R 68, the "first 100 mph motorcycle". The increase in power compared with the R 50 was accompanied by a thorough overhaul and enhancement of the boxer engines. The public, however, preferred the R 69 S over the half-litre model: thus in 1962, after only two years of production, the R 50 S was withdrawn from sale owing above all to the excessive revving of the engine: more than 7,650 revolutions per minute. This high rpm rate had caused a significant amount of vibration that damaged the pistons, and in some cases led even to break the cylinders. After just 1,634 motorcycles had been made, the R 50 S was forced into early retirement. It is worth noting that the R 50 S and its larger sister-bike, the 600cc, were the first to be fitted with a hydraulic steering damper, while from 1965 turn signals made their first appearance. They were mounted on the end of the handlebar and commanded by a highly visible black switch located on the right handlebar (the switch was also used to operate the horn), while on the left handlebar a similar lever served as a light switch and flasher control.

R 50 S

Engine	494cc, two-cylinder, overhead valves
Frame	Tubular welded
Power	35 HP at 7,650 rpm
Transmission	Cardan shaft
Suspension	Front and rear long swingarms with Earles spring assembly/damper
Dimensions, weight	Length 2,125 mm, width 660 mm, height 725 mm (to seat), weight 198 kg
Years of production	1960–62
Chassis serial nos.	From 564001 to 565634
Engine nos.	From 564005 to 565634
Units manufactured	1,634
Spare parts availab.	🏍 🏍 🏍 🏍
Collectors value	🏍 🏍 🏍 🏍 🏍
Price	From 15,000 to 20,000 euros

COLLECTORS CORNER

Despite the limited sales success at the time of its release, the R 50 S is now one of the most popular motorcycles among collectors worldwide. The small number of units produced has turned it into a sort of motorcycle version of what the Penny Black stamp is for philatelists. Due to the high compression ratio, it is a particularly awkward bike to handle and definitely not for novices, but maintains an undeniable charm that many have compared to that of Porsche cars. The difference between demand (large) and supply (very small) has pushed up its value exponentially, so that prices are now far out of proportion to its intrinsic value. Be advised that it is practically impossible to find this particular model outside the world of collectors. While this does nothing to improve supply, the fact that it is now the preserve of collectors does at least offer guarantees on the quality and originality of any pieces that may be made available for sale.

R69S

Certain bikes in the history of Bayerische Motoren Werke, by a happy coincidence of events, aesthetic qualities, performance, sporting successes or fashion trends, have ended becoming icons. So it was for the R 2, the "people's bike", for the R 51 series, "the most beautiful BMWs of all time" and for the R 68, the "100 mph motorcycle". The R 69 S, too, partakes of this happy fate, and became known as the "dream motorcycle": for the fans of the day, that could hardly afford a machine that cost 4,030 Deutsche marks; and for today's collectors, who consider this flagship BMW bike as an essential part of their armoury. Compared with its smaller sister-bike the R 50 S, the 600cc R 69 S was conceived, designed and built with an eye to becoming the reference model for exports, especially to England and the United States – this latter a market BMW still had to conquer. To prevent a repeat of the problems that had caused the removal of the R 50 S from the sales catalogue, namely the dangerous vibrations at high speeds and breakages of pistons and cylinders, as of 1963 the R 69 S added a vibration dampener mounted on the front edge of the camshaft, an operation that was also carried out on the models from previous years and saved the R 69 S from the early demise that befell the R 50 S. The R 69 S immediately won favour with the public because of its eminent suitability for long-range touring – and at amazing average speeds. Speed and reliability had thus been fused into a single machine, which became the new standard-bearer for Bayerische Motoren Werke. Nor was this touring motorcycle above competing in and winning races such as the 1,000 Kilometres of Silverstone (home of its arch-rivals Norton and Triumph) and the Bol d'Or, a 24-hour which it won in 1960 at the Circuit de Montlhéry, breaking the world speed

R 69 S

Engine	594cc, two-cylinder, overhead valves
Frame	Tubular welded
Power	42 HP at 7,000 rpm
Transmission	Cardan shaft
Suspension	Long-armed Earles fork
Dimensions, weight	Length 2,125 mm, width 722 mm, height 725 mm, weight 202 kg
Years of production	1960–69
Chassis serial nos.	From 655001 to 666320
Engine nos.	From 655001 to 666320
Units manufactured	11,317
Spare parts availab.	🏍 🏍 🏍 🏍 🏍
Collectors value	🏍 🏍 🏍 🏍 🏍
Price	From 16,000 to 25,000 euros

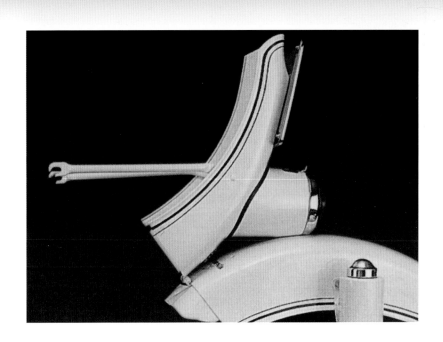

record in its class with an average of 175.9 km/h over 12 hours and 175.8 km/h over 24 hours. In short, if BMW was looking for a response to the commercial strength of the British sports bikes, it certainly found it in the R 69 S. This model was also the first in the history of BMW to have an alternative colour scheme to the traditional black (only the third series of the R 2 had had a two-tone livery thanks to the elegant blue shade of its tank). In fact, the lucky buyers of the R 69 S could choose the Alpen Weiss (white) with black pinstripe edging. This bright white bodywork, applied to just 6% of the models rolled out, was so simple and eye-catching a colour that it earned the R 69 S the nickname of "White Whale". To be strictly accurate, some records indicate that a very small number of R 69 S models were painted red, an unprecedented colour on the BMW palette and a source of some mystery, which only makes it all the more intriguing to collectors. Aesthetically speaking, the two sport bikes (indicated by the "S" in their names) did not diverge substantially. The main differences were in the engine. In a change from the R 50 S, the R 69 S mounted a special damping flywheel to reduce vibrations, but it resulted in so much noise that many owner/users opted to get rid of the flywheel itself. Over the years, only a few improvements were made to R 69 S. Among these, besides the above-mentioned vibration damper of 1963, a grease nipple was added to the cross tube of the swingarm in 1964 (from serial number 658624 on), and stiffer front springs were introduced in 1965 (from serial number 658929 on), a modification that was passed on to all other models equipped with an Earles fork. The R 69 S was also the first BMW to be shipped with a long list of optional extras. Among these, larger fuel tanks (the 24-litre version was

produced by BMW and Hoscke, the 36-litre version by Schorsch Meier), a vast range of alternatives to the standard fitted two-seater saddle designed by former champion "Schorsch" Meier (both Denfeld and Pagusa made a single-seat for rider and passenger, the latter of which came equipped with a handle and adjustable suspension springs, while the back saddle could also be padded and hinged to the main seat to create the so-called *Rennbrötchen*, the "bread loaf"). Again, a chrome arc for the front headlamp, a small VDO tachometer scaled up to 8,000 rpms, the engine guard made from chromed tubes and some engine components polished (including the caps of the foot pegs and the upper hoods of the dampers), a fuel talk cap with lock (the one made by HAMA proved very popular), a leather cover for the fuel tank, a bigger oil sump (the installation of which, however, required an extension of the mouth of the pump), and fairings to improve aerodynamics (the best known and most used were those produced by Heinrich, Peel Engineering and Avon). The handlebar deserves special mention since they came in three different configurations: European standard, American-style (decidedly higher) and the Magura model, where a chromed slat set between the two curves gave a definite off-road air to the bike. Finally, the options included exhaust assembly with two manifolds converging in a tube that, in turn, fed into a raised exhaust pipe on the right side. From 1967 until 1969, the R 69 S was also sold on the American market under the symbol R 69 US (1,003 units), and included all modifications envisaged for the export model: telescopic hydraulic fork instead of the Earles fork, high handlebar, a long seat and a different setup for the support bracket holding the front mudguard.

COLLECTORS CORNER

Frankly, it is hard to grasp fully the renown that this model enjoys among collectors. After all, the reliability of the R 69 S is no better than that of its less powerful and less admired sisters (the R 60 and R 69), and the high performance of the motorcycle, which is comparable to that of a modern bike, is not really in keeping with what one expects when riding a vintage motorcycle. And yet, as with the R 50 S, the gap between the very low supply and the high demand has resulted in a very high final value. Add the unprecedented double colour scheme: black with white pinstripe edging or else white with black pinstripe edging, the latter of which is greatly coveted owing to its rarity. Compared with the 1990s, it is no longer easy to find an R 69 S, unless you have the good fortune to acquire models being decommissioned by public authorities such as the French Gendarmerie or the German police. The most beautiful bikes, however, are almost entirely in the hands of collectors, who will let them go only as part of a trade, or at exorbitant price. At markets and exhibitions, however, you might come across some models whose frames have been cobbled together. In such a case, in light of the high commercial value of the machines and the absence of difficulties in obtaining spare parts, you might even be advised to purchase a bike that is not in a particularly good state of repair. As with the R 50 and R 60, the value of the American version of the R 69 S is in line with that of the European model. It is simply a matter of taste.

R 50/5
R 60/5
R 75/5

In the mid-1960s, realizing the need to offer to BMW customers something that outperformed even the R 69 S, the Munich engineers pushed the 600cc engine to its limits, building a prototype that produced 54.9 HP at 8,000 rpm. It was clear from the first tests, however, that the engine was too complex for mass production. The job of designing the new bike was therefore assigned to a team led by engineer Alexander von Falkenhausen and designer Hans-Günther von der Marwitz, who immediately made their intentions clear: "We want to build a BMW that handle like a Norton Manx". In setting out the challenge, they made a choice as historic as it was revolutionary, and one that broke from the BMW tradition: they planned to free the motorcycle from the constraints imposed by the sidecar. The new models were eagerly awaited, and all the motorcycle magazines in the world were vying with one another to get a scoop. In August 1967, a private photographer succeeded in taking some pictures of a specimen with a completely new shape, which were printed by *Das Motorrad*, the renowned German magazine. This scoop forced the then director of the BMW motorcycle division, Bönsch, to confirm that a new series was under development. Two years later, on 28 August 1969, Bönsch invited the press to Hockenheim and unveiled the new "/5" series. It consisted of three models, the R 50/5, the R 60/5 and the R 75/5, which revolutionized the tradition of Bayerische Motoren Werke. The new series abandoned the rather austere design BMW customers were used to, and indulged in a range of colour schemes for the bodywork that was quite without precedent in the tradition of the Munich company. The engine, meanwhile, breathed new life into the glorious boxer design (BMW divides the production of two-cylinder engines in two different

R 50/5

Engine	496cc, two-cylinder, overhead valves
Frame	Tubular twin cradle
Power	32 HP at 6,400 rpm
Transmission	Cardan shaft
Suspension	Front, telescopic fork with hydraulic dampers; rear, swingarm with springs and hydraulic dampers
Dimensions, weight	Length 2,100 mm, width 740 mm, height 850 mm (to seat), weight 185 kg
Years of production	1969–71 short wheelbase, 1972–73 long wheelbase
Chassis serial nos.	Short wheelbase from 2900001 to 2903623, long wheelbase from 2903624 to 2910000
Engine nos.	Short wheelbase from 2900001 to 2903623, long wheelbase from 2903624 to 2910000
Units manufactured	7,865
Spare parts availab.	🏍 🏍 🏍 🏍 🏍
Collectors value	🏍 🏍 🏍
Price	From 3,500 to 6,000 euros

R 60/5

Engine	599cc, two-cylinder, overhead valves
Frame	Tubular twin cradle
Power	40 HP at 6,400 rpm
Transmission	Cardan shaft
Suspension	Front, telescopic fork with hydraulic dampers; rear, swingarm with springs and hydraulic dampers
Dimensions, weight	Length 2,100 mm, width 740 mm, height 850 mm (to seat), weight 190 kg
Years of production	1969–71 short wheelbase, 1972–73 long wheelbase
Chassis serial nos. and engine nos.	Short wheelbase from 2930001 to 2938704, long wheelbase from 2938705 to 2950000
Units manufactured	22,721
Spare parts availab.	🏍 🏍 🏍 🏍 🏍
Collectors value	🏍 🏍 🏍
Price	From 4,000 to 7,000 euros

groups: those produced in the factories of Munich from 1923 until 1969, and those produced in the new factory in Berlin-Spandau beginning in 1969 with the launch of the "/5" series). Among the major technical innovations, one of the most noteworthy was the new cylinder, which now had a cast aluminium outer surface with fins for heat dispersion. The crankshaft was now one-piece forged, and rotating on plain bearings that ensured a smooth and vibration-free functioning. Drawing inspiration from automobile technology, the lubrication system was operated by a rotating pump driven by the crankshaft. The R 50/5 and the R 60/5 were equipped with a traditional Bing carburettor with fuel float chamber and enrichment pump, but the new 750cc engine made use of a constant velocity carburettor with a diaphragm acceleration pump that kept the engine smooth and progressive even at full throttle. Finally, special mention needs to be made of both the new oval tube double-cradle steel frame, which guaranteed a high lateral stiffness and an appreciable longitudinal elasticity, and of the front suspension, which saw a return to the telescopic fork already in use on the American version of the previous series (R 50, R 60 and R 69 US) in replacement of the controversial Earles fork. With the new "/5" series, a rev counter, integrated into the speedometer, was included for the first time as standard. The turn indicators were also fitted as standard, but above all

R 75/5

Engine	745cc, two-cylinder, overhead valves
Frame	Tubular twin cradle
Power	50 HP at 6,200 rpm
Transmission	Cardan shaft
Suspension	Front, telescopic fork with hydraulic dampers; rear, swingarm with springs and hydraulic dampers
Dimensions, weight	Length 2,100 mm, width 740 mm, height 850 mm (to seat), weight 190 kg
Years of production	1969–71 short wheelbase, 1972–73 long wheelbase
Chassis serial nos. and engine nos.	Short wheelbase from 2970001 to 2982737, long wheelbase from 2982738 to 3000000 and from 4000001 to 4100000 (US market)
Units manufactured	38,370
Spare parts availab.	🏍️🏍️🏍️🏍️🏍️
Collectors value	🏍️🏍️🏍️🏍️
Price	From 6,000 to 9,000 euros

the series boasted a "revolutionary" electric starter, standard on the R 60/5 and R 75/5 and optional on the smaller R 50/5 – although all the bikes retained the traditional kick-start lever. The battery, unfortunately, was at the very limit of capacity for a bike with an electric starter motor. This problem was resolved only in early 1973, when the rear swingarm was extended by five inches, which gave the bike better stability at high speed and provided the space to accommodate a higher capacity battery. The "/5" series was also produced for the American market, with only cosmetic changes such as raised handlebar, a narrow 18-litre tank with inserts in chrome finishing, as well as the side panels. From 1972, with the arrival of the long wheelbase "/5" version, the chrome trim on the side panels and the 18-litre fuel tank were also added to European models (though one year later a different, non-chromed 18-litre fuel tank was introduced). Some other cosmetic differences between the short wheelbase ("SWB") and long wheelbase ("LWB") series included the shape of the passenger handles (the first series had two separate handles, the second had a single, continuous handle). In 1971, a special saddle with longitudinal ribbing became available, along with side-bags (optional, in leather for the first series, rigid – made by Krauser – for the second series, which were to remain a feature of BMW bikes until 1985). The silencers were made slightly straighter, the name of the model was printed on the engine (against a black background from the second series on) and on the rear of the seat.

The "/5" series: radical innovation

Launched in the summer of 1969, the "/5" series consists of three machines, the R 50/5, R 60/5 and R 75/5, each with different displacements and performance, but all three built as touring motorcycles. From drawing board to production took five years, but the designers got just about everything right, managing to retain the essence of the brand that is so important to the legions of enthusiasts. While the massive engine determined the general shape of the machine, these models still had graceful and slightly sporty contours. One of the best things about the new design was that the accessory elements (air filter, alternator and starter motor) were all enclosed with in the ample engine block. The series was the first to offer both an electric starter motor (an optional extra for the R 50/5) and a kick-start lever. The Earles fork was replaced with a more modern and lightweight telescopic fork with hydraulic shock absorbers. The large headlamp, well suited to the "Gran Turismo" vocation of the motorcycles, contained a powerful H4 halogen bulb. The instrumentation included a "motometer", a combination of speedometer and rpm dial, along with all the warning lights. The new two-seat saddle, also a novelty, could be lifted up to reveal a storage space containing equipment from the manufacturer (a tool bag and the user's manual). Another important innovation was the constant velocity Bing carburettor (on the R 75/5 only), a world first on a motorcycle. Such carburettor delivered a smoother power, ideal for a touring bike. Four turn signals encased in aluminium were mounted front and rear on the body of the bike, and not on the handlebar. The "/5" series was an unbelievable success for its day, and in four years 70,000 of them had been produced, helped also by their adoption by police forces almost everywhere in the world.

COLLECTORS CORNER

Of BMW motorcycles aged forty years or more, those of the "/5" series are the only ones still practical for daily use, in particular those fitted with side-bags. No great price difference separates electric starter and kick-starter versions of the R 50/5, nor is there much of a gap between the 500cc and the 600cc, though both are worth less than the R 75/5. The interest of BMW fans is still growing, thanks also to the decent number of these bikes still in circulation. Collectors do, however, draw a distinction between the SWB and LWB versions. "Traditionalists" consider the models from 1969 to 1971 nobler and therefore of greater value, whereas "aesthetes" prefer the 1972 series for its chrome finishing and new colours. As regards colours, the market has a considerable preference for black, ideally in the American version with chrome-trim side covers (worth 500 euros more than the European version of the same), but is also pretty keen on the silver R 75/5 of 1969 with blue edging and the blue R 75/5 of 1972 based on the colours of the Bavarian flag. The 750cc bike is the most prestigious and desired, although before you buy this – or either of the other two – you should check several details. Most important of all, you will want to verify (at least by hearing it) that the engine is running properly, because if not, the repairs might be both time-consuming and costly, though not particularly problematic thanks to the general availability of almost all spare parts. (The only part that cannot be found, because never re-manufactured, is the original fuel tank cap.) Also check the struts holding the central kickstand in place, since they tend to wear out over time, and fixing them requires the removal of the entire engine. Look over the electrics, too (the original system was without fuses), to ensure that previous owners have not botched up the circuitry.

The fuel tank with chrome sides

All the "/5" series was sold with a (small) fuel tank with a capacity of 17.5 litres, including a reserve of 1.25 litres. The large fuel tank with a capacity of 24 litres (reserve of 3.5 litres) was supplied as an optional extra. Also optional was the tank cap with lock. As of 1972, a chrome trim was added to the sides of the fuel tank, especially on the models sold on the American market. The result was what became known affectionately as the "toaster" tank.

THE COLOURS OF THE "/5" SERIES

1970–71
Polarismetallic (grey) with blue border (060/560)
Federweiss (white) with black edging (084/584)
Schwarz (black) with white pinstripe edging (086/590)

1972
Polarismetallic (grey) with blue pinstripe edging (060/560)
Federweiss (white) with black pinstripe edging (084/584)
Schwarz (black) with white pinstripe edging (086/590)
Currymetallic (curry) with black pinstripe edging (029/529
Blaumetallic (metallic blue) with white pinstripe edging (033/533)

1973
Polarismetallic (grey) with blue pinstripe edging (060/560)
Federweiss (white) with black pinstripe edging (084/584)
Schwarz (black) with white pinstripe edging (086/590)
Currymetallic (curry) with black pinstripe edging (029/529
Blaumetallic (metallic blue) with white pinstripe edging (033/533)
Granadarot (red) with white pinstripe edging (023/523)
Grunmetallic (green) with white pinstripe edging (074/574)

data sheet | 1960s

Model	Cylinders	cc	Production years	Units made	Spare parts availability	Collectors value	Price (euros)	Chassis	Engine
R 27	1	247	1960–66	15,364	●●●●●●	●●●	3,000–8,000	From 372001 to 387566	From 372001 to 387566
R 50/2	2	494	1960–69	19,036	●●●●●●	●●●●●	8,000–10,000	From 630001 to 649037	From 630001 to 649037
R 60/2	2	594	1961–69	17,306	●●●●●	●●●●●●	8,000–12,000	From 622001 to 630000	From 622001 to 630000
R 50 S	2	494	1960–62	1,634	●●●●	●●●●●●	15,000–20,000	From 564001 to 565634	From 564005 to 565634
R 69 S	2	594	1960–69	11,317	●●●●●●	●●●●●●	16,000–25,000	From 655001 to 666320	From 655001 to 666320
R 50/5	2	496	1969–71 short wheelb., 1972–73 long wheelb.	7,865	●●●●●●	●●●	3,500–6,000	Short wheelbase from 2900001 to 2903623, long wheelbase from 2903624 to 2910000	Short wheelbase from 2900001 to 2903623, long wheelbase from 2903624 to 2910000
R 60/5	2	599	1969–71 short wheelb., 1972–73 long wheelb.	22,721	●●●●●●	●●●	4,000–7,000	Short wheelbase from 2930001 to 2938704, long wheelbase from 2938705 to 2950000	Short wheelbase from 2930001 to 2938704, long wheelbase from 2938705 to 2950000
R 75/5	2	745	1969–71 short wheelb., 1972–73 long wheelb.	38,370	●●●●●	●●●●	6,000–9,000	Short wheelbase from 2970001 to 2982737, long wheelbase from 2982738 to 3000000 and from 4000001 to 4100000 (US market)	Short wheelbase from 2970001 to 2982737, long wheelbase from 2982738 to 3000000 and from 4000001 to 4100000 (US market)

the 1970s

The arrival on the market of the "/5" series restored prestige to Bayerische Motoren Werke, which in the 1970s transformed itself from a struggling motorcycle company into a commercial powerhouse. BMW motorcycles continued to cost much more than the rivals from Japan – the new competitors on the market that first caught up with and then overtook the prestigious English manufacturers, Triumph above all – but they offered a peculiar trait thanks to their innovations and charm. In 1973, at the Cologne Motor Show, BMW unveiled the R 90 S, a powerful and fast 900cc model with groundbreaking aesthetic and technical standards.

R 60/6
R 75/6
R 90/6

When former journalist Helmut Werner Bönsch, who had always been a passionate road-tester, race-lover and speed fiend, took over the direction of the BMW motorcycle division, a thorough and almost exaggerated dedication to combining safety with high performance became the hallmark of the company. This was the backdrop to the development of a 900cc superbike by BMW designers, during a time the company was working on the "/5" series. Unfortunately, the development of the R 90/5 did not result in the series production of the bike. There were many reasons for this, chief among them being the technical impossibility of ensuring high safety standards given the speed of the machine (above all with brakes, that were still based on drum technology), and because of the limits imposed by the four-speed gearbox, too restricted to take full advantage of the new motor power. Another three years had to pass before BMW could fulfil its dream of mass producing a superbike above 750cc, which it presented at the Oktoberfest of 1973. The bike in question was the flagship model of the new "/6" series, the R 90/6 (which for collectors was to be overshadowed by its sporty sister, the R 90 S). At the time, however, the R 90/6 was a true commercial success; its only drawback, in the eyes of BMW users, was its excessive similarity to the R 75/5, even though in reality the differences between it and its "/5" predecessor were many and substantial. To begin with, the R 90/6 delivered an extra 10 HP, which ensured a top speed of nearly 190 km/h. It also had shallower cups in the hydraulic shock absorbers to reduce vibration and noise. It did, however, retain the 5-cm extension of the swingarm that ensured better road holding (an innovation introduced in the second "/5" series which saw the launch of the long wheelbase, or "LWB",

R 60/6

Engine	599cc, two-cylinder, overhead valves
Frame	Tubular twin cradle
Power	40 HP at 6,400 rpm
Transmission	Cardan shaft
Suspension	Front, telescopic fork; rear, swingarm
Dimensions, weight	Length 2,180 mm, width 740 mm (engine), height 810 mm (to seat), weight 200 kg
Years of production	1973–76
Chassis serial nos. and engine nos.	From 2910001 to 2930000 and from 2960001 to 2970000
Units manufactured	13,511
Spare parts availab.	🏍 🏍 🏍 🏍 🏍
Collectors value	🏍 🏍 🏍
Price	From 3,000 to 5,000 euros

R 75/6

Engine	745cc, two-cylinder, overhead valves
Frame	Tubular twin cradle
Power	50 HP at 6,200 rpm
Transmission	Cardan shaft
Suspension	Front, telescopic fork; rear, swingarm
Dimensions, weight	Length 2,180 mm, width 740 mm (engine), height 810 mm (to seat), weight 200 kg
Years of production	1973–76
Chassis serial nos. and engine nos.	From 4010001 to 4040000
Units manufactured	17,587
Spare parts availab.	🏍️🏍️🏍️🏍️🏍️
Collectors value	🏍️🏍️🏍️
Price	From 4,000 to 6,000 euros

motorcycle). Some very important technical solutions were introduced, including the front disc brake (only the "small" R 60/6 was now being sold with drum-brake technology), and the brand-new five-speed gearbox (rather noisy indeed). The silencers were modified to lower noise, while the hydraulic steering damper was made adjustable to three positions, and could be regulated even while in motion by means of a knob located on the headstock of the steering column. Work was also done on the issue of cold starts, a characteristic defect of the "/5" series, with some small but effective improvements to carburettor settings. Along with the R 90/6, the BMW catalogue also included the aforementioned R 90 S and two rather more sober versions: the R 60/6 (which in fact replaced both the R 60/5 and the R 50/5) and the R 75/6. All the motorcycles, except for the R 90 S which we shall discuss separately, could be purchased in different colours (white, red, black and metallic blue, saffron, metallic green and ice white), with an 18- or 22-litre tank, an optional dual front disc brake (except of course the R 60/6), and the famous rigid side-bags made by Krauser (there were also leather bags available, but they did not meet with great success). All three models also could have an optional cockpit with double instrumentation, like the R 90 S, raised handlebar (also available for the 600cc and 750cc), and a windshield. Produced from 1973 to 1976, the "/6" range was updated in small particulars during its years of manufacture. For example, the first series (up to 1974) had solid-metal disc brakes (from 1975 they were drilled), the turn lights case was aluminium (black from 1975 on), different stanchions and the switches on the handlebar taken from the "/5" generation (from 1975 they were completely re-designed to make them more colourful

R 90/6

Engine	898cc, two-cylinder, overhead valves
Frame	Tubular twin cradle
Power	60 HP at 6,500 rpm
Transmission	Cardan shaft
Suspension	Front, telescopic fork; rear, oscillating swingarm
Dimensions, weight	Length 2,180 mm, width 740 mm (engine), height 810 mm (to seat), weight 200 kg
Years of production	1973–76
Chassis serial nos. and engine nos.	From 4040001 to 4070000
Units manufactured	21,097
Spare parts availab.	🏍 🏍 🏍 🏍 🏍
Collectors value	🏍 🏍 🏍
Price	From 5,000 to 7,500 euros

and ergonomic). As mentioned earlier, the similarity with the "/5" series and the launch of the R 90 S stole the limelight from the other three models of the "/6" series. The R 60/6 offered good performance but was not suited to long journeys, which was something of a distinguishing feature of BMW. For its part, the 750cc was not a great success owing to the closeness of its price with the much higher-performing R 90/6, and customers often ended up going for the larger displacement bike. The R 90/6 did not really suffer from the direct competition with the R 90 S, and managed to sell 21,070 units against 17,455 for its rival, thanks to its high performance, good safety and resilience.

COLLECTORS CORNER

From the collector's point of view, there are no significant differences between the models of the "/6" series. As we enter the 1970s we come into a chronological and technological period closer to the present than to the past, and other factors come into play in our choice of models, one of which is the viability of such bikes for daily use. In this respect, the R 60/6 is in less demand because of its drum brakes and piston carburettors, common to the previous series. The R 75/6 and, especially, the R 90/6 are in more demand because they still provide excellent performance with low fuel consumption and maintenance (apart from an excessive oil consumption). No substantial price difference separates the models with one brake disc from those with two, while the 900cc (R 90/6) commands a higher price than its two sisters. With regard to the colours, it is really a matter of taste. For daily use, the "/6" series beats the "/5" thanks above all to its better safety (disc brakes and longer swingarm), its higher performance and fewer electrical issues (the battery supplied as standard was of higher capacity than that in models produced until 1972, whose batteries were too small for the job). If adopted for frequent use, it also enjoys the many fiscal benefits allowed to vintage machines (depending on the country).

R 90 S

The R 90 S is one of the most controversial of the vintage BMW motorcycles. For some, its prestige and huge popularity – comparable to that of the older single-cylinder models and the R 50 S and R 69 S – are totally undeserved. For others it is an absolute masterpiece and an essential part of any historical collection of BMW motorcycles. Without question, the R 90 S marks a historic turning point not only for BMW motorcycles but for the motorcycle industry all around the world. It signalled a shift from the idea that the choice had to be between either a sports bike or a touring motorcycle and introduced the new concept of a global machine, that could meet the requirements of strength and safety without sacrificing high performance and a top speed of over 200 km/h. The arrival on the market of the R 90 S, the first mass-produced motorcycle in history to include a cockpit as standard, forced the other manufacturers to play a game of catch-up with BMW. The project for a sports bike based on the "/5" series, especially sponsored by the chief designer von der Marwitz, was shelved and the development team spent the first years of the 1970s committed to building a bike that had an adequate braking system with dual front discs, produced about 70 HP, and boasted a stiffer chassis, a steering damper that could be adjusted even while riding, all the same implementing features that would enable the machine to be used for long-range touring trips: a cockpit that enveloped also the handlebar, the "ducktail" extending the rear passenger seat, double dial instruments with clock and voltmeter, and speed performance of the highest level. For the styling of the R 90 S, which had to make a big splash, BMW called in the famous designer Hans A. Muth (who was later to design the futuristic lines of the

R 90 S

Engine	898cc, two-cylinder, overhead valves
Frame	Tubular twin cradle
Power	67 HP at 7,000 rpm
Transmission	Cardan shaft
Suspension	Front, telescopic fork; rear, oscillating swingarm
Dimensions, weight	Length 2,180 mm, width 740 mm (engine), height 810 mm (to seat), weight 205 kg
Years of production	1973–76
Chassis serial nos. and engine nos.	From 4070001 to 4100000
Units manufactured	17,465
Spare parts availab.	🏍 🏍 🏍 🏍 🏍
Collectors value	🏍 🏍 🏍 🏍 🏍
Price	From 7,500 to 12,000 euros

Suzuki Katana). He created a livery that soon became part of the very history of motorcycles the world over. Another noteworthy feature was the new H4 headlights, whose excellent brightness was fundamental at high speeds. BMW motorcycles had now reached such a high degree of reliability that the company management was able to offer, from 1975, a warranty on the same terms and conditions as for a car (one year, unlimited mileage). On road trials, the R 90 S immediately proved more powerful and safer than its Japanese rivals, but also revealed several tuning issues. One very important and at the same time very difficult problem concerned the calibration of sophisticated Dell'Orto carburettors with acceleration pump, which had replaced the traditional Bing units. As with the R 90/6, the R 90 S also underwent a series of updates during its years of production. The first series came with solid rather than drilled front brake discs, the same light switches and the same crankshaft of the "/5" series. The second series, in production from 1975, included a newly designed, more attractive and ergonomic set of lights switches, drilled brake discs to improve stopping performance, especially in rainy conditions, and a reinforced crankshaft, with larger bolts connecting it to the flywheel. Above, we mentioned the aesthetics of the R 90 S, which came in two different colour schemes: smoked Orange Daytona and the cool Imola Silver. Of course all these new additions did not come cheap; however, its unparalleled mix of style, comfort and performance won over many fans its high price notwithstanding. With the BMW R 90 S, the sport-touring motorcycle was born. And, for many years, this was the undisputed icon in its class. These are the main reasons for the status of the R 90 S today as

COLLECTORS CORNER

From the perspective of collectors, the R 90 S is one of the most important machines produced by BMW, comparable in historical significance to models such as the R 6, R 51 and the evolution of the "/3" series, or the R 50 S and R 69 S sports bikes. At the risk of overstatement – indeed many experts in the field do not subscribe at all to this view – we might claim that the technical features, innovative solutions and memorable design make the R 90 S one of the most sought-after bikes ever. Its price has been rising in recent times ever since its inclusion in the catalogue of vintage bikes of historical interest (for Italy at least, where it can be used as a daily means of transport but registered as a vintage motorcycle, with all the fiscal benefits this implies). In light of its evident sports-bike features, which render it "awkward" and unsuited to beginners (it is a vehicle capable of 200 km/h, with safety features well below the current standards for motorcycles of this class), it is much better to collect and keep an R 90 S than to ride it. Further, the maintenance of this model is far more costly and demanding than that of the R 90/6. No particular difference in price exists between the models from the first series and those of the second. Likewise, the colour makes no great difference to the asking price, though the Orange Daytona of the second series is still the most popular on the market. The number of specimens for sale is very small, and owners of this bike are unlikely to part with it easily, which necessarily makes for higher prices.

very popular "historic" piece that is much valued among collectors, also because, in spite of the more than 17,000 units produced, it has become hard to find spare parts in pristine condition.

BMW R 90 S. Three different series for one bike

Between 1973 and 1976, the R 90 S kept its name, but a number of technical and aesthetic features were changed, which have led this model production being divided into three different series:

• "First series": 6,058 units produced between September 1973 and August 1974 with chassis numbers from 4070001 to 4075054 (from 4950001 to 4951005 for motorcycles exported to the USA);

• "Second series": 6,413 units produced between June 1974 and September 1975 with chassis numbers from 4080001 to 4084675 (from 4980001 to 4981738 for motorcycles exported to the USA);
• "Third series": 6,058 units produced between August 1975 and June 1976 with chassis numbers from 4090001 to 4093724 (from 4990001 to 4991260 for motorcycles exported to the USA).

The changes between the first, second and third series
As we saw above, several mechanical and aesthetic differences distinguish the three series of the R 90 S. Leaving out invisible details (though there were many), we can sum up some immediate-impact features that enable us to distinguish one series from another at a glance.
• The first series of the R 90 S has solid front disc brakes, aluminium casing for the turn lights, handlebar switches the same as on the "/5" series, and an almost smooth seat cover.
• The second series has drilled brake discs, new and more modern switches on the handlebar, black plastic casing for the indicator lights, and a cross-stich seat cover.
• The third series retains the characteristics of the second from which it is virtually indistinguishable apart from some minor differences, such as the discontinuation of chrome finishing for nuts and bolts and the number "40" marked on the brake callipers.

R 60/7
R 75/7
R 80/7

The evolution of the "/6" series led naturally to the "/7" series, continuing the naming tradition inaugurated in 1969. The new series was created at the end of 1976, although it did not appear for sale until 1977. There were three basic models: a 600cc version, the R 60/7, which replaced the R 60/6; a revamped 750, the R 75/7; and a brand-new one-litre model, the R 100/7, which we shall look at separately. One year later, the R 75/7 was discontinued to make way for a new version of the 800cc R 80/7, a motorcycle that perfectly embodied the new production philosophy of Bayerische Motoren Werke: more torque, more safety and more comfort. Compared to the previous "/6" series, the new models could count on an improved frame, particularly in terms of the rigidity (with a two-layered upper tube and reinforcements between the descending tubes on the steering column), some minor styling changes (including new square-shaped valve covers, which replaced the now legendary rounded double-ribbed valve covers that had been a BMW feature ever since the R 68 of 1952), and a more complete instrument panel with electronic rpm dial, a speedometer with an anti-vibration hand, and several warning lights including the very useful brake failure warning (indicated by the German "Bremse"), which activated in the event of an insufficient level of brake fluid. From 1979, the motorcycles were equipped with a new cush drive on the Cardan shaft and a new simplex timing belt with hydraulic lash adjustment. Of all the models of the "/7" series, the highest approval rating from both press and public definitely went to the R 80/7 (with over 18,500 units sold). Equipped with a new and better-performing Bing constant velocity carburettor, every detail of the motorcycle was meticulously attended to by the BMW designers with

R 60/7

Engine	599cc, two-cylinder, overhead valves
Frame	Tubular twin cradle
Power	40 HP at 6,400 rpm
Transmission	Cardan shaft
Suspension	Front, telescopic fork; rear, swingarm
Dimensions, weight	Length 2,180 mm, width 740 mm (engine), height 810 mm (to seat), weight 200 kg
Years of production	1976–80
Chassis serial nos. and engine nos.	From 6000001 to 6005517, from 6102001 to 6102014, from 6007001 to 6011412, from 6015001 to 6117273
Units manufactured	11,163
Spare parts availab.	🏍 🏍 🏍 🏍 🏍
Collectors value	🏍 🏍 🏍
Price	From 3,000 to 4,500 euros

R 75/7

Engine	745cc, two-cylinder, overhead valves
Frame	Tubular twin cradle
Power	50 HP at 6,200 rpm
Transmission	Cardan shaft
Suspension	Front, telescopic fork; rear, swingarm
Dimensions, weight	Length 2,180 mm, width 740 mm (engine), height 810 mm (to seat), weight 200 kg
Years of production	1976–77
Chassis serial nos. and engine nos.	From 6020001 to 6024507, from 6220001 to 6220278, from 6222001 to 6222005
Units manufactured	6,264
Spare parts availab.	🏍 🏍 🏍 🏍 🏍
Collectors value	🏍 🏍 🏍
Price	From 3,500 to 6,000 euros

an eye for performance, versatility and fuel consumption. The motorcycle had dual-disc front brake as standard (the smaller-engine versions had the second disc as an option), and an optional single-disc rear brake (which was only available with the alloy wheel option), which guaranteed powerful and safe stopping. The shifting was improved through an external kinematic mechanism giving greater smoothness and accuracy, while ride comfort was enormously enhanced through a further reduction of vibration at high speeds, a reaffirmation of the legendary low noise of the BMW engine and the spacious and comfortable seat. Robust machines from every point of view, the "/7" models gave excellent performance on any terrain with minimal maintenance. Many accessories were available for the "/7" series, the most popular of which were: the tank bag (and its rainproof cover), the traditional Krauser side-bags and rear rack, the engine protection bars, useful in case of a fall, the splash guard for the rear fender, a generous windscreen for enhanced protection of the rider at high speeds and in the rain, the S series sports seat (mounted on the R 100 S as standard), and high handlebar. Less appreciated by BMW customers was the full fairing that could be mounted on all models, a solution that was not aesthetically beautiful and, worse still, very expensive. At the time of the launch of the "/7" series, BMW offered seven metallized colours: cool grey with light-blue pinstripes (silber-metallic), orange (orange-metallic) with gold pinstripes, red (rotmetallic) with gold pinstripes, dark brown (schwarz-metallic) with gold and light-blue pinstripes (blau-metallic) with white pinstripes.

R 80/7

Engine	797cc, two-cylinder, overhead valves
Frame	Tubular twin cradle
Power	50 HP at 7,250 rpm (on request 55 HP at 7,000 rpm)
Transmission	Cardan shaft
Suspension	Front, telescopic fork; rear, swingarm
Dimensions, weight	Length 2,180 mm, width 740 mm (engine), height 810 mm (to seat), weight 200 kg
Years of production	1977–84
Chassis serial nos. and engine nos.	From 6025001 to 6028787, from 6200001 to 6201915, from 6030001 to 6032475, from 6130001 to 6130118, from 6132001 to 6133186
Units manufactured	18,522
Spare parts availab.	🏍🏍🏍🏍🏍
Collectors value	🏍🏍🏍
Price	From 3,500 to 5,000 euros

COLLECTORS CORNER

A premise: the "/7" series stands on the borderline where vintage collectibles meet the ordinary second-hand market. Accordingly, diverse factors need to be considered both from the perspective of the collector and from the perspective of the second-hand buyer. These include mileage, the state of repair and the options and standard fittings that come with the machine, all of which have a bearing on comfort and safety if the motorcycle is destined for everyday use. That said, the most popular model in the series is without a doubt the R 80/7 in the version with spoke wheels, less so the version with alloy wheels. The most interesting for collectors, however, is the R 75/7, by virtue of the fact that fewer units were sold and it is therefore a rarer item. The same goes for the small R 60/7, which was mainly sold to public authorities. The three

models in the "/7" series also suffer from a not-inconsequential disadvantage from the collector's perspective: the range of colours lacks the traditional black, which is always a favourite with fans. To make up for this absence, in the 1970s some owners took matters into their own hands and painted their machines black, but this prejudices the originality and impairs the value of the vehicle. For day-to-day purposes, all models are easy to use and low-maintenance, while the commercial value of the various optionals is small, given that most of them eventually became standard. Some tips when buying: always check the that the brake pump works and, above all, test the integrity of the stand and its attachments, because being forced to replace it means to run into the significant cost of having to remove the engine.

R 100/7
R 100 S
R 100 T

Parallel to the birth of the new "/7" series, and three years after entering the 900cc class with the R 90/7 and R 90 S, BMW launched three models that marked its debut into the one-litre engine class. This historical threshold was finally crossed by the motorcycles of Bayerische Motoren Werke, which was responding promptly to requests from its customers for bikes that could compete with the powerful Japanese models. An anecdote will give some idea of how important this achievement was. It was 15 October 1976, and BMW had organized the official presentation of its new motorcycles to the Italian press in Mugello. For the occasion, an R 100 S and an R 100 RS had left Munich bound for the Mugello racetrack, ridden not by any two ordinary test drivers, but by none other than Horst Spintler and Hans Carl, respectively the Director and Deputy Director of the BMW motorcycle division. The idea was to show how the new flagship BMW could travel long distances, and cater to every category of driver, even top managers. Technically perfected right down to the smallest detail, the models differed from one another at an aesthetic level, each being decked out in a manner that reflected its intended use. The R 100/7 was the "entry-level" one-litre BMW, with essential technical and aerodynamic solutions, and so it remained until replaced by the R 100, while the R 100 S had a very high sporting potential that, however, was at least initially overshadowed by its sister-bike, the full-fairing R 100 RS. In any case, the R 100 S, designated heir of the historic R 90 S, proved the fastest in the range. It featured the cockpit already seen on the 900cc version, which it began to replace as of 1980. At the end of 1978 a limited series of R 100 S models with alloy wheels and rear disc brakes was produced, the last in the line before it was

R 100/7

Engine	980cc, two-cylinder, overhead valves
Frame	Tubular twin cradle
Power	60 HP at 6,500 rpm
Transmission	Cardan shaft
Suspension	Front, telescopic fork; rear, swingarm
Dimensions, weight	Length 2,130 mm, width 630 mm (handlebar), height 820 mm (to seat), weight 200 kg
Years of production	1976–78
Chassis serial nos. and engine nos.	From 6045001 to 6047995, from 6070001 to 6223330, from 6050001 to 6053635, from 6040001 to 6043414
Units manufactured	12,056
Spare parts availab.	🏍 🏍 🏍 🏍 🏍
Collectors value	🏍 🏍 🏍
Price	From 4,000 to 5,500 euros

R 100 S

Engine	980cc, two-cylinder, overhead valves
Frame	Tubular twin cradle
Power	65 HP at 6,600 rpm
Transmission	Cardan shaft
Suspension	Front, telescopic fork; rear, swingarm
Dimensions, weight	Length 2,210 mm, width 630 mm (handlebar), height 820 mm (to seat), weight 205 kg
Years of production	1976–78
Chassis serial nos. and engine nos.	From 6065001 to 6068753, from 6060001 to 6063149
Units manufactured	11,762
Spare parts availab.	🏍 🏍 🏍 🏍 🏍
Collectors value	🏍 🏍 🏍
Price	From 5,500 to 7,000 euros

replaced by the R 100 T. This latter motorcycle was almost identical to its predecessor, but came with alloy wheels designed and built with the American market uppermost in mind. On all the models, the valve lids followed the new angular design, and the only differences lay in the colours: aluminium for the R 100/7, R 100 S, R 100 T and R 80 T and black for the high-end bikes (R 100 RS, R 100 RT, R 100 CS). Lots of features and extras were available for the models: a high windscreen for motorcycles not equipped with fairings, side attachments and the related Krauser side-bags, an engine guard and the useful twin headlights that increased illumination. Additional instruments such as a voltmeter and a clock were available both for bikes with cockpits and for those without any aerodynamic protection.

COLLECTORS CORNER

Of the three one-litre bikes that made up the basic BMW range, the most popular model both then and now is the R 100 S, in part because it was the heir of the famous R 90 S, in part because unlike its smaller sister, it came equipped with the more reliable Bing carburettor in lieu of the sophisticated Dell'Orto type. Some small changes made the R 100 S into a motorcycle that can be still put to everyday use now, as it strikes a fair balance between performance and safety. The R 100/7 does not attract many buyers, because, though set at almost the same commercial value, it does not share the upgrades to the gearbox or the coil ignition that optimizes power delivery. Among the shortcomings of the R 100 S and the successive R 100 T are problems with the clutch, which, in spite of the increased power, had remained unchanged from that mounted on smaller-engined models. The considerable increase in oil consumption is another failing that needs to be noted. Among the several configurations, collectors still prefer the spoke-wheeled version. Also much coveted is the R 100 S with alloy wheels, triple disc brake and red bodywork with black tones. The market for the R 100 T is small to non-existent.

R 100 T

Engine	980cc, two-cylinder, overhead valves
Frame	Tubular twin cradle
Power	65 HP at 6,600 rpm
Transmission	Cardan shaft
Suspension	Front, telescopic fork; rear, swingarm
Dimensions, weight	Length 2,210 mm, width 630 mm (handlebar), height 820 mm (to seat), weight 205 kg
Years of production	1978–84
Chassis serial nos. and engine nos.	From 6110001 to 6110088, from 6115001 to 6115002, from 6050001 to 6053635, from 6040001 to 6043414
Units manufactured	5,463
Spare parts availab.	🏍️ 🏍️ 🏍️ 🏍️ 🏍️
Collectors value	🏍️ 🏍️ 🏍️
Price	From 4,000 to 6,000 euros

R 100 RS
R 100 RT
R 80 RT

In 1976, BMW achieved a new world first in the field of motorcycle production: with the R 100 RS and the R 100 RT, it introduced full fairings fitted as standard, setting a trend that was to be followed soon afterwards by other motorcycle makers, with the Japanese quickest off the mark. The R 100 RT and its smaller-displacement sister, the R 80 RT, were designed for riders who wanted to enjoy long trips, while the R 100 RS was the response of BMW engineers to the insistent demands of customers who had long been waiting for a bike that could compete at every level with the powerful and high-performance Japanese motorcycles. The R 100 RS, therefore, is the last great collector piece in the BMW motorcycle range. It is a machine with an enormous historical significance, as it marked the debut of BMW in the one-litre engine class. The aesthetic of this new flagship was once again the work by the famous designer Hans A. Muth (the brain behind the revolutionary design of the earlier R 90 S), which had focused in the realization of a synthetic protective hull, or "integral cockpit" as it became known, which was then tested in Pininfarina's wind tunnel. The result was so good that the R 100 RS was named "Bike of the Year" by *Das Motorrad*, and was rewarded with strong sales both to the general public and to public authorities, notably the police corps of France and Germany. Silent, ultra-protective and so comfortable that it was nicknamed "the 200 km/h armchair" (the standard was a single-seater, but upon request a two-seater could be fitted at no extra cost, which was less pleasing to the eye but certainly more practical), the R 100 RS was also quiet and came with a rich array of instruments. It was, in all respects, a revolutionary machine. This is why today it is so requested by collectors around the world. From a

R 100 RS

Engine	980cc, two-cylinder, overhead valves
Frame	Tubular twin cradle
Power	70 HP at 7,250 rpm
Transmission	Cardan shaft
Suspension	Front, telescopic fork; rear, swingarm
Dimensions, weight	Length 2,210 mm, width 580 mm (handlebar), height 820 mm (to seat), weight 210 kg
Years of production	1976–92
Chassis serial nos. and engine nos.	From 6080001 to 6085159, from 6086001 to 6092865, from 6075001 to 6396003
Units manufactured	33,648
Spare parts availab.	🏍 🏍 🏍 🏍 🏍
Collectors value	🏍 🏍 🏍 🏍
Price	From 3,500 to 6,000 euros

R 100 RT

Engine	980cc, two-cylinder, overhead valves
Frame	Tubular twin cradle
Power	70 HP at 7,250 rpm
Transmission	Cardan shaft
Suspension	Front, telescopic fork; rear, swingarm
Dimensions, weight	Length 2,210 mm, width 700 mm (handlebar), height 820 mm (to seat), weight 217 kg
Years of production	1978–84
Chassis serial nos. and engine nos.	From 6195001 to 6196851, from 6230001 to 6237516
Units manufactured	18,015
Spare parts availab.	🏍 🏍 🏍 🏍 🏍
Collectors value	🏍 🏍
Price	From 3,500 to 5,500 euros

technical perspective, the R 100 RS marked the return of constant velocity Bing carburettors, which ensured better control at low revs, better fuel consumption (although in proportion to the mass and performance of the bike: no more than 12 kilometres per litre) and reduced pollution. The rear shock absorbers were adjustable to three positions for easy customization by the driver, who could also opt for special HD springs and dampers (standard on the RS and RT models) if intending the bike for a more "sporty" vocation. The steering damper, too, was adjustable to three positions, while the standard instrumentation was the most complete that could be found at the time, with a voltmeter, electric clock and an easy-to-read rev counter and speedometer. Also noteworthy was the excellent redesign work on the fuel tank, starting with the cap, which was rendered flat with no protruding points, came with a security key, and included an overflow system for disposing of excess fuel via a tube that discharged it on the ground. During its sixteen years of production (a record for BMW), the R 100 RS was further refined. The first series (most coveted by collectors) came with spoked wheels, double front disc brake and

COLLECTORS CORNER

The three R-series models that included built-in fairing as standard are now experiencing the law of retaliation. While the inclusion of full fairing was the feature that grabbed the attention of the press and public at the time and met with great success, the presence of this same element is now regarded as a limit to the usability of the motorcycle on the road. At the time, the issues related to the introduction of an integrated shell had been eclipsed by the enthusiasm for the novelty, but now they are regarded as a major drawback. The fairing makes the handlebar tight and limits the steering angle; it increases the weight of the machine, and moreover the feeling about it; conveys the heat from the engine towards the rider; and increases the engine noise working as a resonant chamber. All these negative factors have put off collectors, and the market for the motorcycle is rather stagnant. Another big issue is poor braking (especially in the very first series). Of the three models, the most popular is the

R 100 RS, particularly the 1976 version with spoked wheels and rear drum brake, worth 1,000 euros more than any of the following series whether consisting of the 1977–78 models with alloy wheels and rear drum or of the final 1978 version with rear disc brake. There is little demand for the Classic version (as a result of the questionable choice of colour scheme) and for the R 100 RT and R 80 RT whose fairings are decidedly too voluminous.

rear drum brake; as of 1977 the spoked wheels were replaced by light alloy versions. One year later, a rear disc brake marked the definitive abandonment of the drum. The last major changes, mostly of a technical nature, were effected in 1981, including the introduction of a light alloy jacket for the cylinders, a flat filter in a plastic box, a larger oil sump and a shift assist for the gear pedal. In 1983 a special version of the R 100 RS, called the Classic Series 500 Limited Edition was made (only 500 units thereof). This boasted several aesthetic peculiarities, including Krauser bags matching the paintwork and a special Madison (light-blue) or Blue paint that was then adopted by BMW for the first series of the new K 100 generation. The R 100 RT super-touring bike also underwent some changes during its six years of production, moving from spoked wheels in 1978 with front and rear disc brakes to the almost final version of 1981, which came with new light alloy wheels. A motorcycle designed for long journeys, with broad and protective fairing, an adjustable windshield, seat material matching (on demand) the two-tone body paintwork and a complete instrument range, from 1980 the R 100 RT underwent mechanical improvements such as the inclusion of a more modern ignition timer, a new Bing constant velocity carburettor with a throttle return spring and a very useful cush drive mounted on the final section of the Cardan shaft. In 1981, BMW started making a cheaper 800cc version of this machine, almost exclusively for use by public authorities.

R 80 RT

Engine	797cc, two-cylinder, overhead valves
Frame	Tubular twin cradle
Power	50 HP at 6,500 rpm
Transmission	Cardan shaft
Suspension	Front, telescopic fork; rear, conventional swingarm
Dimensions, weight	Length 2,220 mm, width 930 mm (fairing), height 820 mm (to seat), weight 214 kg
Years of production	1982–84
Chassis serial nos. and engine nos.	From 6420001 to 6425163
Units manufactured	7,315
Spare parts availab.	🏍 🏍 🏍 🏍 🏍
Collectors value	🏍 🏍
Price	From 3,000 to 4,000 euros

R45
R65
R65LS

In 1977, Bayerische Motoren Werke recorded a new high for the sales of its motorcycle division: a total of 31,515. Long gone were the years of crisis when sales were in the order of 5,000 (the sum of 1968 and 1969 was less than 10,000). Riding on the crest of this wave of enthusiasm, but also conscious that it needed to broaden its customer base, BMW management set the engineers to work on designing models that were both more affordable and easier to drive for lay persons. The fabulous one-litre bikes were expensive and difficult to drive, and what was needed now, it was reasoned, were motorcycles suitable also for newcomers to two-wheeled vehicles and for ordinary people who could not afford to spend 12,000 Deutsche marks on an R 100 RS. So it was that at the Cologne Motor Show of 1978 BMW presented to the public the "small" R 45 and R 65, two very similar motorcycles both expressly designed for novices. The former, powered by a 473cc engine delivering 27 HP was eligible for low insurance premiums; the latter, with a 649cc engine was intended for "weekend bikers". The emphasis was on both quality and comfort, with the aim to build two motorcycles that were in every respect BMW machines and met all the high production standards of the company, even though they offered lower performances than the average BMW model (the R 45 had a top speed on just 145 km/h). It was this very commitment to maintaining quality that prevented the company from achieving any substantial reduction of production costs, with the result that the new motorcycles went on sale with price tags not far below those for the more powerful models. Therefore, despite and because of these initial good intentions, the R 45 was to become the most expensive under 500cc motorcycle in Germany, so that, in an effort to spur sales on foreign

R 45

Engine	473cc, two-cylinder, overhead valves
Frame	Tubular twin cradle
Power	27 HP at 6,500 rpm (35 HP at 7,250 rpm)
Transmission	Cardan shaft
Suspension	Front, telescopic fork; rear, swingarm
Dimensions, weight	Length 2,110 mm, width 630 mm (handlebar), height 810 mm (to seat), weight 185 kg
Years of production	1978–85
Chassis serial nos. and engine nos.	From 6195001 to 6196851, from 6230001 to 6237516
Units manufactured	28,158
Spare parts availab.	🏍 🏍 🏍 🏍 🏍
Collectors value	🏍 🏍
Price	From 1,500 to 2,500 euros

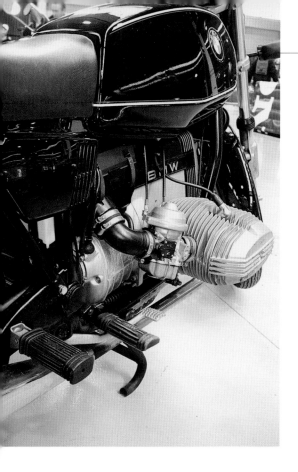

markets, it was offered in a souped-up version with 35 HP. Another factor that weighed heavily on the sales of the R 45 was the rather questionable basic colour scheme available: champagne with gold pinstripes or brown with red pinstripes. The R 65, meanwhile, was basically the same as its less powerful sister: while it delivered 45 HP (50 HP as of 1980), the aesthetic differences were negligible. The frame of both models was almost identical to that of the R 75/7, except that the swingarm had been shortened by 5 cm and the wheels had a radius of 18 inches instead of the traditional 19. The engine case and gearbox assembly were also the same as the R 75/7. The R 45 and R 65 had a new type of seat and fuel tank design that distinguished them from their predecessors. In the case of the latter, the new straight-edged configuration was more in line with the shape of the engine. Similarly the re-designed handgrips proved easier to use, in spite of a slightly overlong travel on the accelerator. The wheels were of light alloy, the front fender was sporty in aspect. The straight-axle fork that replaced the previous leading-axle setup allowed a reduction in the wheelbase and a better balance of masses, which was very much to the benefit of manoeuvrability and stability. The rear hub had numerous self-ventilating holes that allowed for a better cooling of the brake drum, while the front braking system consisted of a traditional ATE-made with dual-piston calipers. The R 65 could be fitted, upon request, with a second disc brake. The options available for both models included two additional instruments (clock and voltmeter) that complemented the already excellent basic cockpit set, and a second horn. To meet the need of customers in search of less traditional styling, a sportier version of the R 65 with more attention to detail was

R 65

Engine	649cc, two-cylinder, overhead valves
Frame	Tubular twin cradle
Power	45 HP at 7,250 rpm
Transmission	Cardan shaft
Suspension	Front, telescopic fork; rear, single-sided swingarm
Dimensions, weight	Length 2,110 mm, width 600 mm (handlebar), height 810 mm (to seat), weight 205 kg
Years of production	1978–85
Chassis serial nos. and engine nos.	From 6340001 to 6349336, from 6310001 to 6413588
Units manufactured	29,454
Spare parts availab.	🏍 🏍 🏍 🏍 🏍
Collectors value	🏍 🏍
Price	From 2,500 to 3,500 euros

introduced in 1981, and named the R 65 LS. It featured some visual and functional improvements, including the addition of a small but effective pod that enclosed both the instrumentation and the headlamp, silencers painted in black, a new seat tail with two solid handles for the passenger, re-designed wheels, larger rear brake shoes and a double front disc brake. Finally, an "enduro" version of the R 65, called the G/S, was also created: virtually identical to the R 80 G/S, it came equipped with an R 65 engine.

R 65 LS

Engine	649cc, two-cylinder, overhead valves
Frame	Tubular twin cradle
Power	50 HP at 7,250 rpm
Transmission	Cardan shaft
Suspension	Front, telescopic fork; rear, single-sided swingarm
Dimensions, weight	Length 2,110 mm, width 600 mm (handlebar), height 810 mm (to seat), weight 205 kg
Years of production	1981–85
Chassis serial nos. and engine nos.	From 6350001 to 6354679
Units manufactured	6,389
Spare parts availab.	🏍 🏍 🏍 🏍 🏍
Collectors value	🏍 🏍
Price	From 2,500 to 4,500 euros

COLLECTORS CORNER

These two small-displacement models made by BMW are of such low appeal to collectors and are of such relatively recent manufacture that they are traded mainly on the ordinary second-hand motorcycle market. Whereas the R 45 is more interesting for being rideable by novice riders, the R 65 LS is another matter, for it may be of some interest to collectors, especially with its "Hennarot" (red) paintwork with white wheels. Easy to handle and particularly well suitable to city driving, it has the added benefit of not requiring too much maintenance work.

1970s

data sheet

Model	Cylinders displ.	cc	Prod. years	Units made	Spare parts av.	Collectors value	Price (euros)	Chassis	Engine
R 60/6	2	599	1973–76	13,511	🏍🏍🏍🏍🏍	🏍🏍🏍	3,000–5,000	From 2910001 to 2930000, 2960001 to 2970000	From 2910001 to 2930000, 2960001 to 2970000
R 75/6	2	745	1973–76	17,587	🏍🏍🏍🏍🏍	🏍🏍🏍	4,000–6,000	From 4010001 to 4040000	From 4010001 to 4040000
R 90/6	2	898	1973–76	21,097	🏍🏍🏍🏍🏍	🏍🏍🏍	5,000–7,500	From 4040001 to 4070000	From 4040001 to 4070000
R 90 S	2	898	1973–76	17,465	🏍🏍🏍🏍🏍	🏍🏍🏍🏍🏍	7,500–12,000	From 4070001 to 4100000	From 4070001 to 4100000
R 60/7	2	599	1976–80	11,163	🏍🏍🏍🏍🏍	🏍🏍🏍	3,000–4,500	From 6000001 to 6005517, 6102001 to 6102014, 6007001 to 6011412, 6015001 to 6117273	From 6000001 to 6005517, 6102001 to 6102014, 6007001 to 6011412 6015001 to 6117273
R 75/7	2	745	1976–77	6,264	🏍🏍🏍🏍🏍	🏍🏍🏍	3,500–6,000	From 6020001 to 6024507, 6220001 to 6220278, 6222001 to 6222005	From 6020001 to 6024507, 6220001 to 6220278, 6222001 to 6222005
R 100/7	2	980	1976–78	12,056	🏍🏍🏍🏍🏍	🏍🏍🏍	4,000–5,500	From 6045001 to 6047995, 6070001 to 6223330, 6050001 to 6053635, 6040001 to 6043414	From 6045001 to 6047995, 6070001 to 6223330, 6050001 to 6053635, 6040001 to 6043414
R 100 S	2	980	1976–78	11,762	🏍🏍🏍🏍🏍	🏍🏍🏍	5,500–7,000	From 6065001 to 6068753, 6060001 to 6063149	From 6065001 to 6068753, 6060001 to 6063149
R 80/7	2	797	1977–84	18,522	🏍🏍🏍🏍🏍	🏍🏍🏍	3,500–5,000	From 6025001 to 6028787, 6200001 to 6201915, 6030001 to 6032475, 6130001 to 6130118, 6132001 to 6133186	From 6025001 to 6028787, 6200001 to 6201915, 6030001 to 6032475, 6130001 to 6130118, 6132001 to 6133186
R 45	2	473	1978–85	28,158	🏍🏍🏍🏍🏍	🏍🏍	1,500–2,500	From 6195001 to 6196851, 6230001 to 6237516	From 6195001 to 6196851, 6230001 to 6237516
R 65	2	649	1978–85	29,454	🏍🏍🏍🏍🏍	🏍🏍	2,500–3,500	From 6340001 to 6349336, 6310001 to 6413588	From 6340001 to 6349336, 6310001 to 6413588
R 65 LS	2	649	1981–85	6,389	🏍🏍🏍🏍🏍	🏍🏍	2,500–4,500	From 6350001 to 6354679	From 6350001 to 6354679
R 100 T	2	980	1978–80	5,463	🏍🏍🏍🏍🏍	🏍🏍🏍🏍	4,000–6,000	From 6110001 to 6110088, 6115001 to 6115002, 6050001 to 6053635, 6040001 to 6043414	From 6110001 to 6110088, 6115001 to 6115002, 6050001 to 6053635, 6040001 to 604341
R 100 RS	2	980	1976–92	33,648	🏍🏍🏍🏍🏍	🏍🏍🏍🏍	3,500–6,000	From 6080001 to 6085159, 6086001 to 6092865, 6075001 to 6396003	From 6080001 to 6085159, 6086001 to 6092865, 6075001 to 6396003
R 100 RT	2	980	1978–84	18,015	🏍🏍🏍🏍🏍	🏍🏍	3,500–5,500	From 6195001 to 6196851, 6230001 to 6237516	From 6195001 to 6196851, from 6230001 to 6237516
R 80 RT	2	797	1982–84	7,315	🏍🏍🏍🏍🏍	🏍🏍	3,000–4,000	From 6420001 to 6425163	From 6420001 to 6425163

the 1980s

The 1980s represented a turning point in BMW history. Partially in response to commercial and technological pressure from Japanese motorcycle makers, the Bayerische Motoren Werke was forced to completely overhaul its range of models. The revolutionary R 80 G/S enduro and the new 1000cc models with full fairing ended up making all the difference with their cutting-edge technology. BMW's reputation of reliability thus gained an aura of prestige and distinction, both off-road and on.

R 100
R 100 CS

The R 100 and R 100 CS represented a completely new direction in boxer-engine BMWs. Available in grey and petroleum blue and featuring all the modifications already incorporated into other models (from the braking system with a dual front disk and rear drum to the sports seat), the R100 was introduced in 1980 to replace the R 100 /7. Meanwhile, the special R 100 CS debuted in 1980 as a powerful, high-speed 70 HP model slightly more than 4,000 bikes sold. The principal differences between these new generation models and their predecessors were mainly technical: starting in 1980, all motorcycles in the range were equipped with electronic ignition and new light alloy Nikasil-coated cylinder liners in place of their cast iron counterparts, a modification that significantly reduced oil consumption (a critical factor for the R 100 S and R 100 T). The engine flywheel was also modified to make it lighter, along with the clutch system, completely redesigned to cut down on the weight of rotating parts. Significant modifications were also made to the drive shaft, including the introduction of a cush drive and a new design for the bevel gears. The chief modifications to the chassis included a completely redesigned front fork and a shift from the traditional ATE brakes with floating calipers to more powerful Brembo brakes with caliper fixed to the fork leg. The brake pump was also moved to the handlebar from under the tank and the air filter housing was flattened to enhance airflow. While the R 100 was the new entry-level BMW into the 1000cc class, with essential standard equipment and nice performance, the R 100 CS was introduced as a modern version of the R 90 S and the R 100 S. It was initially sold with spoke wheels to meet the demand by the more

R 100

Engine	980 cc, two-cylinder, overhead valves
Frame	Tubular twin cradle
Power	67 HP at 7,000 rpm
Transmission	Cardan shaft
Suspension	Front, telescopic fork; rear, swingarm
Dimensions, weight	Length 2,210 mm, width 746 mm (handlebar), height 810 mm (to seat), weight 198 kg
Years of production	1980–84
Chassis serial nos. and engine nos.	From 6035001 to 6401795
Units manufactured	10,111
Spare parts availab.	🏍 🏍 🏍 🏍 🏍
Collectors value	🏍 🏍
Price	From 3,000 to 5,000 euros

R 100 CS

Engine	980 cc, two-cylinder, overhead valves
Frame	Tubular twin cradle
Power	70 HP at 7,250 rpm
Transmission	Cardan shaft
Suspension	Front, telescopic fork; rear, swingarm
Dimensions, weight	Length 2,210 mm, width 630 mm (tank), height 820 mm (to seat), weight 200 kg
Years of production	1980–84
Chassis serial nos. and engine nos.	From 6135001 to 6138864
Units manufactured	4,038
Spare parts availab.	🏍🏍🏍🏍🏍
Collectors value	🏍🏍🏍
Price	From 4,500 to 6,500 euros

COLLECTORS CORNER

Like all BMWs produced starting in the 1980s, the R 100 and the R 100 CS belong to that boundary zone between the vintage market and the used motorcycle market, where the collection value has little weight in assessing the value of individual models. This is even more true when we talk about really fast bikes, like the R 100 CS, a very important machine because of its limited numbers (just over 4,000 produced) and fame as a super-fast boxer model, the only one in the range that could safely do over 200 km/h. As for the R 100, its collection value is practically nil, but it is still highly in demand on the used motorcycle market due to the fact that it is an excellent and safe bike for long trips. Neither motorcycle requires particular maintenance with the exception of modifications to the fuel system to allow the use of unleaded petrol. Getting more into specifics, the most sought-after colours are classic black or gradated red-black.

nostalgic customers, but was soon recalled because of a hub problem that ended up requiring the use of a light-alloy wheel. The R 100 CS was sold in three sports colour schemes: red, black and gradated red-black, all with gold striping.

R 80 G/S
R 80 G/S Paris Dakar

There are models in BMW history that have represented a perfect balance of technology and innovation, not for the German manufacturer alone. Among these, the R 80 G/S touring enduro ("G/S" stands for Gelände/Strasse, i.e. off-road/road) certainly occupies a preeminent position. Developed through the application of BMW's experience in off-road competition (resumed in 1979 after a long hiatus) to series production, this motorcycle made its debut in September 1980, without BMW sales representatives having any points of reference: indeed, at the time, there were no examples of off-road bikes conceived specially for on-road use. The international scene at the time was dominated by increasingly powerful machines with elaborate fairings, designed and built expressly to let customers enjoy the thrill of speed. This was exactly the opposite of the R 80 G/S, a motorcycle with a top speed under 170 km/h (partly because of the aerodynamics of the front fender, which rendered the front end unstable at high speeds) and no aerodynamic appendages: just a deliberately Spartan machine. Furthermore, although shifting the footrests towards the back helped somewhat, the rider's upright position left him exposed to the full force of the oncoming air. But as victories accumulated in the then-pioneering Paris–Dakar race, the BMW enduro was transformed bit by bit into a cult object. People were initially a bit put off or daunted by the innovations of the R 80 G/S, but it wasn't long before sales were booming. This new market niche became solidly established in the late 1980s and early 1990s and the Japanese manufacturers were forced to sit up and take notice. Among the technical features introduced with the R 80 G/S, the Monolever

R 80 G/S · R 80 G/S Dakar

Engine	797 cc, two-cylinder, overhead valves
Frame	Tubular twin cradle
Power	50 HP at 6,500 rpm
Transmission	Cardan shaft
Suspension	Front, telescopic fork; rear, single-sided swingarm
Dimensions, weight	Length 2,230 mm, width 820 mm (handlebar), height 860 mm (to seat), weight 168 kg
Years of production	1980–87
Chassis serial nos. and engine nos.	From 6250001 to 6260000 and from 6281001 to 6292522
Units manufactured	21,864
Spare parts availab.	🏍 🏍 🏍 🏍 🏍
Collectors value	🏍 🏍 🏍 🏍 🏍
Price	From 5,000 to 7,500 euros, from 6,000 to 13.000 euros (Dakar)

single-sided rear suspension was unquestionably the most innovative.
A pioneering design choice in a production bike, it provided extraordinary
comfort over any terrain while also reducing chassis weight (BMW claimed
a total reduction of over 7 kilograms) and facilitating maintenance
(removal and installation of the wheel) as well as shock absorber adjustment.
The advantages of this new solution were affirmed by the adoption of the
Monolever system on other BMW models, including the R 80 RT in 1984,
the R 65 in 1985, the R 100 RS in 1986, the R 100 RT in 1987, and the
entire K series. The R 80 G/S proved its versatility in road tests, offering
extraordinary handling and comfort on all surfaces. The chassis was derived
from the "small" R 45 and R 65 touring bikes with a number of modifications
to the front fork. The front brake was a Brembo disk with asbestos-free
semi-metallic pads, ensuring better braking power on wet roads or in other
situations of poor traction. With its original livery – lobster red two-seater
seat contrasting with the white body and the blue & light blue panels on the
tank – the first, now historic, version of the R 80 G/S certainly did not pass
unobserved. In 1982 a version with blue paint and a black seat was offered,
although the most famous and sought-after version of the R 80 G/S is the
Paris–Dakar celebratory model (the trans-African marathon won in 1981
and 1983 by the Frenchman Hubert Auriol on a BMW) characterized
by the distinctive 32-litre tank and the lobster-red single seat.

COLLECTORS CORNER

The R 80 G/S has never experienced dips in demand in spite of its defects, including the undersized petrol tank (giving it a maximum range of 220 kilometres) and faint braking system, which precluded its use on motorways. Thanks to its versatility and ease of driving, the R 80 G/S has always represented the main entrance into the world of BMW motorcycles. Demand is high for the original version with white body components and also strong for the blue variant. The Paris–Dakar version is highly in demand and hard to find, especially the first series with kick starter; less so the aftermarket, kitted out version.

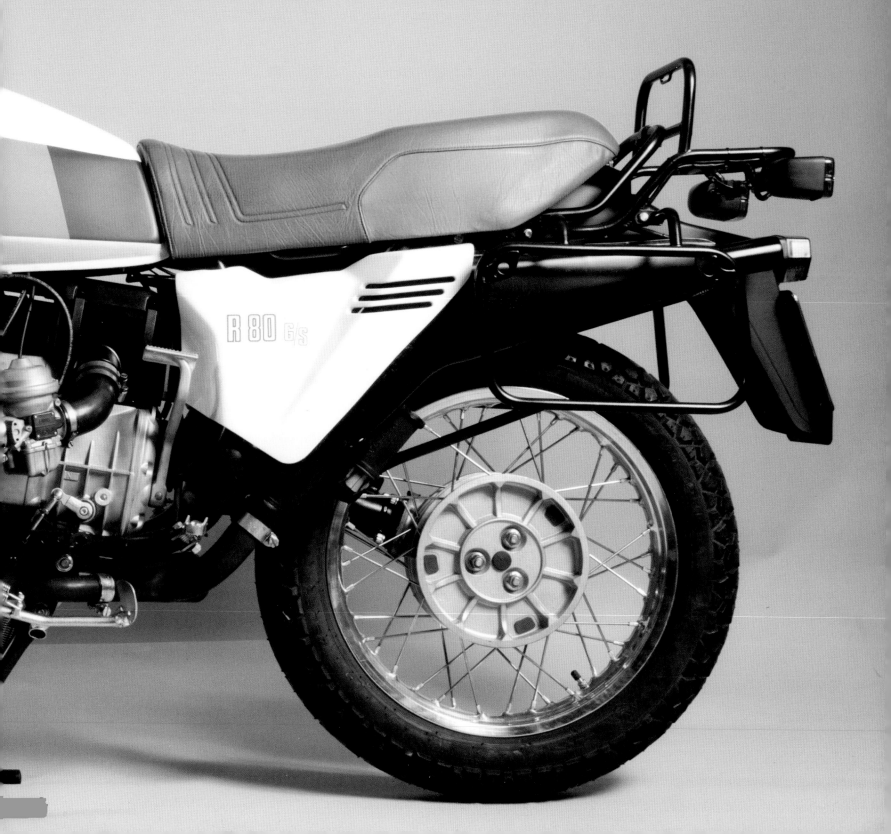

Gaston Rahier's signature decorates
the tank of the R 80 G/S Paris–Dakar

R 80 G/S Paris–Dakar

The R 80 G/S Paris–Dakar is one of the most legendary and beloved bikes among BMW collectors. This is partly because it was the first enduro for grand tours and partly because it gave a taste of Africa to the many lucky enthusiasts who were able to afford this small jewel in 1984. Still highly sought-after today and hard to find in the original version (many exemplars on the market are not "native" Paris–Dakars but ordinary R 80 G/S bikes dressed up with aftermarket components), the R 80 G/S Paris–Dakar was launched on the international market by BMW in 1984, partly to ride the wave of successes on African soil and partly to get a jump on the Japanese rivals in the touring enduro market. The new motorcycle differed from its predecessors precisely in its "grand tour" equipment: the tank was increased from 19.5 to 32 litres (with an autograph by Gaston Rahier painted instead of a sticker) and fitted with two petcocks instead of one. The graphics, dominated by motorsport colours and the words "Paris–Dakar", had greater aesthetic appeal. A one- or two-seater seat was available with integrated luggage rack attached to the closure mechanism of the long seat (in this single-seater version the bike was 3 centimetres taller). The rear fender was painted white to match the rest of the body and the chrome silencer had an integrated heat shield (debuting on the ST version). The bike was also equipped with a larger 12V/20Ah battery and both an electric and a kick starter (optional on the standard model); the front fork had a reinforcement bridge, optional on the standard model. A true off-road touch were the Michelin T61 tyres, very nice to look at but not suited to ride on tarmac.

Given the high demand for motorcycles with Paris–Dakar gear, BMW sold a transformation kit at a rather advantageous price – for the seller: in 1984, the kit cost 1,500 Deutschmarks, one fifth the selling price of the motorcycle. The Paris–Dakar was produced from 1984 to 1987; according to the magazine *Motorrader*, only 3,190 were original (specifically, 770 in 1984, 690 in 1985, 1,100 in 1986 and 630 in 1987). There are various ways to determine whether a motorcycle you are looking at is an original Paris–Dakar or one fitted out with a conversion kit. Some of them are more technical, such as checking for a steering stop (to protect the turn indicators) or whether the engine number is located near the left manifold (for motorcycles with a conversion kit, the number will probably be located near the oil cap). We recommend taking the frame number to a BMW Motorrad dealer, where you can search the database to see if the frame is listed as referring to a "special paint" version, which indicates that it is an original Paris–Dakar and not one fitted out post-production with a conversion kit. Regarding optionals that may be found or installed on a Paris–Dakar, in addition to the classical racks, Krauser touring bags, shielded rubber spark plug caps, clocks and temperature monitors, we also mention in particular the steel shock absorber identical to the one mounted on the original G/S series but with a supplementary oil tank. In addition, it was rather common practice to install the round valve covers deriving from the R 69 S and R 68 series instead of the standard square-shaped ones.

BMW at the Paris–Dakar

Paris–Dakar. Two words. Two goals. One dream. For motorcyclists, for BMW enthusiasts, for those who have adventure in their hearts and arms. Many long years have passed since the first edition of a race that, in spite of the recent changes in track, everybody considers to be the African rally raid par excellence.

Over three decades have passed since the summer of 1979, when contestants set out to brave more than 9,500 km of what were probably the world's most challenging and dangerous roads, over 70% of them crossing deserts and sand. It is a true elimination race, which has unfortunately claimed the lives of some riders and even that of its founder, Thierry Sabine. Names of men and women who have lived their great passion for this impossible dream to the utmost. And no motorcycle brand has a history more closely associated with this great endurance race than BMW. The idea for the Dakar Rally originated during the Abidjan–Nice race, when Thierry Sabine got lost on his motorcycle in the Libyan desert. After returning from Africa, he decided to create a rally raid that would not simply be a motorcycle race, but a true and timeless adventure: a man and his motorcycle against the desert and its captivating perils. Sabine imagined a route starting in Paris and finishing on the long Senegalese beach at Dakar, passing through many African countries and their immense deserts.

The first edition of the Paris–Dakar started on 26 December 1979 from the Place du Trocadéro. 170 competitors set out to reach Dakar, some 10,000 km away. Along with the winner Cyril Neveu on his Yamaha was the French photographer, journalist and driver Jean-Claude Morellet, known famously by his nickname "Fenouil". He achieved impressive placements on a BMW bike, the R 800. Fenouil competed in five Dakar Rallies on a BMW customized by HPN of Seibersdorf, a firm that worked closely with BMW Motorsport. Thanks to its experience in numerous sports competitions, including off-road endurance races, HPN laid the technical groundwork

Above, Hubert Auriol and Gaston Rahier, the 1984 winners; right, Richard Sainct in 2000

for the Bayerische Motoren Werke's first victory in the Dakar Rally. The year was 1981 and Herbert Auriol, leader of the BMW team that also included Bernard Neimer and Fenouil, was the first across the line at Dakar on a R 80 G/S. BMW achieved the final victory again in 1983, in part thanks to the extraordinary prep work carried out by the former BMW driver Herbert Scheck, who boosted the power of the G/S using a new 980 cc, 70 HP engine. Hubert Auriol would pass the baton on to the legendary Gaston Rahier the following year. Belgian, fierce competitor, motocross champion in spite of his diminutive stature, in 1984 Rahier crossed the line just ahead of his teammate Auriol. BMW celebrated this outstanding first and second place finish by launching the R 80 G/S Pais–Dakar on the international market, prominently sporting Rahier's signature on the tank. This special Dakar version remained on the market through 1984, and Gaston Rahier's victory the following year (astride the legendary white and orange BMW with the number 101, which would forever be known as the "Dakar BMW") was more than perfect. It was BMW's fourth Paris–Dakar victory in five years.

Top to bottom: the no. 100 BMW, winner of the 1981 Paris–Dakar race; Gaston Rahier's no. 101 from 1985; and Rahier in 1984

And these victories were accompanied by others in major races such as the Rallye des Pharaons, and the Baja 1000 in California.

In 1987, BMW decided not to be present with an official team at the Dakar Rally starting line in Paris, but continued to provide support to a group of independent drivers who were as numerous as they were competitive. Outstanding among them was Eddy Hau, winner of the Paris–Dakar in the stock bike category in 1988 and 1992. And the exploits of Jutta Kleinschmidt, BMW engineer and winner of the Dakar Rally in the women's category, are also quite noteworthy.

After a ten-year hiatus, BMW Motorrad celebrated its official return to the race to Dakar in 1998. Abandoning the powerful two-cylinder engines that had written the history of the African marathon, BMW staked everything on new one-cylinder models based on the F 650. The first year back in the race was not particularly glorious for the Bavarian motorcycle maker. However, the following year, benefiting from a wealth of accumulated experience, the Frenchman Richard Sainct brought home BMW's fifth victory. The following year, 2000, marked BMW's most impressive triumph, dominating the race by sweeping the top four places. Richard Sainct was first across the line once again ahead of his teammates Oscar Gallardo, Jean Brucy and Jimmy Lewis, the latter winning third place on his R 900 RR. Although the year 2001 marked BMW's final official participation in the Dakar Rally, BMW and Dakar are two names that will always be strongly intertwined in the history of competitive motorcycling.

R 80 ST
R 80 RT

In the wake of the success of the R 80 G/S, fans began demanding an equally sleek and agile machine with the same captivating look but more suited to city use and with room for a passenger. BMW responded with the R 80 ST, which many consider the best-designed motorcycle of its time. The 797.5cc engine used for the R 80 G/S was installed on the entire R 80 series, which added the R 80 RT and the R 80 ST in the autumn of 1982. The R 80 ST was the direct descendant of the success and experience of the R 80 G/S. After the obvious initial surprise at the stylistic, conceptual and technical innovations of the maxi enduro, BMW customers requested and obtained a version expressly designed for road use. The design was very similar to the original project with just a few minor exterior modifications (for example, the new "enclosed" tailpipe, the front fender, the handlebar) and mechanical tweaks. While keeping the same chassis as the R 80 G/S, a number of extremely apt changes were introduced to enhance handling, especially on mixed routes. The 19" front wheel, straight axle fork (as on the R 45 and R 65) and raised but narrower handlebar enhanced the fantastic handling of an already excellent frame. The two new colours, red and grey with striping and matching rear fender, gave the bike a more elegant and finely finished look. The model also featured the R 45 and R 65 dashboard with tachometer and odometer. The ST's chrome tailpipe with metal heat shield was later installed on the R 80 G/S Paris–Dakar. The well-tested 800cc engine was also used on the R 80 RT, a bike mostly wanted by the police and armed forces in different countries. It was a grand touring bike at a competitive price. Its main external characteristic was the broad, comfortable and

R 80 ST

Engine	797 cc, two-cylinder, overhead valves
Frame	Tubular twin cradle
Power	50 HP at 6,500 rpm
Transmission	Cardan shaft
Suspension	Front, telescopic fork; rear, single-sided swingarm
Dimensions, weight	Length 2,180 mm, width 790 mm (handlebar), height 845 mm (to seat), weight 183 kg
Years of production	1982–84
Chassis serial nos. and engine nos.	From 6054001 to 6058984
Units manufactured	5,963
Spare parts availab.	🏍 🏍 🏍 🏍 🏍
Collectors value	🏍 🏍 🏍 🏍
Price	From 4,000 to 6,500 euros

enveloping fairing, which was subjected to exhaustive testing in the Pininfarina Wind Tunnel. The windscreen could be adjusted manually to suit the rider by means of knobs located on the inner side of the fairing. It also featured a rack that could take loads of up to 5 kg and a handle to improve passenger stability and safety. The two waterproof 35-litre hard side-bags, large enough to hold two full-sized helmets, left no doubt that this was a touring machine. The side-bags could be removed and remounted using a single lockable clasp. The R 80 ST was sold in two colours: red or blue.

R 80 RT

Engine	797 cc, two-cylinder, overhead valves
Frame	Tubular twin cradle
Power	50 HP at 6,500 rpm
Transmission	Cardan shaft
Suspension	Front, telescopic fork; rear, conventional swingarm
Dimensions, weight	Length 2,220 mm, width 746 mm (handlebar), height 820 mm (to seat), weight 168 kg
Years of production	1982–84
Chassis serial nos. and engine nos.	From 6420001 to 6425163
Units manufactured	7,315
Spare parts availab.	🏍 🏍 🏍 🏍 🏍
Collectors value	🏍 🏍
Price	From 3,000 to 4,000 euros

COLLECTORS CORNER

The R 80 ST should be considered one of the most innovative BMW bikes of the 1980s. However, it never sold as well as it should have, partly because it was too far ahead of its time and overshadowed, in any case, by the R 80 G/S. But while its enduro sister-bike was easy and enjoyable to drive, the modified chassis of the ST made it more precise in holding a line and more stable at medium and high speeds. Another of the elements adding to the quality of the ST is the heat guard on the tailpipe to enhance passenger comfort. A good portion of the STs were sold in the United States, a market where fashion is relatively unimportant and the focus is on the quality and personality of the bikes. The R 80 RT, on the other hand, is quite similar in its aesthetics to the R 100 RT, differing only in terms of displacement and the lack of a rear disk brake. While not delivering exhilarating performance, the 800cc engine made it for a good grand tourer that was particularly coveted in countries where big engines are subject to extra taxes and much more expensive insurance coverage. The R 80 RT is suitable for touring couples who do not need outstanding performance.

K 100
K 100 RS
K 100 RT
K 100 LT

BMW Motorrad celebrated its 60th anniversary in 1983 with the presentation of the K 100, the first model in the K series and the first motorcycle in the world to adopt the latest in automobile technology. It represented a radical turning point, a bike with an absolutely novel and revolutionary engine design that broke with all the classic schemes: the BMW Compact Drive System. The power plant featured a one-piece engine block, transmission and crankshaft in line with the direction of travel, and everything hung from a bridge frame. The elimination of carburettors in favour of Bosch LE Jetronic digitally controlled fuel injection (deriving from automotive technology) brought excellent performance coupled with lowered fuel consumption, and made it possible to install a catalytic converter on a motorcycle exhaust. In the following years, this very innovation would turn out to be decisive in the popularity of BMW motorcycles among the police forces in many countries. The initial "K" stood for "Kompact", referring to the engine and drive train configuration. The heart of the K 100 was a longitudinal four-cylinder, water-cooled, twin-cam, two-valve engine laid on its left side. It was nicknamed "flying brick" for the way it looked. The creators of this small technological wonder thus wrote a new page in the history book of world motorcycling. The team of engineers included Stefan Pachernegg, project leader, Josef Fritzenwenger, mechanical design leader, Günter Schier, chassis design, Martin Probst, engine design, Richard Heydenreich, design director and Klaus Volker Gevert, the style director. BMW invested significant resources in development and testing this highly innovative project. Before going onto the assembly line, the K 100 underwent over

K 100

Engine	987 cc, four-cylinder, in-line engine rotated 90° left
Frame	Tubular bridge frame, open below
Power	90 HP at 8,000 rpm
Transmission	Cardan shaft
Suspension	Front, telescopic fork; rear, single-sided swingarm
Dimensions, weight	Length 2,220 mm, width 730 mm (handlebar), height 810 mm (to seat), weight 239 kg
Years of production	1983–87
Units manufactured	11,549
Chassis serial nos.:	From 0000001 to 0010000, from 0033001 to 0033027, from 6308101 to 6309422
Spare parts availab.	🏍 🏍 🏍 🏍 🏍
Collectors value	🏍 🏍
Price	From 1,000 to 1,500 euros

K 100 RS

Engine	987 cc, four-cylinder, in-line engine rotated 90° left
Frame	Tubular bridge frame, open below
Power	90 HP at 8,000 rpm
Transmission	Cardan shaft
Suspension	Front, telescopic fork; rear, single-sided swingarm
Dimensions, weight	Length 2,220 mm, width 800 mm, height 810 mm (to seat), weight 253 kg
Years of production	1983–89
Units manufactured	34,804
Chassis serial nos.:	From 0010001 to 0020000, from 0080001 to 0090000, from 0140001 to 0149896
Spare parts availab.	🏍 🏍 🏍 🏍 🏍
Collectors value	🏍 🏍
Price	From 1,000 to 2,000 euros

650,000 km of tests. Over one hundred technicians were involved in the R&D effort. To get the K project going, the Bayerische Motoren Werke decided to build what was then Europe's most modern motorcycle factory, completely redesigning and overhauling the Berlin-Spandau production plant, in operation since 1928. Innovation of the production process was an essential component in the success of this model, whose engine cost less than a 1000cc boxer engine at the time because it took fewer people to build one. A very significant feature of the new engine design was enhanced accessibility, making it possible to perform major operations, such as valve adjustment, without having to spend time removing and reinstalling portions of the fairing or performing other preliminary operations. Riding the wave of success, the basic version (without fairing) was immediately joined by the RS as a high-speed touring machine and by the RT, where comfort and protection from the elements were much appreciated by long-distance touring aficionados. The LT version differed only in its colour scheme, with striping, matching side-bags and top-case, instrumentation complete with radio, and self-adjusting shocks.

K 100 RT

Engine	987 cc, four-cylinder, in-line engine rotated 90° left
Frame	Tubular bridge frame, open below
Power	90 HP at 8,000 rpm
Transmission	Cardan shaft
Suspension	Front, telescopic fork; rear, single-sided swingarm
Dimensions, weight	Length 2,220 mm, width 916 mm, height 810 mm (to seat), weight 263 kg
Years of production	1984–88
Units manufactured	22,335
Numeri di serie:	From 0020001 to 0030000, from 0090001 to 0097829
Spare parts availab.	🏍 🏍 🏍 🏍 🏍
Collectors value	🏍 🏍
Price	From 1,000 to 2,000 euros

K 100 LT

Engine	987 cc, four-cylinder, in-line engine rotated 90° left
Frame	Tubular bridge frame, open below
Power	90 HP at 8,000 rpm
Transmission	Cardan shaft
Suspension	Front, telescopic fork; rear, single-sided swingarm
Dimensions, weight	Length 2,220 mm, width 916 mm, height 810 mm (to seat), weight 272 kg
Years of production	1986–91
Units manufactured	14,899
Chassis serial nos.:	From 0170001 to 0180000, from 0190001 to 0193272
Spare parts availab.	🏍 🏍 🏍 🏍 🏍
Collectors value	🏍 🏍
Price	From 1,000 to 2,500 euros

COLLECTORS CORNER

Outstanding bikes in all respects, the K 100s are tough, reliable and have low operating and maintenance costs. Indeed, the robustness of the engine eventually spawned the legend that the reason BMW abandoned this project was precisely because it was putting their mechanics out of a job... Oil consumption is practically zero, even after tens of thousands of kilometres, and rarely is anything more than routine maintenance required. In spite of some minor defects, the transmission and driveshaft are practically eternal. The electronics are simple and reliable. Fuel consumption easily ranks with that of more modern bikes. The only problem – if one can even call it that – is the risk of keeping the bike for show instead of for use. If not used with some frequency, the various electrical and mechanical components tend to deteriorate and the cost of restoring them can be even higher than the value of the bike itself. The parts that are most subject to problems as a result of non-use are the fuel pump, the combined oil/water pump, the brake pump and the injectors.

K 75
K 75 C
K 75 S
K 75 RT

BMW studied both three- and four-cylinder engines right from the beginning of the K series design process. The choice to launch on the market the K 100 first was dictated more by marketing than by technical considerations. Motorbikers were only able to see the three-cylinder K 75 two years after the debut of its older sibling, but the three-cylinder models were also an immediate hit, exceeding all expectations with some 20,000 built in the first two years. The use of a counter-rotating balance shaft allowed BMW engineers to develop the very first vibration-free three-cylinder engine. Especially in the S version, the K 75 was very successful for its sports performance and elegant styling. Its suspension, stiffer than that on the K 100, gave the bike better road performance in spite of its lower power and also greater range thanks to better fuel efficiency: nearly 30 kilometres per litre (70 mpg). These models also had the advantage of weighing less than the K 100; for instance, between the K 100 LT and the K 75 the weight difference was around 40 kg. The basic model of the first K 75 series was the K 75 C, the only bike in the K series with a rear drum brake. This bike was joined, and in 1990 replaced, by the K 75, with rear disk brake. In 1985 the K 75 S was introduced. It was a sports touring model with a half-fairing fastened to the chassis and a higher top gear ratio. In 1988 an optional under-engine spoiler became available. Finally, in 1989 the K 75 RT was introduced; it was similar to the K 100 RT, with the same fairing, electrically controlled windscreen and side-bag mounts, although the side-bags themselves did not come as standard equipment. It was adopted by police departments in many countries for its high manoeuvrability.

K 75

Engine	740cc, three-cylinder, in-line engine rotated 90° to the left
Frame	Tubular bridge frame, open below
Power	75 HP at 8,500 rpm
Transmission	Cardan shaft
Suspension	Front, telescopic fork; rear, single-sided swingarm
Dimensions, weight	Length 2,220 mm, width 710 mm (handlebar), height 810 mm (to seat), weight 228 kg
Years of production	1985–96
Units manufactured	18,485
Chassis serial nos.:	From 0120001 to 0120615, from 0250001 to 0256066, from 6215001 to 6220000, from 6426001 to 6430000
Spare parts availab.	🏍 🏍 🏍 🏍 🏍
Collectors value	🏍 🏍 🏍
Price	From 1,000 to 1,500 euros

K 75 C

Engine	740cc, three-cylinder, in-line engine rotated 90° to the left
Frame	Tubular bridge frame, open below
Power	75 HP at 8,500 rpm
Transmission	Cardan shaft
Suspension	Front, telescopic fork; rear, single-sided swingarm
Dimensions, weight	Length 2,220 mm, width 710 mm (handlebar), height 810 mm (to seat), weight 228 kg
Years of production	1985–90
Units manufactured	9,556
Chassis serial nos.:	From 0110001 to 0116424
Spare parts availab.	🏍 🏍 🏍 🏍 🏍
Collectors value	🏍 🏍 🏍
Price	From 1,000 to 1,500 euros

K75S

Engine	740cc, three-cylinder, in-line engine rotated 90° to the left
Frame	Tubular bridge frame, open below
Power	75 HP a 8,500 rpm
Transmission	Cardan shaft
Suspension	Front, telescopic fork; rear, single-sided swingarm
Dimensions, weight	Length 2,220 mm, width 620 mm (handlebar), height 810 mm (to seat), weight 235 kg
Years of production	1985–95
Units manufactured	18,649
Chassis serial nos.:	From 0100001 to 0110000, from 0210001 to 0214049
Spare parts availab.	🏍️ 🏍️ 🏍️ 🏍️ 🏍️
Collectors value	🏍️ 🏍️ 🏍️
Price	From 1,000 to 2,000 euros

K75RT

Engine	740cc, three-cylinder, in-line engine rotated 90° to the left
Frame	Tubular bridge frame, open below
Power	75 HP at 8,500 rpm
Transmission	Cardan shaft
Suspension	Front, telescopic fork; rear, single-sided swingarm
Dimensions, weight	Length 2,220 mm, width 620 mm (handlebar), height 810 mm (to seat), weight 258 kg
Years of production	1989–96
Units manufactured	21,264
Chassis serial nos.:	From 0220001 to 0230000, from 0370001 to 0374860, from 6018001 to 6020000
Spare parts availab.	🏍️ 🏍️ 🏍️ 🏍️ 🏍️
Collectors value	🏍️ 🏍️ 🏍️
Price	From 2,000 to 3,000 euros

COLLECTORS CORNER

There is still a bigger market today for K 75s than for K 100s. This is partly due to their smaller dimensions and lower weight but mainly because of their decidedly more modern and well-proportioned lines. However, they are getting very difficult to find due to growth in a lateral market: pilots of ultra-light aircraft keep buying them up so they can disassemble them and use the excellent engines on their aeroplanes. As well as being highly reliable, the K 75 engine offers the best power/weight ratio among multi-cylinder engines. Furthermore, its fuel injection system is unaffected by altimetric pressure differences.

K1
K100 RS 16V

The 1988 Cologne motor show featured the debut of a truly futuristic bike. Encased in a sleek aerodynamic fairing that covered both the front wheel and the tail, the BMW K 1 marked a radical turning point in the Bayerische Motoren Werke's conception of a sports motorcycle. While the original idea had been to design a sportier version of the K 100 RS, increases in engine performance by competitors forced the BMW engineers to make some significant changes to the K 100 design. The object was not to design an entirely new motorcycle, but to create a more powerful variant of the K series. So the focus was on the engine. While keeping the same transmission and driveshaft, modifications were made to the cylinder head, adopting a four-valve configuration and incorporating a Motronic digital fuel system thanks to BMW automotive experience. A torque of 100 Nm at 6,750 rpm, coupled with an exceptionally low drag coefficient for a motorcycle, allowed the K 1 to compete with its more powerful rivals. A determining factor in this sense was the one-piece fairing designed for high cruising speeds while offering maximum protection from atmospheric agents to both driver and passenger. The technical developments went beyond the induction of the four valves. Indeed, for the first time, the dual pivot swingarm "Paralever", introduced with the R 100 GS, was applied to a road bike, as was the new front fork and the newly designed three-spoke wheels. Engine power was limited to 100 HP to comply with German law, which prohibited the sale of more powerful motorcycles. The bike also came with a range of driver safety features. The fairing and the plastic cover over the tank, for example, were designed to absorb impact and project the driver up and over an obstacle in the event

K1

Engine	987cc four-cylinder, in-line engine rotated 90° left
Frame	Tubular bridge frame, open below
Power	100 HP at 8,000 rpm
Transmission	Cardan shaft
Suspension	Front, telescopic fork; rear, single-sided swingarm
Dimensions, weight	Length 2,250 mm, width 875 mm, height 1,210 mm, weight 259 kg
Years of production	1989–93
Units manufactured	6,921
Chassis serial nos.:	From 6372001 to 6378246
Spare parts availab.	🏍 🏍 🏍 🏍 🏍
Collectors value	🏍 🏍 🏍
Price	From 3,500 to 6,000 euros

K 100 RS 16 V

Engine	987cc four-cylinder, in-line engine rotated 90° left
Frame	Tubular bridge frame, open below
Power	100 HP at 8,000 rpm
Transmission	Cardan shaft
Suspension	Front, telescopic fork; rear, single-sided swingarm
Dimensions, weight	Length 2,320 mm, width 800 mm, height 800 mm (to seat), weight 259 kg
Years of production	1990–93
Units manufactured	12,666
Chassis serial nos.:	From 0200001 to 0206575, from 6405001 to 6410000
Spare parts availab.	🏍 🏍 🏍 🏍 🏍
Collectors value	🏍 🏍 🏍
Price	From 2,000 to 3,500 euros

of a frontal collision. Taking advantage of the fantastic BMW K 1 engine, the idea was also to capitalize on the success of the K 100 RS. Thus, in the winter of 1990, the K 100 RS 16V was born, with just a few modifications to the chassis (larger section frame), aesthetics (wider and more comfortable handlebar) and position of the rear-view mirrors. In practical terms, the new bike had the heart of a K 1 transplanted into the body of the K 100 RS. It was the right mix of technology and classic styling. And it was an immediate hit, its success being partly due to the fact that in addition to the indispensable side-bags, it also offered the possibility of mounting a rear top case.

COLLECTORS CORNER

The bike sold well initially (more than 4,000 K 1s in the first six months). However, sales fell off after the initial enthusiasm partly due to disappointment at the fact that the K 1 was the first BMW that could not take hard side-bags. BMW attempted to stimulate sales by adding a Club version in metal-flake black to the two original colour schemes of blue-yellow and red-yellow. This new version was decidedly less showy and more elegant. As for the K 100 RS 16V, it is still an extremely up-to-date touring machine but not very practical for day-to-day transportation needs, especially in the city. The engine tends to overheat in stop-and-start driving while the low handlebar is more tiring for the arms and makes low speed manoeuvring more difficult. The proverbial reliability is a plus only for those who use the bike continuously. Long periods of disuse may compromise the operation of electrical and mechanical pumps.

R100 GS
R100 GS Paris Dakar
R100 R

A motorcycle riding the wave of victories: this is a fitting description of the R 100 GS in its various versions, given that it made its debut on the heels of the four thrilling consecutive victories by BMW in the Paris–Dakar, considered to be the most selective race in the world. Seizing the moment, Bayerische Motoren Werke presented a 1000cc bike with striking aesthetics and colours at the 1988 Cologne motor show: the R 100 GS Paris–Dakar. Its introduction ushered in a new concept of touring bike: powerful, stable and easily able to handle motorways and rough roads, and even, as the name suggests, the arduous challenges of desert lands. It featured a particularly well thought-out set of accessories and guards to protect against off-road spills, as well as an exceptional cargo capacity with a solo seat. In 1990 it was joined by a version of the R 80–R 100 GS, which still had a fairing but was less extreme in its lines and equipment, making it more appetizing to road riders. The year following the debut of these off-road versions witnessed the arrival of the R 80 R and R 100 R, and 1993 the R 100 Mystic. As in previous models, the substance had not changed. The sole rationale for the modifications was to make the bike more roadworthy. The front wheel was reduced from 21 to 18 inches in order to increase its directional stability at high speeds. Wider section tyres were also used and a second front disk brake was added (standard equipment on the 100s, optional on the 80s). The R 100 Mystic differed from the others only for its aesthetics and "Mystic Red" colour scheme, whence its name.

R 100 GS

Engine	980 cc, two-cylinder, overhead valves
Frame	Tubular twin cradle
Power	60 HP at 6,500 rpm
Transmission	Cardan shaft
Suspension	Front, telescopic fork; rear, single-sided swingarm
Dimensions, weight	Length 2,290 mm, width 830 mm (handlebar), height 850 mm (to seat), weight 210 kg
Years of production	1986–94
Chassis serial nos. and engine nos.	From 6276001 to 6280000, from 6331001 to 6336417, from 6461501 to 6468515
Units manufactured	34,007
Spare parts availab.	🏍️🏍️🏍️🏍️🏍️
Collectors value	🏍️🏍️🏍️
Price	From 5,000 to 7,500 euros

COLLECTORS CORNER

In spite of the fact that almost thirty years have passed since it made its first appearance, this motorcycle is still very popular among the new generation of bikers, who are justifiably convinced that they are buying a vehicle with exceptional touring qualities, limited operations and maintenance costs and an enduring market value. Indeed, the Paris–Dakar version sells at prices comparable to recently built bikes. The other models exhibit only slight differences in terms of quality, the main one being in how they are used. There were just a few modifications to the chassis to meet the needs of widely varying motorcyclists: from adventure-seeking off-roaders to those who use the bike to get to work every day. For two people going on a tour with baggage, the R versions are to be preferred over the GS for stability and safety in braking.

R 100 GS Paris-Dakar

Engine	980 cc, two-cylinder, overhead valves
Frame	Tubular twin cradle
Power	60 HP at 6,500 rpm
Transmission	Cardan shaft
Suspension	Front, telescopic fork; rear, single-sided swingarm
Dimensions, weight	Length 2,290 mm, width 830 mm (handlebar), height 850 mm (to seat), weight 210 kg
Years of production	1988–96
Chassis serial nos. and engine nos.	From 6415001 to 6417557, from 0065001 to 0070000, from 0340001 to 0341218
Units manufactured	8,772
Spare parts availab.	🏍️🏍️🏍️🏍️🏍️
Collectors value	🏍️🏍️🏍️🏍️
Price	From 7,000 to 8,500 euros

R 100 R

Engine	980 cc, two-cylinder, overhead valves
Frame	Tubular twin cradle
Power	60 HP at 6,500 rpm
Transmission	Cardan shaft
Suspension	Front, telescopic fork; rear, single-sided swingarm
Dimensions, weight	Length 2,210 mm, width 1,000 mm, height 1,190 mm, weight 218 kg
Years of production	1991–95
Chassis serial nos. and engine nos.	From 0125001 to 0169000, from 0240001 to 0250000, from 6469000 to 6470000
Units manufactured	20,589
Spare parts availab.	🏍️🏍️🏍️🏍️🏍️
Collectors value	🏍️🏍️🏍️
Price	From 3,500 to 5,500 euros (Mystic from 5,000 to 6,500 euros, Classic from 6,000 to 8,000 euros, 80 R from 3,000 to 4,500 euros)

1980s
data sheet

Model	Cylinders displ.	cc	Prod. years	Units made	Spare parts availability	Collectors value	Price (euros)	Chassis
R 100	2	980	1980–84	10,111	🏍🏍🏍🏍🏍	🏍🏍	3,000–5,000	From 6035001 to 6401795
R 100 CS	2	980	1980–84	4,038	🏍🏍🏍🏍🏍	🏍🏍🏍	4,500–6,500	From 6135001 to 6138864
R 80 G/S, R 80 G/S Dakar	2	797	1980–87	21,864	🏍🏍🏍🏍🏍	🏍🏍🏍🏍🏍	5,000–7,500 6,000–13,000	From 6250001 to 6260000, 6281001 to 6292522
R 80 RT	2	797	1982–84	7,315	🏍🏍🏍🏍🏍	🏍	3,000–4,000	From 6420001 to 6425163
R 80 ST	2	797	1982–84	5,963	🏍🏍🏍🏍🏍	🏍🏍🏍🏍	4,000–6,500	From 6054001 to 6058984
K 100	4	987	1983–87	11,549	🏍🏍🏍🏍🏍	🏍🏍	1,000–1,500	From 0000001 to 0010000, 0033001 to 0033027, 6308101 to 6309422
K 100 RS	4	987	1983–89	34,804	🏍🏍🏍🏍🏍	🏍🏍	1,000–2,000	From 0010001 to 0020000, 0080001 to 0090000, 0140001 to 0149896
K 100 RT	4	987	1984–88	22,335	🏍🏍🏍🏍🏍	🏍🏍	1,000–2,000	From 0020001 to 0030000, 0090001 to 0097829
K 100 LT	4	987	1986–91	14,899	🏍🏍🏍🏍🏍	🏍🏍	1,000–2,500	From 0020001 to 0030000, 0090001 to 0097829
K 75	3	740	1985–96	18,485	🏍🏍🏍🏍🏍	🏍🏍🏍	1,000–1,500	From 0120001 to 0120615, 0250001 to 0256066, 6215001 to 6220000, 6426001 to 6430000
K 75 C	3	740	1985–90	9,556	🏍🏍🏍🏍🏍	🏍🏍🏍	1,000–1,500	From 0110001 to 0116424
K 75 S	3	740	1985–95	18,649	🏍🏍🏍🏍🏍	🏍🏍🏍	1,000–2,000	From 0100001 to 0110000, 0210001 to 0214049
K 75 RT	3	740	1989–96	21,264	🏍🏍🏍🏍🏍	🏍🏍🏍	2,000–3,000	From 0220001 to 0230000, 0370001 to 0374860, 6018001 to 6020000
K 1	4	987	1989–93	6,921	🏍🏍🏍🏍🏍	🏍🏍🏍	3,500–6,000	From 6372001 to 6378246
K 100 RS 16 V	4	987	1989–93	12,666	🏍🏍🏍🏍🏍	🏍🏍🏍	2,000–3,500	From 0200001 to 0206575, 6405001 to 6410000
R 100 GS	2	980	1986–94	34,007	🏍🏍🏍🏍🏍	🏍🏍🏍	5,000–7,500	From 6276001 to 6280000, 6331001 to 6336417, 6461501 to 6468515
R 100 GS Paris-Dakar	2	980	1988–96	8,722	🏍🏍🏍🏍🏍	🏍🏍🏍🏍🏍	7,000–8,500	From 6415001 to 6417557, 0065001 to 0070000, 0340001 to 0341218
R 100 R	2	980	1991–95	20,589	🏍🏍🏍🏍🏍	🏍🏍🏍	3,500–5,500	From 0125001 to 0169000, 0240001 to 0250000, 6469000 to 6470000

the | 1990–2000s

At the beginning of the 1990s, Bayerische Motoren Werke found itself in a situation similar to what had happened thirty years earlier: the boxer-engine models were no longer able to effectively compete with their rivals. Once again the company made the right choices in responding. After redesigning an updated boxer, BMW Motorrad decided to expand out of the high-end bike market and introduce models in the medium displacement range. As before, the determining element was a highly innovative power plant that marked an even greater break with BMW tradition than the one caused with the introduction of the K series. At the turn of the millennium, BMW focused not only on further development of the boxer engine, but also on increasing the engine size of the K series.

K 1100 LT
K 1100 RS

The K series witnessed a boost in engine size to 1100cc at the beginning of the 1990s while still remaining under the 100 HP threshold enforced by German law until 1995. The developments of the previous decade were implemented to increase engine torque. This choice brought a series of positive outcomes, both technical and in terms of comfort. For example, the small but significant modification to the engine boosted power output while also significantly reducing vibrations, especially at cruising speeds. The increased displacement was supported by a Bosch electronic Multipoint Motronic injection system, yet another example of BMW successfully applying automotive technology to motorcycles. The K 1100 LT (for "Luxury Touring") was an immediate hit, and not merely for the inevitable media hype regarding the largest BMW engine ever made. Users and the specialized media were completely taken by its features and it was quite rightfully ranked as one of the world's most comfortable and high performing touring motorcycles at the time. The engine was completely hidden by a full fairing designed to create a cone of air as the motorcycle moved, eliminating bothersome and dangerous turbulence, even when fully loaded. Stock equipment included ABS, removable hard side-bags that matched the fairing for maximum elegance, and a high-capacity top case. The fairing offered the utmost in rider protection at the time and featured a Plexiglas windscreen that could be adjusted while driving by means of a three-way switch originally mounted on the dash, but then integrated into the left-side handlebar switches. This made it possible to adjust the windscreen angle to suit speed. The K 1100 RS sports version was the fruit

K 1100 LT

Engine	1092cc, four-cylinder, in-line engine rotated 90° left
Frame	Tubular space frame
Power	100 HP at 7,500 rpm
Transmission	Cardan shaft
Suspension	Front, telescopic fork; rear, single-sided swingarm
Dimensions, weight	Length 2,250 mm, width 915 mm, height 810 mm (to seat), weight 290 kg
Years of production	1989–99
Units manufactured	22,757
Spare parts availab.	🏍 🏍 🏍 🏍 🏍
Collectors value	🏍 🏍 🏍
Price	From 2,500 to 3,500 euros

of BMW's experience with all the previous versions. Initially viewed as models for a narrow niche market, they were such a commercial success that more than 30,000 LTs and RSs were sold.

K 1100 RS

Engine	1092cc, four-cylinder, in-line engine rotated 90° left
Frame	Tubular space frame
Power	100 HP at 7,500 rpm
Transmission	Cardan shaft
Suspension	Front, telescopic fork; rear, single-sided swingarm
Dimensions, weight	Length 2,230 mm, width 802 mm, height 810 mm (to seat), weight 268 kg
Years of production	1992–96
Units manufactured	12,179
Spare parts availab.	🏍 🏍 🏍 🏍 🏍
Collectors value	🏍 🏍 🏍
Price	From 2,500 to 3,500 euros

COLLECTORS CORNER

If you are lucky enough to chance upon any K 1100 model without a lot of miles under its belt, you will be sure to have a fantastic touring bike offering excellent performance and reliability without having to spend an arm and a leg. However, as we explained above regarding K series bikes, before you buy one you need to be sure you are actually going to use it. These motorcycles have to be used with a certain regularity; disuse will result in deterioration of the electrical and mechanical components and tyres.

R 1100 RS

Seventy years after the introduction of the first motorcycle with a boxer engine, the R 32, BMW unveiled the R 1100 RS. This bike was built around a completely redesigned and reconceived boxer, the engine that had written the bulk of the Bavarian motorcycle manufacturer's history. The R 1100 RS was a two-cylinder road bike revolutionary in many ways. The first and most important innovation was the engine known as Project R 259, that introduced the following features: 4 valves per cylinder, electronic injection, separated gearbox, and a power of 90 HP at 7,250 rpm. It also featured completely novel aesthetics and chassis. After being previewed in photos published in the specialized media to stir up anticipation, the R 1100 RS debuted officially at the International Motorcycle, Scooter and Bicycle Fair in Cologne in September 1992. The only thing the new boxer had in common with its predecessors was the configuration of the cylinders. New emission regulations prompted the use of electronic injection and three-way catalytic converters. Furthermore, with this model the engine became an integral part of the chassis, a load-bearing frame element providing exceptional stability without any increase in weight. The Telelever suspension system was also adopted for the front fork, and a Paralever rear swingarm encased the Cardan shaft drive train. Owners had plenty of possibilities for customizing their machines thanks to a broad range of optionals, from heated handgrips to adjustable windscreen, handlebar and seat, as well as a wide selection of side-bags and top cases. In spite of its anything-but-irrelevant weight of 239 kg, the motorcycle did handle very well, and thanks to the innovative chassis it performed well both on low and high speed roads.

R 1100 RS

Engine	1085-cc, two-cylinder boxer
Frame	Tubular steel frame with load-bearing engine
Power	90 HP at 7,250 rpm
Transmission	Cardan shaft
Suspension	Front, Telelever; rear, Paralever swingarm
Dimensions, weight	Length 2,175 mm, width 920 mm, height 800 mm (to seat), weight 239 kg
Chassis serial nos.	From 0290001 to 0300000, from 0410001 to 0412292 (the data are available only up to 1995. After that year, with the introduction of custom elements specific for each model, frame numbers were no longer made public in compliance with EU privacy law)
Years of production	1992–2001
Units manufactured	26,403
Spare parts availab.	🏍️ 🏍️ 🏍️ 🏍️ 🏍️
Collectors value	🏍️ 🏍️ 🏍️
Price	From 1,800 to 3,500 euros

COLLECTORS CORNER

The R 1100 RS is an excellent motorcycle that can be found on today's market at a good quality/price ratio. The series originally had a few issues with the gearbox, and the clutch was a bit undersized. When buying, it is better to avoid models with ABS. As the motorcycle ages, the ABS may cause problems and require replacement – at costs that may actually be higher than the value of the bike itself. High oil consumption, on the other hand, is to be expected on motorcycles that have covered a lot of road.

R 1100 GS
R 850 GS
R 1100 R
R 850 R

From the moment it unveiled the R 1100 RS, BMW made no mystery of its plans to update all its boxer models. However, when the decision was made to lay hands on the GS, the towering enduro breed of BMW's triumphs in the Paris–Dakar, it seemed like things might be going a little too far. The R 1100 GS made its official entrance in the autumn of 1993, in a special section of the Frankfurt Auto Show dedicated to motorcycles. The visitors were impressed and captivated by the enormous bike with its futuristic lines and knobby tyres. It was an exceptional success, selling well beyond the most optimistic forecasts: almost 45,000 units, and with unimaginable pre-order times. In spite of its anything-but-affordable price tag, this huge BMW bike exerted a strong appeal and people were willing to wait months to have one. The model had all it took to seize the imagination of venturesome spirits, starting from its dimensions. Someone wrote that when it was hoisted on its centrestand it looked like "a two-wheeled pachyderm". Equipped with cutting-edge technology, the bike had a first-rate brake system with dual front disk brakes, a rear disk brake and an optional switchable ABS. It was also equipped with the latest Telelever and Paralever suspension. The booming sales were attributed to a number of elements that had won more people over than the Bayerische Motoren Werke had anticipated: the captivating lines, the bold colours and, most importantly, apt technological innovations and top rate comfort. Towards the end of the production period, it was joined by its little sister, the R 850 GS. Even though the new model sold for nearly the same price, buyers were anything but scarce, especially in countries where maxi-bikes were subject to higher taxes. An R 850 GS made an appearance in 2000 in the action flick *Romeo Must Die*, directed by

R 1100 GS

Engine	1085cc, two-cylinder boxer
Frame	Tubular steel space frame with load-bearing engine
Power	80 HP at 7,250 rpm
Transmission	Cardan shaft
Suspension	Front, Telelever longitudinal arm with central shock absorber; rear, Paralever swingarm
Dimensions, weight	Length 2,189 mm, width 920 mm, height 840/860 mm (to seat), weight 243 kg
Chassis serial nos.	From 0057001 to 0060000, from 0430001 to 0433065, from 6366001 to 6370000 (the data are available only up to 1995. After that year, with the introduction of custom elements specific for each model, frame numbers were no longer made public in compliance with EU privacy law)
Years of production	1993–99
Units manufactured	39,842
Spare parts availab.	🏍 🏍 🏍 🏍 🏍
Collectors value	🏍 🏍 🏍
Price	From 3,000 to 4,500 euros

R 850 GS

Engine	848cc, two-cylinder boxer
Frame	Tubular steel space frame with load-bearing engine
Power	70 HP at 7,000 rpm
Transmission	Cardan shaft
Suspension	Front, Telelever longitudinal arm with central shock absorber; rear, Paralever swingarm
Dimensions, weight	Length 2,196 mm, width 920 mm, height 840/860 mm (to seat), weight 243 kg
Years of production	1996–2001
Units manufactured	2,242
Spare parts availab.	🏍 🏍 🏍 🏍 🏍
Collectors value	🏍 🏍 🏍
Price	From 2,800 to 3,800 euros

R 1100 R

Engine	1085cc, two-cylinder boxer
Frame	Tubular steel space frame with load-bearing engine
Power	80 HP at 6,750 rpm
Transmission	Cardan shaft
Suspension	Front, Telelever longitudinal arm with central shock absorber; rear, Paralever swingarm
Dimensions, weight	Length 2,197 mm, width 898 mm, height 780/800 mm (to seat), weight 235 kg
Chassis serial nos.	From 0360001 to 0363665 (the data are available only up to 1995. After that year, with the introduction of custom elements specific for each model, frame numbers were no longer made public in compliance with EU privacy law)
Years of production	1993–2001
Units manufactured	26,073
Spare parts availab.	🏍 🏍 🏍 🏍 🏍
Collectors value	🏍 🏍 🏍
Price	From 3,000 to 4,500 euros

COLLECTORS CORNER

Differing mainly in engine size, the R 1100 GS and the R 850 GS are both to be considered absolutely sturdy and reliable bikes. If you are looking to buy one of these models, be sure to check the odometer reading (the lower the mileage, the better) and make sure a complete maintenance record is available. Then have a look at the components to make sure that the muffler, disk brakes and other gear are original. The same can generally be said for the R 1100 R and the R 850 R regarding both the positive characteristics and the care that must be taken when choosing one to buy. Today the most sought-after models are those with spoke wheels, which were originally only available as optionals. The R 850 R is the most saleable of the two-cylinder models for its relatively low operation and maintenance costs.

Andrzej Bartkowiak. As for the previous series with the old boxer engine, after the R 1100 sports and enduro versions had come out, it was time for the "naked" model, stripped of all frills and oriented to those who use their motorcycle during the week to get to work and on weekends for short or medium-range outings. This was the four-valve R 1100 R and its little sister-bike the R 850 R, with lines characterized by the large fuel tank and a saddle very similar to those used on horses.

R 850 R

Engine	848cc, two-cylinder boxer
Frame	Tubular steel space frame with load-bearing engine
Power	70 HP at 7,000 rpm
Transmission	Cardan shaft
Suspension	Front, Telelever longitudinal arm with central shock absorber; rear, Paralever swingarm
Dimensions, weight	Length 2,196 mm, width 920 mm, height 840/860 mm (to seat), weight 243 kg
Chassis serial nos.	From 0350001 to 0351697 (the data are available only up to 1995. After that year, with the introduction of custom elements specific for each model, frame numbers were no longer made public in compliance with EU privacy law)
Years of production	1995–2001
Units manufactured	Not available
Spare parts availab.	🏍 🏍 🏍 🏍 🏍
Collectors value	🏍 🏍 🏍
Price	From 3,000 to 4,300 euros

F650 GS carb
F650 ST carb
F650 GS
F650 GS Paris Dakar

In 1993, with the ambition of opening up new market segments, BMW went to work on a new motorcycle at an affordable price, one that would offer good fun without excessive operating costs. The objective was to create a bike designed mainly for young riders on a relatively tight budget. Hence the F 650, a single-cylinder model produced jointly with Italian Aprilia, using an Austrian Rotax engine and, for the first time in the history of BMW, a chain drive. The F 650 was designed to allow the power delivery to be reduced on customer request, making it an option for freshly licensed drivers. Additionally, like its big sister, it was designed to accept such accessories as side-bags and a catalytic converter. The GS and ST versions differed only in equipment. The GS had a 19-inch front wheel and off-road tyres, while the ST had an 18-inch front wheel. The ST also had a slightly lower seat than the GS. There were some in the motorcycle world who were a bit sceptical. The idea of marketing a "low-budget BMW" in a fiercely competitive segment seemed to be a recipe for trouble. But the sales data wiped away all doubt. The F 650 was an enormous commercial success. Six years after its initial introduction, BMW decided to market an updated version of the successful single-cylinder bike, this time without outsourcing anything, producing instead the entire bike at its Berlin plant. Unlike its carburettor predecessor, the new F 650 had a fuel injection engine. However, given that the first- and second-generation models had the same name, the qualifier "carb" was added to the former to distinguish it from its fuel injected successor. Otherwise, the new models presented the same traditional configuration, the GS having an enduro vocation and the GS Dakar a more

F 650 GS · F 650 ST (carb)

Engine	652 cc, single-cylinder
Frame	Square tube single beam frame split into double cradle
Power	48 HP at 6,500 rpm
Transmission	Chain
Suspension	Front, telescopic fork; rear, dual swingarm, central spring strut
Dimensions, weight	Length 2,180 mm, width 880 mm, height 800 mm (to seat), weight 191 kg
Chassis serial nos.	Not available
Years of production	1993–2000
Units manufactured	51,405
Spare parts availab.	🏍 🏍 🏍 🏍 🏍 🏍
Collectors value	🏍 🏍 🏍
Price	From 1,000 to 1,900 euros (GS) and 2,500 euros (ST)s

accentuated off-road identity. The fuel injection engine was also outfitted with a catalytic converter while the fuel tank was placed in the triangular space under the seat. It was only slightly more powerful than its predecessors, but with greatly improved power delivery. Offered as an option on the first series, the ABS was later included in the price as standard equipment.

F 650 GS

Engine	654cc, single-cylinder
Frame	Double side beam frame
Power	48 HP at 6,500 rpm
Transmission	Chain
Suspension	Front, telescopic fork; rear, dual swingarm, central spring strut
Dimensions, weight	Length 2,175 mm, width 910 mm, height 780 mm (to seat), weight 175.4 kg
Chassis serial nos.	Not available
Years of production	Since 1999
Units manufactured	Not available
Spare parts availab.	🏍 🏍 🏍 🏍 🏍
Collectors value	🏍 🏍 🏍
Price	From 2,000 to 3,000 euros

COLLECTORS CORNER

The F 650 carb engine operating costs are anything but exorbitant. These models may be kept in running order using non-original components purchased at competitive prices because they share the engine with various other makers and models. Difficulties may be encountered, on the other hand, with certain details of the body and chassis. After the expiration of the agreement between BMW and Aprilia, no one made an effort to keep spare parts available. Of course, this issue does not exist for the F 650 GS and F 650 GS Dakar. These motorcycles are extremely easy to handle, particularly well suited to daily use and recommended for beginners because the excellent weight distribution greatly facilitates their use even in the hands of inexperienced riders. The power/weight ratio is also excellent.

F 650 GS Dakar

Engine	652cc, single-cylinder
Frame	Double side beam frame
Power	50 HP at 6,500 rpm
Transmission	Chain
Suspension	Front, telescopic fork; rear, dual swingarm, central spring strut
Dimensions, weight	Length 2,189 mm, width 910 mm, height 870 mm (to seat), weight 192 kg
Chassis serial nos.	Not available
Years of production	Since 1999
Units manufactured	Not available
Spare parts availab.	🏍🏍🏍🏍🏍
Collectors value	🏍🏍🏍
Price	From 2,000 to 3,000 euros

R80GS Basic

Above being a great bike in its own right, the R 80 GS Basic was a sort of monument to a model that had written an important part of BMW history. It was also a brilliant piece of marketing, enjoying immediate success. Produced for just a few months in a limited series, in spite of the objectively prohibitive price – even for incurable BMW history buffs – all 2,995 exemplars of the R 80 GS Basic sold without difficulty. Appropriately dubbed "Basic", this model echoed the look of the glorious G/S of 1980 although it was outfitted with totally up-to-date technology. Designers chose the glorious colour scheme of white fenders and tank with light blue frame, the same as the BMWs that proved their mettle in the major world enduro races of the 1970s. The last ones were sold with a 24-litre tank in place of the original 19.5-litre tank, to enhance the somewhat mysterious allure of long distance off-road motorcycles. In some parts of the world, the version with the larger tank was sold under the name "Kalahari". It has a very high collection value.

R 80 GS Basic

Engine	797cc, two-cylinder boxer
Frame	Tubular twin cradle
Power	52 HP at 6,500 rpm
Transmission	Cardan shaft
Suspension	Front, telescopic fork; rear, single-sided swingarm
Dimensions, weight	Length 2,230 mm, width 820 mm, height 900 mm (to seat), weight 192 kg
Chassis serial nos.	Not available
Years of production	1996–97
Units manufactured	2,995
Spare parts availab.	🏍️🏍️🏍️🏍️🏍️
Collectors value	🏍️🏍️🏍️🏍️🏍️
Price	From 10,000 to 12,000 euros

COLLECTORS CORNER

This is the shining star for collectors, an object of desire, a model that may drive collectors to do crazy things. It is a great motorcycle with a grand allure and perhaps the only two-wheeler whose value is constantly increasing. There are many reasons for its success, starting with the fact that it belongs to a limited series, has a very evocative, noteworthy look and is very agile and drivable. When we consider that this was the last motorcycle produced with the classic two-valve engine, it is understandable that its collector's value is so high that it is difficult to put a number on it.

K 1200 RS
K 1200 LT

In the mid-1990s, BMW technicians decided to focus again on the four-cylinder K series engine. The result was the K 1200 RS. In spite of its name, it did not represent an evolved form of the K 1100 RS but rather a completely new motorcycle, starting with its engine, although it preserved the basic arrangement of the Kompact (K) with a dual camshaft, straight-four configuration rotated 90° around the longitudinal axis. The new features included a hydraulic clutch and six-speed gearbox. But the truly radical innovations were made to the chassis. The K 1100 RS had an aluminium alloy single beam frame. Like its sister-bikes in the new-born R series, it had a Telelever front fork with hydraulic shock absorber and an aluminium Paralever swingarm in the rear with a single arm and a gas shock absorber adjustable in preload and rebound. The brand new silent-block mounts – a BMW first – reduced vibrations from the 130 HP (at 8,750 rpm) engine. One of the innovations that attracted greatest attention was the over-the-top ergonomics, where the seat, handlebar and footrests position could be adjusted like a tailor-made suit in just a few minutes to fit driver height, driving style and tastes. The bike held the road perfectly, its brakes responded promptly, and the engine provided quick and lively but smooth power. From the core of this bike the K 1200 LT was born in 1999; it is considered one of the most comfortable and reliable motorcycles for people who love long road trips. The revolutionary engine and frame of the K 1200 RS were incorporated perfectly into a true grand touring chassis. In spite of its daunting 380 kg of weight, the new bike was immediately recognized for its ease of handling and rich array of accessories, including a sound system with

K 1200 RS

Engine	1171cc, longitudinal in-line four-cylinder
Frame	Single-beam aluminium bridge frame
Power	130 HP at 8,750 rpm
Transmission	Cardan shaft
Suspension	Front, Telelever longitudinal arm with central shock absorber; rear, Monolever swingarm
Dimensions, weight	Length 2,250 mm, width 850 mm, height 800 mm (to seat), weight 380 kg
Chassis serial nos.	Not available
Years of production	Since 1996
Units manufactured	Not available
Spare parts availab.	🏍 🏍 🏍 🏍 🏍
Collectors value	🏍 🏍 🏍 🏍
Price	From 2,500 to 3,500 euros

a cassette deck and controls on the dashboard and handlebar. A CD changer could also be installed in one of the side-bags and a GPS unit, deriving from automobile use, could be installed in the other. The EVO ABS brake system, with brake booster, dynamically distributed braking pressure between the front and rear wheels. The bike was reworked in 2004, with the new version benefiting from greater horsepower. In 2007, the K 1200 RS made an appearance in Russell Mulcahy's film *Resident Evil: Extinction*, where it was Alice's (Milla Jovovich) ride.

K 1200 LT

Engine	1171cc, inclined in-line four-cylinder, rotated 90° left
Frame	Single-beam aluminium bridge frame
Power	98 HP at 6,750 rpm
Transmission	Cardan shaft
Suspension	Front, Telelever longitudinal arm with central shock absorber; rear, Monolever swingarm
Dimensions, weight	Length 2,508 mm, width 1,080 mm, height 800 mm (to seat), weight 345 kg
Chassis serial nos.	Not available
Years of production	Since 1999
Units manufactured	Not available
Spare parts availab.	🏍️ 🏍️ 🏍️ 🏍️ 🏍️
Collectors value	🏍️ 🏍️ 🏍️ 🏍️
Price	From 4,000 to 6,000 euros

COLLECTORS CORNER

The K 1200 RS was and remains an excellent bike for long distance touring. Comfortable, performing and reliable, it provides for carefree touring without having to make difficult compromises between desire and reality. The only problem is that it is getting harder and harder to find ones for sale with fewer than 100,000 miles (150,000 km) on the odometer. They are worthy machines, but with all the problems of vehicles at the end of a long and honoured career. The most critical point here is the ABS system. The same problems characterize the K 1200 LT, although things are a bit more complicated because of its wealth of high-tech components. With its grand endowment, this motorcycle suffers greatly from age and wear and in some cases, the replacement of worn out components such as the clutch, gearbox and brake system ends up costing more than the bike is worth.

R 1200 C

The "C" stands for Cruiser, and also for Custom, two terms that conjure images of long sunlit roads, adventure, strong emotions, dust and distant horizons, and a sense of total freedom. When BMW decided to explore the theme of cruisers in 1997, it did it in an absolutely original way, regaling fans with the R 1200 C, a model that was different from any other BMW bike but also from the Harleys and their innumerable imitations. The BMW Cruiser range was introduced to the world with an extremely original motorcycle for people who love the wind in their faces and wide-open spaces in front of them. Since the development of the new boxer engine in 1993, the Bavarian motorcycle manufacturer planned to install it on a new motorcycle that would open up new market segments. Four years later, the R 1200 C made its debut. It was a brand new motorcycle departing significantly from the traditional BMW canons. The fully tried and tested two-cylinder engine was also redesigned for this model, adapting it to the "ride to live" style, where speed is of secondary importance with respect to torque and flexibility. The motorcycle was also totally new in aesthetical terms, even for a custom bike. The beautifully elegant anodized aluminium A-arm connecting to the Telelever fork plays a prominent role in the aesthetics. The motorcycle was officially presented as follows: "We gave our engineers a simple yet incredibly ambitious task: build a cruiser that exceeds all expectations. Marked by high technology and high feeling. A motorcycle with a forthright personality and unmistakable origin: an authentic BMW". The outcome of the effort was a model that evoked the sensations of long trips but was sufficiently well balanced to be used for everyday purposes, a concept that hitherto had only rarely been associated with a motorcycle of this

R 1200 C

Engine	1170cc, two-cylinder boxer
Frame	Single-beam aluminium frame with load-bearing engine
Power	61 HP at 5,000 rpm
Transmission	Cardan shaft
Suspension	Front, Telelever longitudinal arm with central shock absorber; rear, Monolever swingarm
Dimensions, weight	Length 2,340 mm, width 1.050 mm, height 740 mm (to seat), weight 236 kg
Chassis serial nos.	Not available
Years of production	Since 1997
Units manufactured	Not available
Spare parts availab.	🏍 🏍 🏍 🏍 🏍
Collectors value	🏍 🏍 🏍 🏍
Price	From 3,000 to 6,500 euros

COLLECTORS CORNER

All versions of the R 1200 C (Basic, Avantgarde, Independent, and the more recent Montauk) are beautifully elegant, although collectors appear to strongly favour the first series for its classic colours and spoke wheels. The availability of a nearly infinite range of accessories to personalize the bike with taste and elegance helps support its continuing popularity. It is not a bike that passes unobserved, but it does demand a special passion for this type of machine.

type. With respect to its competitors, the R 1200 C was endowed with a range of optionals that allowed it easily to be adapted to the needs of the buyer. The perfect harmony between functionality, high-quality materials and style was a fundamental element in the enduring success of the model. In 1997, an R 1200 C had a cameo in the James Bond movie *Tomorrow Never Dies*, and in 2002 was featured in a high-speed chase with Tom Cruise and Gwyneth Paltrow in the opening scenes of *Austin Powers in Goldmember*.

R 1100 S

No boxer engine motorcycle prior to the R 1100 S had ever boasted such power. The project for a two-cylinder model with a clear high-performance sports vocation kept BMW designers and engineers fully occupied. Starting from the R 1100 RS, they decided to work along two apparently contradictory lines: preserve the touring character that is one of the fundamental elements of the German motorcycle maker's tradition while also exalting the sporting capabilities of a high-performance speed machine. The result was the R 1100 S, which was put on the market in 1998. Its rugged lines, low handlebar and tailpipe tucked high up under the rear end to keep it out of the way on the curves and optimize weight distribution were the elements of a chassis created specially to handle the power increase. It was the birth of a motorcycle with a sporting heart, bright and lively but controllable and safe thanks to its sophisticated engineering that gave new life to the legendary BMW boxer engine. Impetuous, dynamic, capable of reaching high cruising speed, it provided generous power and maximum fun. Every detail had its functional dimension. A hard cover was available for the passenger seat, transforming the bike into an aggressive single-seater with harmonious lines and dynamic design. It immediately met with great enthusiasm for its ability to couple the best in the boxer engine with the unmistakable character of a grand BMW motorcycle. The BMW R 1100 S represented a perfect balance between form, function and sportiness. Its lines were strongly influenced by wind tunnel testing during the design phase, which produced the enveloping partial fairing with its innovative incorporated mirrors. Starting in 2001, it could be equipped with the new EVO brakes and also had the option of the new sports I-ABS. Its performance in the mono-brand Boxer Cup, created specially by the mother company, contributed to its commercial success.

R 1100 S

Engine	1085cc, two-cylinder boxer
Frame	Aluminium frame with load-bearing engine
Power	98 HP at 7,500 rpm
Transmission	Cardan shaft
Suspension	Front, Telelever longitudinal arm with central shock absorber; rear, Monolever swingarm
Dimensions, weight	Length 2,180 mm, width 880 mm, height 800 mm (to seat), weight 229 kg
Chassis serial nos.	Not available
Years of production	Since 1998
Units manufactured	Not available
Spare parts availab.	🏍 🏍 🏍 🏍 🏍
Collectors value	🏍 🏍 🏍 🏍
Price	From 3,000 to 4,500 euros

COLLECTORS CORNER

Elegant and balanced, the R 1100 S is a sports touring motorcycle that gives its best with a single rider. Its finest features include a perfect weight distribution and suspension that can be customized to suit the type of use and the owner's driving style. The built-in sports ABS is also excellent. The tastefulness and elegance of design are important factors in its enduring popularity. It is not a bike that passes unobserved, but it does demand a special passion for this type of machine. The version in highest demand is the Boxer Cup Replika, which is more aggressively sporty, created specially for the mono-brand championship, where it played a strong protagonist role.

R 1150 R
R 1150 RS
R 1150 RT
R 1150 GS
R 1150 GS Adventure
R 1150 R Rockster

Six years after its introduction, the displacement was increased from 1085 to 1130 cc on the four-valve boxer engine to optimize power output and reduce bothersome vibrations while cruising. A hydraulic clutch was adopted, smoother when engaging and simpler to build. This marked the birth of the R 1150 series, very similar yet also very different from the 1100s. The first models to use the new engine were the R and RS versions, with their unmistakable lines and notable improvements in performance, comfort and driving pleasure. It was the right compromise between sport and comfort. The attention of enthusiasts was focused on the model that had taken the place of the previous, historic BMW R 1100 GS enduro. The GS version of the new series was unveiled in June 1999. A new member was thus added to the GS class, the historical initials marking the Bavarian motorcycle maker's presence in the mixed-use bike market, initiated with the R 80 G/S in 1980. It was a motorcycle with changes that were more a question of substance than form. It differed from its predecessors mainly in its front end, where the fender was modified and its upper section enclosed part of the oil cooler circuit as well as providing addition protection to the driver. A dual asymmetrical headlamp was also installed in place of its rectangular counterpart on the R 1100 GS. In 2002, in keeping with tradition, the normal version was joined by a more adventurous sister-bike, the R 1150 GS Adventure, with equipment inspired by desert rallies and particularly the dusty Paris–Dakar. The R 1100 R also had a much sportier version: the R 1150 R Rockster. Aggressive and fascinating, the Rockster completed the BMW Motorrad range in the segment of the naked bikes, making an impression by its clearly nonconformist look, thanks to the

R 1150 R

Engine	1130cc, two-cylinder boxer
Frame	Tubular steel space frame with load-bearing engine
Power	85 HP at 6,750 rpm
Transmission	Cardan shaft
Suspension	Front, Telelever longitudinal arm with central shock absorber; rear, Monolever swingarm
Dimensions, weight	Length 2,170 mm, width 940 mm, height 800 mm (to seat), weight 238 kg
Chassis serial nos.	Not available
Years of production	Since 1999
Units manufactured	Not available
Spare parts availab.	🏍 🏍 🏍 🏍 🏍
Collectors value	🏍 🏍 🏍
Price	From 3,000 to 4,000 euros

R 1150 RS

Engine	1130cc, two-cylinder boxer
Frame	Tubular steel space frame with load-bearing engine
Power	95 HP a 7,250 rpm
Transmission	Cardan shaft
Suspension	Front, Telelever longitudinal arm with central shock absorber; rear, Monolever swingarm
Dimensions, weight	Length 2,170 mm, width 920 mm, height 810 mm (to seat), weight 246 kg
Chassis serial nos.	Not available
Years of production	Since 2000
Units manufactured	Not available
Spare parts availab.	🏍 🏍 🏍 🏍 🏍
Collectors value	🏍 🏍 🏍
Price	From 2,500 to 3,500 euros

particular colour combinations of opaque black and citrus or opaque black and orange, not to mention its eye-catching aesthetics. The features of this model included painted rims and a particular headlamp set with a small windscreen and full instrumentation. In 2003, the BMW R 1150 R Rockster played a role in the film *Paycheck*, directed by John Woo and starring Ben Affleck and Uma Thurman; the R 1150 RT made an appearance in *The Italian Job* directed by Felix Gary Gray, and the R 1150 GS had a cameo in *Timeline*, director Richard Donner. In 2006, it was the R 1150 R's turn to play a starring role on the screen in Ultraviolet by Kurt Wimmer.

R 1150 GS

Engine	1130cc, two-cylinder boxer
Frame	Tubular steel space frame with load-bearing engine
Power	98 HP at 6,750 rpm
Transmission	Cardan shaft
Suspension	Front, Telelever longitudinal arm with central shock absorber; rear, Monolever swingarm
Dimensions, weight	Length 2,189 mm, width 980 mm, height 840 mm (to seat), weight 246 kg
Chassis serial nos.	Not available
Years of production	Since 1999
Units manufactured	Not available
Spare parts availab.	🏍️ 🏍️ 🏍️ 🏍️ 🏍️
Collectors value	🏍️ 🏍️ 🏍️ 🏍️
Price	From 3,000 to 4,500 euros

R 1150 GS Adventure

Engine	1130cc, two-cylinder boxer
Frame	Tubular steel space frame with load-bearing engine
Power	85 HP at 6,750 rpm
Transmission	Cardan shaft
Suspension	Front, Telelever longitudinal arm with central shock absorber; rear, Monolever swingarm
Dimensions, weight	Length 2,180 mm, width 980 mm, height 900 mm (to seat), weight 253 kg
Chassis serial nos.	Not available
Years of production	Since 2001
Units manufactured	Not available
Spare parts availab.	🏍 🏍 🏍 🏍 🏍
Collectors value	🏍 🏍 🏍 🏍 🏍
Price	From 6,000 to 7,000 euros

R 1150 RT

Engine	1130cc, two-cylinder boxer
Frame	Tubular steel space frame with load-bearing engine
Power	95 HP at 7,250 rpm
Transmission	Cardan shaft
Suspension	Front, Telelever longitudinal arm with central shock absorber; rear, Monolever swingarm
Dimensions, weight	Length 2,230 mm, width 898 mm, height 810 mm (to seat), weight 279 kg
Chassis serial nos.	Not available
Years of production	Since 2002
Units manufactured	Not available
Spare parts availab.	🏍 🏍 🏍 🏍 🏍
Collectors value	🏍 🏍 🏍
Price	From 4,000 to 5,000 euros

R 1150 R Rockster

Engine	1130cc, two-cylinder boxer
Frame	Tubular steel space frame with load-bearing engine
Power	80 HP at 6,750 rpm
Transmission	Cardan shaft
Suspension	Front, Telelever longitudinal arm with central shock absorber; rear, Monolever swingarm
Dimensions, weight	Length 2,170 mm, width 920 mm, height 835 mm (to seat), weight 239 kg
Chassis serial nos.	Not available
Years of production	Since 2002
Units manufactured	Not available
Spare parts availab.	🏍 🏍 🏍 🏍 🏍
Collectors value	🏍 🏍
Price	From 3,000 to 4,000 euros

COLLECTORS CORNER

In all its models, the R 1150 series is one of the most coveted by BMW enthusiasts thanks partly to its fame as the "last keeping BMW original philosophy". The reasons for this enduring success should probably be sought not only in their reliability but also in a design concept that does not feel the weight of time and also stands up well to the evolution of fashion. The appraisals are very good and in some cases hit notable figures for fully fitted-out models with low mileage.

data sheet | 1990–2000s

Model	Cylinders displacement	cc	Production years	Units made	Spare parts availability	Collectors value	Price (euros)	Chassis
K 1100 LT	4	1092	1989–99	22,757	🏍🏍🏍🏍🏍🏍	🏍🏍🏍	2,500–3,500	Not avail.
K 1100 RS	4	1092	1992–96	12,179	🏍🏍🏍🏍🏍🏍	🏍🏍🏍	2,500–3,500	Not avail.
R 1100 RS	2	1085	1991–2001	26,403	🏍🏍🏍🏍🏍🏍	🏍🏍🏍	1,800–3,500	From 0290001 to 0300000, 0410001 to 0412292 *
R 1100 GS	2	1085	1993–99	39,842	🏍🏍🏍🏍🏍	🏍🏍🏍	3,000–4,500	From 0057001 to 0060000, 0430001 to 0433065, 6366001 to 6370000 *
R 1100 R	2	1085	1993–2001	26,073	🏍🏍🏍🏍🏍🏍	🏍🏍🏍	3,000–4,500	From 0360001 to 0363665 *
R 850 GS	2	848	1996–2001	Not avail.	🏍🏍🏍🏍🏍🏍	🏍🏍🏍	2,800–3,800	Not avail.
R 850 R	2	848	1995–2001	2,242	🏍🏍🏍🏍🏍🏍	🏍🏍🏍	3,000–4,300	From 0350001 to 0351697 *
F 650 GS, ST Carb	1	652	1993–2000	51,405	🏍🏍🏍🏍🏍🏍	🏍🏍🏍	1,000–1,900	Not avail.
F 650 GS	1	654	Since 1999	Not avail.	🏍🏍🏍🏍🏍🏍	🏍🏍🏍	2,000–3,000	Not avail.
F 650 GS Dakar	1	652	Since 1999	Not avail.	🏍🏍🏍🏍🏍🏍	🏍🏍🏍	2,000–3,000	Not avail.
R 80 GS Basic	2	797	1996–97	2,995	🏍🏍🏍🏍🏍🏍	🏍🏍🏍🏍🏍🏍	10,000–12,000	Not avail.
K 1200 RS	4	1171	Since 1996	Not avail.	🏍🏍🏍🏍🏍🏍	🏍🏍🏍🏍	2,500–3,500	Not avail.
K 1200 LT	4	1171	Since 1999	Not avail.	🏍🏍🏍🏍🏍🏍	🏍🏍🏍🏍	4,000–6,000	Not avail.
R 1200 C	2	1170	Since 1997	Not avail.	🏍🏍🏍🏍🏍🏍	🏍🏍🏍🏍	3,000–6,500	Not avail.
R 1100 S	2	1085	Since 1998	Not avail.	🏍🏍🏍🏍🏍🏍	🏍🏍🏍🏍	3,000–4,500	Not avail.
R 1150 R	2	1130	Since 1999	Not avail.	🏍🏍🏍🏍🏍🏍	🏍🏍🏍	3,000–4,000	Not avail.
R 1150 GS	2	1130	Since 1999	Not avail.	🏍🏍🏍🏍🏍🏍	🏍🏍🏍🏍	3,000–4,500	Not avail.
R 1150 RS	2	1130	Since 2000	Not avail.	🏍🏍🏍🏍🏍	🏍🏍🏍	2,500–3,500	Not avail.
R 1150 GS Adventure	2	1130	Since 2001	Not avail.	🏍🏍🏍🏍🏍🏍	🏍🏍🏍🏍🏍🏍	6,000–7,000	Not avail.
R 1150 RT	2	1130	Since 2002	Not avail.	🏍🏍🏍🏍🏍	🏍🏍🏍	4,000–5,000	Not avail.
R 1150 R Rockster	2	1130	Since 2002	Not avail.	🏍🏍🏍🏍🏍	🏍🏍	3,000–4,000	Not avail.

* The data are incomplete. With the introduction of specific custom features for each model, frame numbers are no longer publicized in compliance with EU privacy law.

The joy of sidecars

No other motorcycle brand in the world has so associated its name with the sidecar as BMW. Thanks to its collaboration with companies with unparalleled design genius such as Steib, what was originally conceived as merely a system of multiple transport was soon to become a veritable form of art.

Bayerische Motoren Werke had always made robust, reliable and powerful machines that were ideal for combination with a sidecar. Although BMW itself never directly manufactured sidecars, in the collective imagination its name is indelibly associated with them, ever since its very first motorcycle, the R 32. The first sidecar, adopted by BMW in 1924, was produced by another Munich-based company called Royal. The collaboration between them was to burgeon either on production models – such as the legendary Royal-BMW S 49, designed for touring, or the Royal BMW Sport, a streamlined, bullet-shaped sidecar designed for sports bikes – or on motorcycles participating in world competitions.

R 51/3 with Steib S 501

R 51/2 with Steib TR 500

R 11 with Royal

R 17 with Steib Nr. 28

Over time, what had originally been nothing more than a means for carrying an extra passenger became an increasingly refined and complex object, full of fascinating detail, the source of innovative design and state-of-the-art options (an unforgettable example being the Royal Tourism sidecar which included a fixed windshield along with optional side windows and a fold-over roof). Some of the solutions were truly memorable, such as, for example, the completely closed sidecar with hinged door and aerodynamic fin. Thanks to the practicality of the sidecar, BMW was able to cater to the particular requirements of different police forces, the German Postal Office of the 1930s and 1940s (Reichpost), the International Red Cross and other public services such as the Fire Brigade (with a version that more closely resembled a small van than a sidecar). The sidecar became a mainstay of German military campaigns, the classic example being the one attached to the R 12 and R 75 motorcycles. Commissioned by the Wehrmacht during the Second World War, the model adopted here was the 286/1 built by Steib, and renamed the BW43 by BMW. Depending on the theatre of war and

R 68 with Steib LS 200

R 50 S with Steib TR 500

R 75 with Steib Einheitswagen Model B2

R 24 with Steib S 350

R 12 with Steib Einheitswagen Model B1

the military corps for which it was intended, this model came in several different colours.

Royal may have been the original sidecar supplier for BMW, but collectors are particularly fond of those produced by Steib, which went on sale from the mid-1930s, along with those made by the less well-known Stoye company. Steib had been founded in 1914 by Josef Steib Sr., and had become a leading specialist in bodywork and upholstery. Upon receiving a major contract from Ardie-Werk, in 1925 the company focused its energies on the manufacture of sidecars. Thanks to its increasingly integrated collaboration with BMW in the late 1940s and early 1950s, Steib became the undisputed leader in the sidecar manufacturing business, thanks also to its intelligent and effective modernization and revival of some of the great Steib classics from the 1930s. An outstanding example is the Standard model of 1950, which was ideal for pairing with single-cylinder BMWs, and the Special, an evolution of the Standard, which was paired in particular with the R 67.

R 47 with Royal

R 51/3 with Steib S 250

R 12 with Steib Nr. 14

R 25 with Steib LS 200

R 12 with Royal

The 1950s and 1960s saw the production of a number of new models, among the most famous of which was the Steib TR 500, another development of the Standard usually coupled with the R 50 and R 60 motorcycles (those with the Earles fork). The Steib LS 200 was another successful model, most associated with single-cylinder motorcycles, while the Steib S 250 and Steib S 500 were memorable for their elegance and their unmistakable elongated barrel form. The closing of the Steib company in the mid-1960s forced BMW to produce its own sidecars, at least until the beginning of the 1970s, in particular for several public bodies such as the Post Office, the Police and ADAC, whose "Strassenwacht" breakdown rescue sidecars were nicknamed "Angels of the Road". With the arrival of the "/5" series, the sidecar ceased to be an essential element for the company, but in the hearts of BMW fans it still lives on.

R 69 S with Steib S 501

R 25/3 with Steib LS 200

R 60/2 with Steib S 350

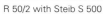

R 50/2 with Steib S 500

BMW Racing Team

Since the early 1920s, the Bayerische Motoren Werke placed a great deal of importance on world motorcycle competitions, from off-road endurance races to world speed records interspersed with a host of victories on the road and in the legendary Tourist Trophy. This chapter presents the history of BMW in sports competitions together with some of the models that have helped write it.

Win. Surprise. Be ahead of the times. Reach the highest peak. Pursue excellence in its purest state, associated with sports performance. This has been BMW's credo right from the beginning. The Bayerische Motoren Werke has always developed its stock bikes in step with motorcycle competitions, in spite of the fact that up until the middle of the past century there was no true world championship either on or off road. The first one would take place in 1949, the World Speed Championship, with the first trophy in the 500 class won by the Briton Leslie Graham on an AJS E90 "Porcupine". However, the most prestigious races were the individual Grand Prix, and preeminent among them the legendary Tourist Trophy on the Isle of Man, the most important competition on the entire international racing calendar.

BMW had actually debuted in competitions before it even officially put its first motorcycle on the market. It was 5 May 1923, and the person who took the prototype 500cc (which would be the basis for the future R 32) onto the track was the engineer Max Friz. Why was BMW so concerned with taking part in races and winning world records? The answer is simple: in the past, even more so than today, races were a fabulous way do advertise a vehicle.

Rudolf Schleicher and the racing R 37

Friz was an ardent proponent of BMW's participation in motorcycle races. The flathead engine was powerful, there were no significant problems in developing it and it appeared to have infinite possibilities for improvement. Friz developed new racing motorcycles, entrusting them to his production manager and tester Rudolf Reich, the bicycle dealer Franz Bieber, and to the Austrian Rupert Karner. The early experiences were however very disappointing, as the BMWs were forced to withdraw from the important Solitude race. A change was yet soon to come, as a result of a less embarrassing defeat of the

BMWs by a prototype motorcycle built by the German engineer and rider Rudolf Schleicher. After the event, Friz did not hesitate to hire the young engineer, entrusting him not only with representing BMW in competitions but also with developing the second model in BMW history, the R 37. The first victory came then on 1 February 1924 in the Munich–Garmisch race, which Schleicher covered in 1 hour and 59 minutes, only 6 minutes more than the first-placed automobile. The following day, Rudolf Schleicher completed the job, achieving the best time for the day at an average speed of 45 km/h. On 15 June that same year, after a triplet in the Solitude race, Bieber won the German road Championship. The R 37 was soon joined by the one-cylinder R 39 and it was this motorcycle, driven by Joseph Stelzer, that won the German Championship for the category. In spite of the

Left, two R 47s, stars of the 1930s;
right, a 1920s "Racing" BMW;
below, a beautiful R 66 racing version

series of victories in the various German Championships, BMW's fame did not expand abroad, where the superior British machines reigned unchallenged.

The decisions of Max Friz and the debut of the 255 Kompressor

As BMW geared up to be competitive also on the international level, its bikes won a host of German Championship races. In the hands of top-notch drivers such as Sepp Stelzer and Ernst Henne, BMWs won at home over 300 races in the years 1926–29. Furthermore, Henne set speed records in 1929 and in the 1930s. The 1920s witnessed an alternation on tracks and on city streets of stock bikes (piloted by independent drivers) such as the R 37, R 47 and R 57,

and fabulous prototypes characterized by numerous modifications (shorter frame, supplementary strap-on fuel tank, custom-designed saddles) and entrusted only to official drivers. Friz's choice to focus on stock models compromised however the development of competition bikes. This decision ultimately led to Schleicher's abandonment of BMW in 1927. Fortunately, at the end of the decade, probably "disturbed" by the growth of German competitors such as DKW and NSU, Max Friz rethought BMW's strategy regarding sports. He first authorized engineer Sepp Hopf to experiment with compressors on racing motorcycles, as was happening with airplane engines, and then in 1931 he called back Rudolf Schleicher. It was the beginning of a new era, which achieved its first moment of glory in 1935 when a new 500cc motorcycle debuted on the AVUS track driven by Ludwig "Wiggerl" Kraus, who came in second at an

The spectacular Type 255 Kompressor of 1938, the bike to beat for the British and Italian motorcycle makers in world-class competition

average speed of over 170 km/h. The motorcycle was not only redesigned in terms of power plant and equipped with an overhead camshaft, but also featured a drum brake on the rear wheel, a telescopic oil-damped front fork and a four-speed pedal-operated gearbox. The carburettors were placed just before the cylinders and the compressor was shifted to a position ahead of the engine block. It was the lightest motorcycle in its category and its weight would continue to decrease down to a minimum of 137 kg. Unlike other compressor-equipped motorcycles, such as NSU, AJS, DKW and Moto Guzzi, the BMW had a low compression ratio. Going by the name of Type 255 Kompressor, this was the bike to beat at the international level towards the end of the 1930s, and it would remain BMW's premier competition bike into the 1950s.

BMW triumphs outside of Germany and on the Isle of Man

1936 marked BMW's first really important triumphs, in particular in the Grand Prix of Sweden, where the BMW Kompressors piloted by Otto Ley and Karl Gall, in that order, succeeded in defeating, for the first time, the official Norton, FN and DKW teams. The same riders were the number one winners in Europe the following year, when their bikes were further improved with the adoption of the plunger suspension, which enhanced the transmission of power to the road. BMWs were then chosen by British racers. Jock West won the important Grand Prix of Ulster after having failed chasing the Senior Tourist Trophy only because of a broken fuel tank (he finished sixth). 1938 was the year of BMW's international consecration, partly thanks to the participation in road races of the off-road specialist Georg "Schorsch" Meier, who won several Grand Prix and the first European Championship. But the greatest glory arrived in 1939, when Schorsch Meier's RS 500 Kompressor won the Senior Tourist Trophy ahead of teammate West and the pack of British Nortons and Velocettes. The legendary "number 49" bike was fitted out to perfection in every detail, with a number of critical tweaks such as the simultaneous pedal activation of the front and rear brakes. This would remain the most important road victory for BMW. In the meantime, independent racers continued to compete on naturally aspirated

The rarest BMW in history: the R S 500,
winner of the 1939 Senior TT with
"Schorsch" Meier

The BMW R 51 RS was the most powerful
motorcycle allowed in the hands of
independent racers in the 1930–40s

engine motorcycles deriving from stock models,
such as the R 5 SS and the R 51 SS, but the
gap between them and official, supercharged
bikes was too wide. Thus, in 1939, the top
independent racers were offered a R 51 RS
equipped with compressor.

The post-war period and the debut in the MotoGP World Championship

After the conclusion of the Second World War,
the Germans resumed organization of
motorcycle races in West Germany, where
BMW played the part of the lion – partly due
to a scarcity of worthy competitors. On the
other hand, German racers and manufacturers were momentarily excluded from
races organized by FIM (Fédération Internationale des Motocyclettistes) and so
they had little choice but to organize races within the national boundaries.
Towards the end of the 1950s, the Kompressor made its final appearance,
concluding almost fifteen years of grand successes, which will remain the most
important ones for BMW in road races. The final races of 1950 had already
witnessed the appearance of new racing models with naturally aspirated engines
in preparation for participation in the 500cc class of the World Championship.
BMW prepared two different 500cc bikes for the 1951 World Championship:
one derived from the Kompressor, with two carburettors but no supercharging,
known as the 251; the other was an experimental motorcycle designed by
Sepp Hopf and dubbed Mustang. These bikes were assigned to Schorsch Meier,
to his brother Hans and to a young budding racer named Walter Zeller, who
won the National Championship that year.

The results in the World Championship were modest. There was a
significant power gap between the BMWs and their competitors, particularly
with the four-cylinder Gilera. BMW thus dedicated the year 1952 to trying out
new options under the direction of the engineer Alex von Falkenhausen, even
skipping a few races. But Hans Baltisberger won BMW its first World
Championship point in the Grand Prix of Germany. BMWs were thus present
at the opening of the 1953 World Championship with a shorter wheelbase and
reworked suspension. The bikes had earlier been outfitted with a rear swingarm,
and Walter Zeller arrived on the Isle of Man with a motorcycle equipped with
an Earles front fork, which would also be adopted by the multi-race-winning
Italian motorcycle manufacturer MV Agusta.

The RS 54 Rennsport, the "dream motorcycle"

BMW's placements in the World Championships remained unimpressive, never
reaching any near the podium. But the motorcycle manufacturer continued to
experiment with new mechanical (for example, fuel injection) and aerodynamic
(full and partial fairings) innovations, introducing these versions while also still
racing their more traditional counterparts. This alternation was due to the fact that
the full fairing was advantageous on fast courses, but significantly compromised

A 1960s competition R 50 S; below,
two magnificent 1950s and 1970s racing
bikes at the BMW Museum of Munich

handling on slower ones. A huge innovation arrived in 1954 with the introduction of the Rennsport, also known as the RS 54. Available as a limited series to independent contestants, this motorcycle was a replica of the ones used by the official team, which were the outcome of the previous years' experimentation. It had a dual overhead cam, provided 45 HP to the wheel at 8,000 rpm, weighed 130 kg dry and was clocked at over 200 km/h (240 km/h with full fairing). This was the BMW response to the overwhelming domination by the Italian Gileras and MV Agustas with their four-cylinder engines, which had displaced the British bikes that had dominated the first editions of the World Championship: Norton, AJS and Velocette. Nevertheless, the results were not overly impressive. Zeller managed to win at Hockenheim in front of Pagani's MV and at Schotten ahead of Ray Amm's Norton; but these races were not included in the World Championship, where in fact BMW did not manage to win a single point. In 1956, in spite of the fact that the absolute dominator, John Surtees, was forced to withdraw from the Championship as a result of an accident, Zeller still only finished second in the final for the 500cc class, a bitter fruit but nevertheless the best placement of any BMW racer in the history of the GP World Championship.

BMW officially abandons the GP World Championship

Zeller's second place finish represented the swan song of the Rennsport, and of BMW generally as a contestant in the World Championship. Indeed, partly due to the difficult economic conditions of the Bavarian manufacturer, no further technical progress was made and 1959 was the last year that BMW, represented by Dale and Ernst Hiller, participated in any significant way in the Championships. Some riders continued to race BMWs independently, with Jäger winning points in 1961. On the national level, on the other hand, a number of Rennsports were still winning races, especially in the hands of Hans-Otto Butenuth, who also participated in some editions of the World Championship, winning a few points in 1970 and 1971. He also raced this

One of the last racing BMWs, the 1978
R 90 S; right, the beautiful Dahms racing
sidecar on a 1954 R S 54 Renngespan

motorcycle in the Tourist Trophy in the early 1970s. The history of BMW
would witness a new chapter in 2007: on 30 November, BMW Motorrad issued
a press release announcing its participation in the World Superbike
Championships starting with the 2009 season.

And not just two-wheelers: the BMW sidecar tradition

It was rather common in the first half of the twentieth century to add a sidecar
to a motorcycle, and BMWs always lent themselves particularly well to this
union. Indeed, almost all BMW motorcycles produced up to 1969 were
designed to accept a sidecar. Of the various sidecars chosen by BMW owners
over time, the most famous were those produced by Steib, which also often
made the sidecars used in competitions.

Such competitions have always been part of the motorcycle racing calendar,
and while the category has not been much applauded or attended, it has
brought a great number of victories to BMW, with a series of 19 World
Championship wins in 21 years from 1954 through 1974, of which the first 14
were consecutive, as well as all 21 corresponding world titles for manufacturers.
The first major race victory came in 1925, after Rudolf Schleicher built a
competitive sidecar and attached it to a R 37. This first victory was achieved by
the rider Theo Schoth in the Buckow Triangle Race. Others were added in the
following years, although there were many fewer races for this type of vehicle
than for individual motorcycles. Particularly important in BMW racing history
was Klaus Enders, who won six World Championships in eight years, almost
always in team with Ralf Engelhardt. His saga, and that of BMW, reached its
culmination in 1974 when he managed to edge out the two-stroke König
piloted by the team Schwärzel and Kleis by a mere two points.

Some of the sidecars that have written
pages of BMW sports history from
the 1950s to the 1970s

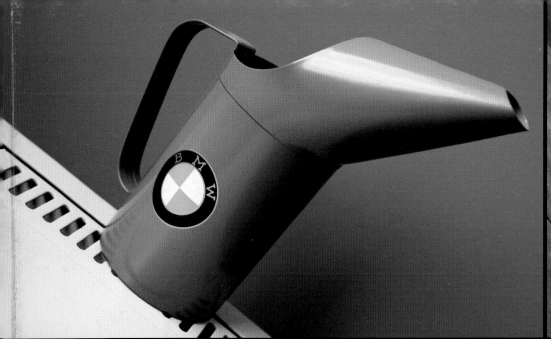

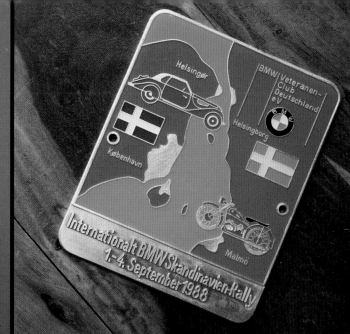

Internationalt BMW Skandinavien-Rally
1.–4. September 1988

BMW Motorrad: Die ersten 75 Jahre. München '98.

7. INTERNAT. ADAC
HESSEN-RHEINLAND-NÜRBURGRINGFAHRT
MSC WÜRSELEN

Motorrad
WANEK
FURTH i. Wald
Tel. 280

100 000 km

Select bibliography

Claudio Somazzi and Massimo Bonsignori, *BMW Passione d'altri tempi* (Novara: Emmelibri, 2003).

Ian Falloon, *Original BMW Air-Cooled Boxer Twins 1950-1996* (St Paul: MBI Publishing Company, 2003).

Roy Bacon, *BMW Twins and Singles*, first ed. 1982 (London: Osprey, 1986).

L. J. K. Setright, *Bahnstormer. The Story of BMW Motorcycle* (London: Transport Bookman, 1978).

Darwin Holmstrom and Brian J. Nelson, *BMW Motorcycles*, first ed. 2002 (Minneapolis: MotorBooks and MBI Publishing Company, 2009).

Kevin Ash, *BMW Motorcycles: The Evolution of Excellence* (Whitehorse Press, 2006).

Ian Falloon, *The BMW Story: Production and Racing Motorcycles from 1923 to the Present Day* (Haynes Publishing, 2004).

Stefan Knittel, *BMW Motorräder*, Semefilm (Milan, 1989).

Bmw Profiles: Motorcycles from Munich, 1923–1969 (BMW Mobile Tradition Historica, 1997).

Motociclismo racconta la storia della BMW (Edisport Editoriale, 2001).

Jean Yves Fenautrigues, *Les BMW à fourches Earles* (Motorportrait, 2005).

Specialized press

Cycle World (USA)
Das Mottorrad (Germany)
The Motor Cycle (UK)
Moto Revue (France)
Motociclismo d'Epoca (Italy)
Moto Storiche e d'Epoca (Italy)
Legend Bike (Italy)

Websites

BMW Historic Archive (www.historischesarchiv.bmw.de)
Military motorcycles in the Second World War (www.motos-of-war.ru)
Wikipedia (www.wikipedia.com)